Law's Interior

Legal and Literary Constructions of the Self

KEVIN M. CROTTY

Cornell University Press

ITHACA AND LONDON

First published 2001 by Cornell University Press
Printed in the United States of America

Library of Congress Cataloging-in-Publication Data
Crotty, Kevin, b. 1948
    Law's interior: legal and literary constructions of the self/
Kevin M. Crotty.
        p. cm.
    Includeds index.
    ISBN 0-8014-3856-X (cloth: acid-free paper)
    1. Law—Philosophy. 2. Personality (Law) 3. Autonomy (Psychology) 4.
Liberty. 5. Individualism—Social aspects. I. Title.
    K230.C76 A35 2001
340'. 1—dc21
                                                    00-011828

Cornell University Press strives to use environmentally responsible suppliers and materials to the fullest extent possible in the publishing of its books. Such materials include vegetable-based, low-VOC inks and acid-free papers that are also recycled, totally chlorine-free, or partly composed of nonwood fibers. Books that bear the logo of the FSC (Forest Stewardship Council) use paper taken from forests that have been inspected and certified as meeting the highest standards for environmental and social responsibility. For further information, visit our website at www.cornellpress.edu.

Cloth printing   10 9 8 7 6 5 4 3 2 1

FSC FSC Trademark © 1996 Forest Stewardship Council A.C.
     SW-COC-098

To Anna Brodsky

Contents

Preface

I began researching and writing this book during a happy year
spent at the Frances Lewis Law Center at the Washington & Lee School
of Law. I am deeply appreciative of the opportunity to explore a subject
that had long fascinated me—to articulate some persistent misgivings
about current legal theory and to explore some new ways of thinking
about it. A Glenn Grant from Washington & Lee University enabled me
to complete work on the manuscript. Winston Davis read two of the
chapters and encouraged me throughout the writing process. Victor
Bers read the first chapter and offered helpful comments and suggestions. Thanks as well to the referees for Cornell University Press for
their suggestions, and to Bernhard Kendler for advice and support.
Quotes from Wallace Stevens are reprinted by permission of Random
House Inc. and Faber and Faber Ltd. John Rawls's "The Idea of Public
Reason Revisited" appeared too late for me to discuss it. There, Rawls offers some clarifications of his argument in *Political Liberalism*, as well as
some amendments to it. While I would have liked to address some of
these changes, I believe that the discussion adequately describes the essentials of Rawls's argument and identifies the problems it poses. My
deepest debt is to Anna Brodsky, and to her I dedicate this book.

K. M. C.

Law's Interior

Introduction

Law is everywhere around us. It is the charter of our state institutions, and it provides the structure and cement of countless transactions everyday. It registers and reflects ongoing conceptions of the extent and kind of duties citizens owe one another. It is inextricably linked to the getting and use of wealth, and underlies and guides the relation between society and its environment. Indeed, an important feature of our legal system is that it extends to all aspects of social life, so that for every conceivable situation there exists case precedent that is at least arguably relevant. There are few subjects, it seems, on which law is wholly silent.

Law's reach is as deep as it is broad: it can reach down into even highly intimate decisions about the course one's life will take. Even where the Constitution directs that such decisions be left to individual choice, that freedom of choice exists because the law so requires. Law's pervasiveness has not only a horizontal dimension (spreading across the spectrum of our social lives), but a vertical one as well, for however varied its forms and the ways it has been conceived, it seems to be a well-nigh universal feature of human societies down through the ages. Law roots even late capitalist, postmodern societies in a thickly layered past. To be sure, we are all positivists now: we cannot help but think of law as something citizens hammer out among themselves. The reigning positivist conception of law, however, is but the latest intellectual model of a perennial practice. This essentially forward-looking view of law cannot disguise the persistence of the past even in an untraditional (not to say antitraditional) society like ours.

1

Law, in short, seems to be one of the most characteristic of human activities, and as essential and inevitable as language. As such, it is not simply a set of commands, but an important way of thinking about ourselves: it illuminates the kind of beings we are. To think of law statically as a set of commands, as some prestigious theorists of law have done, is a bit like thinking of language as a set of grammatical rules. Rather, law is something we *do*—indeed, something that we have always done, and that (despite any millennial aspirations to the contrary) we no doubt always shall do. That is because law, like language, reflects the irreducibly social aspect of our nature. To extend Wittgenstein's famous observation, a wholly private legal system, like a wholly private language, would be a contradiction in terms. Law resembles language in that we are always already inside it. It is a part of the world we encounter and assimilate, and in doing so we become who we are. The order, cooperation, and mutual understanding law makes possible are features that mark it as something internal to us, and indispensable to the formation of identity. Law is too deeply at the heart of society and the political community to be an institution that is, from the individual's point of view, simply "out there" and at arm's length. The duty to obey the law (or, at least, the habitual obedience the law exacts) is a part of our "contents": it partly makes us who and what we are.

Law (like language) points to a paradox at the very heart of the idea of a "self": we attain a sense of our individuality—our distinctive and unique self—only through and by means of shared and age-old public practices. The classic image of the social contract—a group of individuals who create law—is misleading in the picture it presents of a wholly deliberate institution that is fully and uncontroversially responsive to human desires and reason. Rather, law is a practice we carry on partly because we cannot avoid it. More deeply, we are inside this practice; it partly contains us and forms us. Law, then, is not a set of straightforward commands directed outward. It has its own intricate inside. *We* are law's interior.

It is a considerable simplification to say that law respects the individual's autonomy, as if autonomy were something that existed apart from the law, or prior to it. Instead, autonomy is something that gets produced in part by legal means. For autonomy entails self-respect, and requires a certain confidence that one's goals can be realized. It requires education and an economic sufficiency. It will not thrive in a society where grave social disparities are entrenched or condoned. Law has played an increasingly important role in the education and economic prospects of its citizens. It has had a disgraceful history of perpetuating unjust social divisions that discourage or frustrate individual autonomy. It has also been an essential tool for wiping out such divisions.

But the relation between law and autonomy is yet more intricate, for, once autonomy gets produced by social institutions (among them law), law must then respect it. Law poses a kind of "Pygmalion paradox," for the state partly brings about the individual, autonomous agent—who is then endowed with rights on which the state may not infringe. Society and self, then, like *langue* and *parole*, mutually produce each other.

The intricacy of the relation between the individual and the law is ignored by legal positivism, which holds that law is simply the rules that get laid down by the sovereign. According to positivist thinkers, the laws harbor no deeper mystery, and reflect no higher truths. But this seems to oversimplify by treating law as nothing more than the product of individual human wills—as though we simply invented its meanings. On the view taken here, however, we are fashioned by the law—we are "within" it, as a practice we cannot help but carry on. The most significant developments in American law over the last fifty years have continually reflected this aspect of law—without, however, quite articulating it. Yet a watershed decision such as *Brown v. Board of Education*[1] ultimately rests on the perception that the state, far from merely respecting the innate "autonomy" of its citizens, actively brings about or discourages that autonomy. State-run schools had the power to contribute to, or to frustrate, the self-respect of the students, who were, ultimately, being trained for citizenship. Public schools in turn crystallized a broader sense of the law's role in actively forming the autonomy it was supposed to respect. *Brown,* then, points to the model of the law to be presented here: law as containing us and forming us; law as part of our contents. After *Brown,* a view of law as something "laid down" by the sovereign seems simplistic and insufficient, because it fails to capture some of the most important facets of the relation between the citizens and their laws.

To apply this different model of law requires us to rethink some of the most familiar ideas about law. For example, a characteristic claim of legal positivism is that law is an autonomous enterprise in its own right, and is not to be confused with morality. In its most sophisticated versions, legal positivism asserts that a legal system is autonomous in that it rests on a rational basis independent from the diverse and inconsistent moral visions animating citizens in a pluralistic society.[2] It aims at something less lofty than justice, and is satisfied with more modest and more workable ideals

---

1. 347 U.S. 483 (1954).

2. This is the argument elaborated by John Rawls in *Political Liberalism* (New York: Columbia University Press, 1993).

such as "integrity" or "fairness."[3] This view posits a clear boundary between a public realm of shareable reasons and a private realm of comprehensive, yet diverse and inconsistent views of the world. Law is then conceived as a way of sidestepping the profound disagreements within a pluralistic society; it is a separate, public realm where consensus is possible, even within the prevailing dissensus about ultimate matters. To be sure, people will disagree about the laws and judicial decisions, and painful choices will sometimes be necessary, but these disagreements are simply part of a coherent political community that rests on certain articulable principles.

On this view, law is a realm of freedom, in which individual citizens step back and away from the concrete particulars of their lives—the received traditions that may have largely shaped their identity—to make arguments about social arrangements based solely on reason. Law, in other words, is *separate from* morality: it rests on reasons that exist apart from any particular vision of the world and of the ultimate questions of existence. There are several ways to picture this separateness. One formulation has it that law addresses the "right," which is prior to and distinguishable from the "good."[4] Or, law is the embodiment of public reason,[5] which is the object of an "overlapping consensus" among diverse and otherwise inconsistent comprehensive belief systems.[6] Law, in other words, is a kind of "module" that can be inserted into a variety of otherwise inconsistent beliefs: whatever the ultimate model of reality espoused by a particular belief system, it ought to be able to recognize the great good of a stable and tolerant state. That law constitutes a separable realm is a tribute to the ability and willingness of a sophisticated citizen body to confine itself to publicly shareable reasons when arguing about public matters, and expressly to avoid recourse to each one's fundamental moral beliefs. The laws, then, are the deliberate, rational enactments of the political community; to ensure that they *are* in fact deliberate and rational requires good faith and a considerable degree of sophistication on the part of citizens.

Such is the most recent version of legal positivism. It is in many ways an attractive vision, but, it seems to me, an implausibly optimistic one—above all in its rationalistic bias that behavior is motivated by articulate beliefs

3. On the legal system as aiming at integrity (rather than justice), see Ronald Dworkin, *Law's Empire* (Cambridge: Harvard University Press, 1986), 164–68, and Chapters 6 and 7. On justice construed as the more modest and workable ideal of "fairness," see the first chapter of John Rawls, *A Theory of Justice* (Cambridge: Harvard University Press, 1971).

4. See Rawls, *Political Liberalism*, 173–211.

5. Ibid., 212–54.

6. Ibid., 39–40, 150–54, 170–71.

that can be provisionally set aside when the occasion demands. It overestimates reason and underestimates the importance of such subrational and not easily articulated features as race and gender in shaping identity and behavior. Here, actual developments in case law over the last fifty years (when race and gender have become increasingly central issues) seem to have outrun theory. Thus, it is open to question whether citizens can in fact step outside their personalities to inhabit a more purely rational realm. Even more controversial is the extent to which this ideal of deliberative rationality is an attractive one: for this model, rather than embodying some universal feature inherent in all of us, may be subtly selective and discriminatory, favoring those who best fit the profile. It seems to rest on the bland assumption of a universally shared rationalistic "core," and to ignore or soften the potential divisiveness of the subrational aspects of identity.

The complexity of the relations between self and law is far from academic. Developments within American law in the twentieth century have made it difficult to see law as merely respecting citizens' innate, independently existing autonomy. This model was no doubt always simplified, but was perhaps at one time workable. Its usefulness is rapidly dwindling in a legal environment sensitized to the pervasive role government inevitably plays in forming not only the expectations of its citizens, but even their sense of identity and self-respect. It has come to seem less and less plausible that the state confronts a well-bounded private zone, or that it is strictly neutral in regard to private decisions.

The waning of a powerful and easily understood paradigm is unsettling: the idea of rights seems ineradicable in our legal system, but the readiest model for understanding those rights (a self innately possessed of rights over against the state) is at odds with our current legal reality. It may seem, as some commentators have urged, that we are stuck in the absurd situation of arguing legal cases in terms of a now essentially meaningless concept of "rights."[7] At any rate, our inability to account for our practices in a really credible way is troubling. Controversial court decisions become badly and perhaps needlessly divisive when they are based on reasons, or use assumptions, that no longer command much conviction. An inability to give a compelling account of our practices leaves them uncomfortably exposed to attacks that reduce them to nothing more than power politics.[8]

7. Louis Michael Seidman and Mark V. Tushnet, *Remnants of Belief: Contemporary Constitutional Issues* (New York: Oxford University Press, 1996), chapter 1. See also below, Chapter 3, Section 3.

8. This, I think, is the kernel of truth in the claim made in Richard Weisberg's *Poethics* (New York: Columbia University Press, 1992), 7–9, that even correct judicial opinions will

A more persuasive account, I believe, would present law as itself existing within tension among our ethical aims. Max Weber's celebrated distinction between "the ethics of responsibility" (*Verantwortungsethik*) and "the ethics of conviction" (*Gesinnungsethik*) is relevant here.[9] Weber's distinction addresses some of the same ethical realities as do positivist accounts of law, yet it draws a strikingly different picture of them. He presents two different ethical attitudes. On the one hand is the disposition to act in conformity with one's personal convictions, whatever the toll on oneself or others. This "ethics of conviction" is premised on the view that morality should not bend to questions of expedience or even of the practical effects of one's "moral" conduct in the actual world.

Weber contrasts this ethics of conviction with a different set of ethical commitments in which expedience takes on a far more urgent and ethically compelling aspect. Within this "ethics of responsibility," moral agents have the ethical task of considering the likely effects their actions will have on the world, and the way their behavior will affect their fellows. The point is that to consider expediency and the practical effects of one's actions is not to step outside the bounds of ethical behavior, but is itself an important ethical stance.

Weber's distinction between two ethical dispositions is richly suggestive. For my purposes, however, it suffices to point out that the duty in a pluralistic society to base one's arguments on publicly shareable reasons is a form of his "ethics of responsibility," for it rests on the agent's acknowledgment of the need (in a pluralistic society) to consider the effect of his actions and arguments on others—in particular, others' ability to respond to the argument in kind. Confining oneself to publicly shareable reasons exemplifies "responsibility ethics" in its commitment to preserving others' ability to respond. "Conviction ethics," in turn, corresponds to the private zone of multifarious individual beliefs, where each one is free to act on the basis of his own convictions.

By identifying each of these as *ethical* stances, Weber indicates the possibility of a genuine conflict between them—that is, an unresolvable rift in our ethical commitments, and in particular between personal conviction and public responsibility. It is just this rift that the sophisticated versions of legal positivism seem to deny, positing instead a more manageable set

---

not survive unless they are conveyed in effective and persuasive language. Weisberg has in mind the correct, but unsatisfactorily reasoned, decisions in *Brown v. Board of Education*, 347 U.S. 483 (1954) and *Roe v. Wade*, 410 U.S. 113 (1973). I discuss *Brown* and *Roe* in Chapter 3, Section 3.

9. Max Weber, "Politics as a Vocation," in *From Max Weber: Essays in Sociology*, trans. H. H. Gerth and C. Wright Mills (New York: Oxford University Press, 1946), 118–28.

of duties that can then be assigned priorities. Abortion is perhaps the most familiar example of a conflict between conviction and responsibility ethics. According to sophisticated versions of legal positivism, it emerges as a foregone conclusion that these individual convictions must yield to the more publicly responsible position of respecting others' decisions in an essentially private matter.

In contrast, Weber's distinction of two ethical attitudes better captures the painful sense of authentic conflict that has made the abortion question such a long-lived and apparently unresolveable issue. It underscores the difficulty of deliberately *not* acting on one's most intense convictions. On this view, then, law does not end-run ethical conflict, but is one of the sites in which such conflicts are played out.

We can approach this conflict from another direction. It is possible to give an account in which private and public autonomy look completely consistent and mutually supportive. Public autonomy here means the democratic ideal of citizens deciding together the rules that will govern their life in common. This ideal may be said to call forth, in turn, the complementary ideal of private autonomy, a commitment to seeing each of the citizens as equal and autonomous individuals. This private autonomy is a necessary presupposition for that public autonomy that requires discourse and debate among equals. I am here paraphrasing Jürgen Habermas, who presents autonomy as consistent and coherent in its private and public aspects.[10]

But autonomy seems a rather more conflicted ideal than Habermas apparently allows. Individual autonomy is closely associated with what Charles Taylor has called the "ethics of authenticity"—the ethically compelling need to be just who and what one most authentically is, in one's own terms.[11] But that authentic sense of self may be inconsistent with the more rationalistic model of individual autonomy, which may come to feel like a distortion of one's authentic self, and therefore subtly oppressive. Even supposing that it is spawned by the ideal of public autonomy, then, "private autonomy" seems to transcend its origins, and open the possibility of a real conflict between one's individual sense of personal authenticity and the more public version of rational, equal autonomy. Women's rights present perhaps the most familiar form of this tension between authenticity and autonomy. The rationalist ideal of equal, autonomous citi-

---

10. Jürgen Habermas, *Between Facts and Norms: Contributions to a Discourse Theory of Law and Democracy*, trans. William Rehg (Cambridge: MIT Press, 1996), 84, 88–89, 103–4.

11. See Charles Taylor, *The Ethics of Authenticity* (Cambridge: Harvard University Press, 1991), and his *Sources of the Self* (Cambridge: Harvard University Press, 1989), 368–90, 456–93.

zens appears on inspection to be covertly male, and therefore subtly, but pervasively, prejudicial to women's interests.

The point for now is that law does not quite manage to set conflict aside or to keep it at bay. Rather, it inhabits a tension between divergent and sometimes inconsistent ethical aims. It does not constitute a realm separate from the deep and inconsistent ethical lives of its citizens. To be sure, law in this country has aspired to be autonomous and set apart from the flow and flux of everyday life. The challenge to legal theory is to treat the autonomy of law precisely as an aspiration—something that influences our practices, but is never fully possessed by them. In this book I present a model of law as a practice that aspires to a separateness it can never achieve. Rather than progressing toward an ever greater objectivity (the picture Oliver Wendell Holmes memorably drew in his book *The Common Law*), it traces a more cyclical path: a movement now toward objectivity (simple rules that are easily followed and administered), and now toward incorporating more of what I will call the ethical complexity of its citizens. Put another way, law veers between aiming at a simplified model of the person (in the interests of clarity and efficiency) and articulating a more comprehensive and nuanced view (in the interests of being truly expressive and therefore less unjust). These diverse movements within the law partly reflect competing intuitions about ourselves—as being at the same time outside society and deeply inside it.

Law, then, has two commitments—to simplify social life to a set of readily understood and administered rules; and to ensure that these rules safeguard and promote whatever is felt to be genuinely vital to human interests. These two commitments ensure that the body of law is unstable and continually evolving; more particularly, they ensure that the line between public and private is not drawn permanently, and that it is open to renegotiation. To say that law is separate from morality—to say that a stable line divides public discourse from private commitments—is to distort our picture of the practice of law. For, as I try to show in Chapter 1, law not only simplifies, but attempts to do so in a way that does not violate or ignore anything truly vital to human flourishing.

Law must respect citizens, but the relevant features of the person as citizen have become increasingly controversial. Once upon a time, the most pertinent aspects were rationality and autonomy. Such a view of the citizen comported a distinct vision of society as a kind of supercontract among autonomous beings. But now race, gender, and sexual orientation have come to seem increasingly relevant and ineradicable attributes. Law has had to change in order to accommodate these evolving views of citizenship. It can no longer be premised on a single, universal model of the self, then, but needs to respond to a pluralism of different selves, distinguished (and divided) by physical features that shape or color identity, expectations, and world-view. I explore in Chapter 2 the difficulties law has had in incorporating more complex ideas of the self.

The idea of a right has, in consequence, become elusive. Individual rights can no longer be plausibly conceived as inhering in the individual. More plausibly, they are understood as arising together with the democratic practice of hammering out in common the laws that govern our lives together. Even this formulation, however, gives too static a notion of rights. For as I have suggested, the self is unstable and dynamic: it is contingent, local, partisan, mutable—immersed in its historical circumstances. One disturbing aspect of this immersion is that the self is in large part produced by the state that is supposed to respect it. Also, ideas about the essential attributes of the person as citizen expand and change: no longer confinable to rationality, to autonomy, they now necessarily include race, gender, sexual orientation. Physical attributes, the bodies of citizens are now pertinent features of citizenship. In this environment, the idea of an individual right necessarily changes: it does not grow from, reflect, or protect some immutable feature of the person or some necessary, static role played by the individual citizen within a democracy. Nor can a right be plausibly understood as drawing a sacred circle around the individual—a circle into which the state may not intrude (for the state actually forms the rights-bearing individual). To be persuasive, the idea of a right must be as fluid as the idea of the citizen. This is deeply unsettling. Rights, we feel, are the brakes that prevent government overreaching; to make them open-ended, mutable, contingent may seem to destroy them. And, indeed, some writers have argued that the idea of rights has become largely meaningless.

In Chapter 3 I sketch a theory of rights that seems implicit in the most important constitutional decisions of the last half-century, but that legal theory (it seems to me) has not quite managed to bring to the surface. Those decisions have reflected a sense that the state does not simply respect individual rights. Rather, it actually plays a role in bringing about the kind of individual autonomy that makes having rights a significant fact about us. The Constitution, if it is to remain a meaningful document, cannot ignore this increasingly vivid perception of the role played by law and the state in shaping autonomy. Rights, then, cannot be confined to those explicitly spelled out in the text of the Constitution. These latter I think of as "membership rights"—those rights belonging to anyone as a member of the political community. In addition to those, however, courts have come round to recognizing (without, however, quite articulating) what might be called "entry rights"—rights to become a member of the political community of autonomous individuals. Decisions reflecting this perception often invoke equal protection as their rationale. The Equal Protection clause, however, does not seem to me fully to capture the import of these decisions, because they reflect the sense not merely that law protects everyone equally, but that law must root out those forces and trends that frustrate or impede the development of fully autonomous citizens. The autonomy that seemed inherent in individuals now looks more like a question of the individual's social circumstances. The Constitution, therefore, must now actively bring about the autonomy presupposed in it.

This theoretical sketch of rights points in turn to a new account of the relations between the judiciary and the legislature. The model of this relation has been the excessively unidirectional one of courts sitting in judgment of the legislators, testing legislative enactments against the requirements set forth in the Constitution. On the view offered here, courts look to such enactments as one way of understanding the ongoing and changing relation that exists between citizens and the Constitution that structures their political community. Legislative developments, in other words, are one powerful indicator of what constitutional rights have become, and how they have evolved. The judiciary and the legislature, then, mutually inform and guide each other. Legislation reflects and forges the evolving relation between state and citizen; the judiciary projects this relation into an account of rights.

Constitutional adjudication, then, is sometimes a matter not simply of interpreting this or that phrase within the document, but, more deeply, of construing the relation between the Constitution and "we, the people"—and, in particular, the reason why the Constitution is authoritative and, so to speak, "constitutive." On this reading, some of the watershed opinions from the Supreme Court have been to a significant degree "poetic," in the sense that, while entailing expertise in interpreting legal language, they were essentially efforts to find a persuasive model of the relations between citizen and state.

Can theory, by itself, quite articulate a persuasive model of rights, once rights have gotten to be so complex? There is reason to think that it cannot. Theory simplifies our practices in order to make them more intelligible; it is like a map that flattens the world to two dimensions, but does so in order to make it more easily navigated. The simplifications impose a cost (the loss of concrete particulars), but confer a substantial benefit: they enable us to situate fleeting and unrepeatable particulars within an encompassing frame. A good theory confers an articulable significance on concrete instances, by marshaling them into a coherent and consistent scheme. Ideally, too, it has predictive power: it should enable us to return to the real world with a better sense of how things are. At its best, it illuminates individual cases, and helps us see features of them that might otherwise have escaped our notice. Such is the aspiration, for example, of a legal theory such as Ronald Dworkin's, which has distinct implications for the way judges approach individual cases.

Recent legal theory, however, is in a curious situation, for, as developments in constitutional adjudication have made clear, it is just the marginal, the other, the heterodox—in short, the very elements that tend to get filtered out by theory—that seem theoretically central: no theory that sidelines them can seem complete or wholly satisfying. Jurisprudence now faces a reality that not merely resists theory, but seems hostile to it, as imposing simplifications whose apparently inevitable effect is to enshrine a particular model of reality. Just by doing what it is supposed to do, theory risks falsifying in serious ways the sprawling reality it seeks to illuminate.

To be persuasive, an account of law must capture what I will call its "permeability": its aspirations at once to separateness and to responsiveness; its attempt to be clear and straightforward on the one hand, and truly expressive on the other. Partly to correct for the tendency of theory to isolate its subject, I have built my discussion around treatments of three imaginative works—Aeschylus' *Oresteia,* St. Augustine's *Confessions,* and the poetry of the American writer Wallace Stevens. I do not see this as an "interdisciplinary" approach, since that term apparently presupposes that law is a well-bounded "discipline." That is in fact just what I want to dispute; I want to situate law within the social amalgam of which it is such a vital and pervasive part.

The pertinence of literature to law lies essentially in the way it sets law within a human context: it presents law as an activity to which people have recourse for reasons that can be appreciated only in the broader context of their lives. In part because of its ceremonial character, law (more particularly, legal procedure) is a powerful device for focusing pervasive human qualities—cunning intelligence, mercy, cruelty. The agonistic structure of the legal process, moreover, affords writers an especially dramatic context in which to explore these qualities. The *jurisprudential* point of studying law through literature is to emphasize these multiple and intricate connections between law and the world around and within it.

The philosophy of law tends to treat it as something static and apart, with its own determinate nature. Literature, it seems to me, can illuminate our understanding of law by treating our legal practices as woven into the broader social fabric, rather than as an autonomous, static thing in its own right. One of the most important features of law is its openness to change. To isolate and identify what law timelessly "is" is to miss the importance of law's constant movement, which reaches far down even to deep and formative matters such as the way the relation between law and citizen is understood. The central feature of law, as presented in literature, is not its separability from other pursuits, but the links joining it to the rest of the world: therein lies the pertinence of literature to the study of law. Literature should help us correct for the tendency of theory to arrest the free flow of a continually evolving practice.

We have to do here, perhaps, with the latest avatar of what Plato once famously called the "ancient dispute between poetry and philosophy." Plato, notoriously, tipped the balance in favor of philosophy, and would have banished the tragedians from his ideal state. More recently, however, the claims of poetry have received a more attentive hearing: the very passions that seemed to Plato to make tragedy a debased and noxious influence in the city may now well be felt to correct for the excessive, and so potentially distorting, rationality of theory.

This book, then, belongs to the rapidly burgeoning field of law and literature. Law and literature are two of the most important things we do with language, and the affinity between them is an ancient one, going back at least as far as the first written laws—composed in a style meant to be memorable, authoritative, and impressive.[12] Indeed, some of the most characteristic works of ancient literature—for example, the orations of Demosthenes in Greek and of Cicero in Latin—were originally intended for the law courts. This tradition of forensic rhetoric was an important influence in the formative years of American law, too, in the eighteenth and early nineteenth centuries.[13]

In the 1970s James Boyd White made the first fledgling efforts to repair the bridges that had so long existed between law and literature, and to restore to law something of its stature as a humane and civilized pursuit.[14]

12. For example, the language of the Twelve Tables of Rome—the earliest codification of Roman law, and dating to the mid-fifth century B.C.E.—is clipped, direct, and unforgettable. We know that Roman schoolchildren still memorized them in Cicero's day, more than 350 years after they were first promulgated. See Alan Watson, *Rome of the Twelve Tables* (Princeton: Princeton University Press, 1975).

13. Robert A. Ferguson, *Law and Letters in American Culture* (Cambridge: Harvard University Press, 1984).

14. See James Boyd White, *The Legal Imagination* (Boston: Little, Brown, 1973). White has continued to explore the relations between law and literature in *Justice as Translation: An Essay in Cultural and Legal Criticism* (Chicago: University of Chicago Press, 1990); *Heracles' Bow: Essays on the Rhetoric and Poetics of the Law* (Madison: University of Wisconsin Press, 1985); *When Words Lose Their Meaning: Constitutions and Reconstitutions of Language, Character and Community* (Chicago: University of Chicago Press, 1984).

Interest in the possibilities of law and literature grew considerably during the 1980s. Ronald Dworkin, for example, in *Law's Empire* (1986), presented law as an interpretive practice akin to literature: modes of literary criticism, therefore, were potentially suggestive for understanding the way judges interpret statutory law and case precedent in deciding cases.[15] Other studies asserted that literature could correct for law's tendency to fussy legalism, by expressing the idiosyncrasies and painfulness of individual, subjective experience in a vivid and compelling way. Because law almost inevitably uses broad generalizations, it tends to assimilate individuals to a common, supposedly universal stereotype. By showing the specialness of women's and minorities' experience, for example, literature potentially contests and corrects the law's need for rough-and-ready (not to say crude) generalizations.[16] Literary critical methods of the 1980s (most prominently deconstruction) were also applied to legal texts, in order to debunk them by showing their "indeterminacy" and deep, internal contradictions; deconstruction showed how authoritative legal texts were merely fictional.[17] Law and literature has continued to flourish in the 1990s.[18] One of the most striking signs of the continued vigor and new legitimacy of this approach is the 1998 revised edition of Richard Posner's 1988 book, originally titled *Law and Literature: A Misunderstood*

15. Dworkin, *Law's Empire*, 45–86, 228–38.

16. See, e.g., Carolyn Heilbrun and Judith Resnik, "Convergences: Law, Literature, and Feminism," *Yale Law Journal* 99 (1990): 1913–53; Deborah Rhode, "Feminist Critical Theories," *Stanford Law Review* 42 (1990): 617–38; Robin West, "Authority, Autonomy, and Choice: The Role of Consent in the Moral and Political Visions of Franz Kafka and Richard Posner," *Harvard Law Review* 99 (1985): 1449–56.

17. See, e.g., Mark Tushnet, "Critical Legal Studies and Constitutional Law: An Essay in Deconstruction," *Stanford Law Review* 36 (1984): 632–47; J. Balkin, "Deconstructive Practice and Legal Theory," *Yale Law Journal* 96 (1987): 743–86; Clare Dalton, "An Essay in the Deconstruction of Contract Law," *Yale Law Journal* 94 (1985): 997.

18. Among the notable studies that have recently appeared, see Richard A. Posner, *Law and Literature,* revised edition (Cambridge: Harvard University Press, 1998); Theodore Ziolkowski, *The Mirror of Justice: Literary Reflections of Legal Crises* (Princeton: Princeton University Press, 1997); Bruce L. Rockwood, ed., *Law and Literature Perspectives* (New York: Peter Lang, 1996); Martha Nussbaum, *Poetic Justice: The Literary Imagination and the Public Life* (Boston: Beacon Press, 1995); Ian Ward, *Law and Literature: Possibilities and Perspectives* (Cambridge: Cambridge University Press, 1995); Robin West, *Narrative, Authority, and Law* (Ann Arbor: University of Michigan Press, 1993); Richard Weisberg, *Poethics and Other Strategies of Law and Literature* (New York: Columbia University Press, 1992), and the same author's *The Failure of the Word* (New Haven: Yale University Press, 1984); Thomas C. Grey, *The Wallace Stevens Case* (Cambridge: Harvard University Press, 1991). Ward (*Law and Literature,* 3–27) offers a useful overview of this burgeoning field. Some of the "classics" of the law-and-literature school are collected in Lenora Ledwon, ed., *Law and Literature: Text and Theory* (New York: Garland, 1996).

Relation. In the new edition, Posner has dropped the pejorative subtitle, and emphasizes his support of the law-and-literature movement and his wish to see it flourish.[19]

A persistent and characteristic claim in "law and literature" studies is that lawyers and judges can learn useful moral lessons about their practice from novels, plays, and poems. This is the idea animating such studies as Richard Weisberg's *Poethics* or Martha Nussbaum's *Poetic Justice,* to name just two of the most distinguished.[20] I have several doubts about such an approach, however. First, the assumption appears to be that law is inherently fussy, petty, and repressed, and needs to be supplemented and corrected by the humane values of literature. To be sure, it is always useful for lawyers to be reminded of the human toll exacted by insensitive application of legal rules. But why assume that literature is the only, or even an especially privileged source of moral illumination? A moral philosopher like Martha Nussbaum may well find literature a particularly suggestive supplement to the conceptual rigors of philosophy. But why might not lawyers find religion or even moral philosophy a source of illumination in their professional lives? (The poet Wallace Stevens, himself a lawyer, writes of a religious pamphlet by a judge in Pennsylvania Dutch country, which began: "Indeed when Spinoza's great logic went searching for God, it found Him in a predicate of substance.")[21] Moral illumination can come from far less intellectual sources than either philosophy or literature: an incident on the subway, a chance encounter on the street, a happy time with one's family—any or all of these, or any number of other experiences can touch the conscience and expand the sensibilities.

More deeply, the problem with studies urging the salubrious ethical effects of literature is that they are rather more optimistic about literature than writers themselves have tended to be. An artist like Vladimir Nabokov finds a culminating image of the artist in the damnable figure of a child molester—Humbert Humbert in *Lolita.* When Nabokov insists at the conclusion of the novel that *Lolita* has no moral in tow, that is partly because art (as personified in the monstrous Humbert) has only a precarious claim to moral authority.[22] Theodor Adorno famously asked whether art was

---

19. Posner, *Law and Literature,* 7.

20. Further references are given in Chapter 1, Section 3.

21. Wallace Stevens, *Letters of Wallace Stevens,* ed. Holly Stevens (New York: Alfred A. Knopf, 1981), 415.

22. See Anna Brodsky, *Strategies of Bliss,* forthcoming. The account of *Lolita* in Richard Rorty, *Irony, Contingency, and Solidarity* (Cambridge: Cambridge University Press, 1989), though moving and interesting, seems finally too optimistic in its assertion that readers learn valuable moral lessons from reading it.

even possible after Auschwitz. Even in his mature view, after he had retracted his flat-out denial of the possibility of art,[23] Adorno considered it a mark of genuine art that it questioned its own existence—that it did not blithely assume its own moral soundness. "True art challenges its own essence," he wrote.[24] More recently, Iris Murdoch has cautioned that one of the dangers of art—with its powerful intimations of beauty, its "rounded wholes"—is that it may convince its audience that they are better than they really are.[25] In other words, the moral lessons audiences think they draw from art—the benefit they believe they derive from it—may in fact be a way they delude themselves. There is no guarantee that people will draw the lessons from literary works that ethical critics think they should. Literature is a form of instruction by *anamnesis*—it teaches you what you already know. Art, it seems, confirms people in their rooted convictions, rather than challenging them to a genuinely more embracing moral purview.

For these reasons, it seems unsatisfying to present literature as shedding rays of spiritual truth on the benighted practice of law. That is to present the relation between law and literature as a one-way street. Far better, it seems to me, to present law and literature as two different, but in many ways cognate human practices, each open to criticism and, more particularly in our time, each racked with self-doubt. It may be that the function of jurisprudence nowadays is not to remove these doubts, or to assure us that law is the coherent, perfectly comprehensible practice we would like it to be. Rather than ridding law of its tensions and ambiguities, the purpose of contemporary jurisprudence might be to help us explore them more deeply, and—perhaps most important—to avoid the temptation of nihilism. Artists have had to address some potent political forces in this century that threatened to undermine the very idea of art and the autonomy of the artist. The ways they have done so may help us to see, in turn, the continued vitality of the idea of rights (in a time when the same or similar political forces have threatened to undermine the very idea of the individual). Our inability to frame a fully cohesive and integrated theory of law does not mean that law is moonshine or merely politics; that literary artists struggle with similar doubts about the vitality of art should help us to see that this is so. Our predicament may be that

23. Theodor W. Adorno, *Negative Dialectics,* trans. E. B. Ashton (New York: Seabury, 1973), 362–63: "[I]t may have been wrong to say that after Auschwitz you could no longer write poems. But it is not wrong to raise the less cultural question whether after Auschwitz you can go on living."

24. Theodor W. Adorno, *Aesthetic Theory,* trans. C. Lenhardt (London: Routledge, 1984), 2.

25. Iris Murdoch, *Metaphysics as a Guide to Morals* (London: Penguin, 1992), chapter 1.

we must carry on a practice without a fully formed theory explaining it. Comparing law and literature, I hope, will show why theoretical quandaries do not paralyze our ongoing practice.[26]

One of the most important, indeed foundational, texts for law and literature is the *Oresteia*, because (as I will show in Chapter 1) it is to an important extent precisely about the intricate relation between law and life. More specifically, it is about the emergence of a separate and autonomous institution that holds out (precisely because of its separateness and autonomy) the hope of freeing people from the passionate emotions of vengeance and the blistering imperatives of justice. Because of its narrative structure, however, the final achievement of an autonomous legal order remains an equivocal one: the portrayal of the fierce emotions and imperatives in the earlier plays makes the climactic equilibrium seem precarious at best. In dramatizing the origins of law, the *Oresteia* underlines the significance of law's wish to be autonomous and genuinely separate from the world around it, even as it casts doubt on the ability of law (or any human institution) to achieve it.

I set the *Oresteia* against John Rawls's recent account of the origins of the liberal state. The story Rawls has to tell bears a surprisingly close resemblance to that enacted in the *Oresteia*. Where Rawls, however, sees a liberal state as inhabiting a well-defined territory that cleanly separates public from private, the boundary that emerges in the *Oresteia* appears shifting and blurred. It is the blurriness of this line that makes the *Oresteia* the pertinent text it is: it helps us think through what is implausible in some very attractive recent accounts of the liberal state and of law as the "public reason" of the liberal state.

Even when it does not specifically address law, literature is an important supplement to the simplifications law inevitably introduces in its conception of persons. In Chapter 2 I turn to St. Augustine's *Confessions*, which, like the *Oresteia*, is a foundational text—a charter, so to speak, for the complex self. The arc of the story Augustine tells climaxes in book 8 with the achievement of a model of the self finally adequate to the intricate, internal, mutually inconsistent drives that make up anyone's subjective experience. Of course, lives had no doubt always been complex, but

---

26. See the suggestive comments by Charles Taylor, "To Follow a Rule," in *Philosophical Arguments* (Cambridge: Harvard University Press, 1995), 165–80. Taylor urges the primacy of practice over the ability to formulate the rules guiding the practice. He writes: "The person of real practical wisdom is less marked by the ability to formulate rules than by knowing how to act in each particular situation. There is a crucial 'phronetic gap' between the formula and its enactment, and this . . . is neglected by explanations that give primacy to the rule-as-represented" (177).

Augustine was arguably the first to find a literary vehicle able to reveal a purely internal, psychological depth to experience. The *Confessions* is in some ways strikingly modern: to a twentieth-century reader, it inevitably suggests Freud and his theories of depth psychology. Augustine's explosion of an apparently well-bound ego into countless disparate desires will recall postmodern skepticism about the self.

Law has not been able to evade this psychological intricacy. The American law of custodial confessions, for example, poses in a legal context many of the same issues of voluntariness, susceptibility, and mixed motives that Augustine wrestled with at a theological level. The watershed Supreme Court decision *Miranda v. Arizona*[27] illustrates the problems the law has in incorporating a fully complex psychological model of the person, even as it is under pressure to do so. In Chapter 2 I want to bring these two very different forms of confession into a single focus, in order to study the tension between the law's commitment to a simplified model of the self and the pressure on it to asssimilate a more complex model.

A major strand in law and literature studies is to present law itself as a kind of literature—a linguistically self-conscious practice that, at its best, builds up and strengthens community. Ronald Dworkin uses the affinities between law and literary practice partly to show law as the most characteristic activity of a political community, in which citizens offer reasoned arguments about what the formative principles underlying the community require in any given situation.[28] James Boyd White, too, has stressed the rhetorical nature of the legal opinion, and has argued that one of the most important tasks judicial decisions perform is to articulate the animating principles of the political community.[29] Literature builds up community, then, by affording especially sensitive and nuanced portrayals of individual ethical choices, as well as by providing the community with common stories.

A major problem with such studies is that they are more confident about the community-building potential of literature than literary artists themselves have been. Dworkin and White, for example, both seem to presuppose a smooth and unconflicted relation between the self and the community. On their view, the artist produces the literary works that foster the bonds constituting the community—and this is a model of what judges do, as well. But in fact this is an implausibly ideal account of artistic production, for there exists a palpable tension between the artist's

27. 384 U.S. 436 (1966).
28. Dworkin, *Law's Empire*, 45–86, 228–58.
29. This idea suffuses White's writings, but see, e.g., his *Heracles' Bow*, 28–48.

commitment to his own vision and the communal aspects of his work. Lyric poetry—traditionally the product of a uniquely sensitive and talented individual—may seem fatally out of touch, hermetic, irrelevant. It has not been easy for poets to be true to their gift and at the same time to heed the demand for pertinence. Negotiating the tensions between self and community has been at best difficult, and at worst—as for example in Stalinist Russia—downright catastrophic. One of the great virtues of the twentieth-century poet Wallace Stevens is that he has taken on these issues, and subjected the continued possibility of lyric poetry to a really searching examination. Stevens makes poetry from his questioning of poetry: he does not blandly assume the community-building properties of art, but takes seriously the question of whether poetry is outmoded and discredited precisely because it cannot build community—that it is merely the (self-indulgent) expression of an idiosyncratic personality. Stevens's poetry grows, in important part, from this crisis in the status of the individual talent.

Stevens's examination of the poet in many aspects parallels contemporary developments in the theory of individual rights in Constitutional jurisprudence. Lyric poetry and legal rights alike seem to presuppose a firm sense of the individual. Many developments in the twentieth century, however, have conspired to make the idea of an individual far more complex and problematic. The challenge both to poetry and to law, then, has been to articulate a plausible model of the individual—one that takes into account these pressing historical developments. Chapter 3 takes up and elaborates this parallel between poetic and legal developments in the twentieth century.

Here, my hope is that these two practices—legal and literary—will illuminate each other: that the best theory of rights throws light on Stevens, and that Stevens, in turn, may help articulate some features a theory of rights must incorporate to be really persuasive. The idea, however, is not to replace our confusion with confidence, but to explore more deeply the contours of the tensions troubling the surface of law.

Each of the literary works examined in this book comes from a transitional period, and reflects the ambiguities and tensions of such periods. As Theodore Ziolkowski has put it, literary works produced in such transitional eras do not simply refer to law, but tend to call legality itself into question.[30] As such, they are very suggestive for jurisprudence, and cast a

---

30. Ziolkowski, *Mirror of Justice*, 14–19. Such works reflect "those moments of crisis in the evolution of law when the entire system is being challenged" (16). These are works, he writes, in which "it is not the facts that are in question but the values by which the facts are to be judged."

distinctive light on the central jurisprudential question "what is law?" Thus, Aeschylus' *Oresteia,* addressed in Chapter 1, was first performed just as Athens was entering the period of high classicism: the *polis* (city) was taking over from traditional, tribal forms of social organization. At the same time, the mythic concept of the hero that hailed from earlier times was sufficiently vital to make the values of the city seem ambiguous and partial.

Eight hundred years later, St. Augustine elaborated his spiritual program of confession in a period when the "classical" world was on the wane and Christianity was becoming increasingly influential. Christian beliefs provided an external perspective from which the contours, the limits and blind spots of classicism could be assessed. Finally, Wallace Stevens wrote when America was becoming an ever more industrialized and secular mass society, and less and less the rural, Christian America of his youth.

Perhaps because of their transitional status, Aeschylus, Augustine, and Stevens all share a concern with evil—a theme that corrects for what I take to be the excessive optimism of much recent legal theory. Greek tragedy is perhaps the literary genre of evil par excellence: it draws much of its power and fascination from its narratives of laudable human projects fatally undermined and ruined by forces beyond the protagonist's control. The pictures it presents of human life and hopes are at striking odds with the models we find in legal theory. Tragedy has taken on a new relevance as a way of thinking about the flaws and limitations of rationalist confidence in the power to direct one's life as one judges best.[31]

Augustine initially developed his theory of the will in order to explain the origins of evil—to justify the ways of God to man, and to place the blame squarely on humanity's shoulders. But his account became far richer, and ultimately came to look like an interior version of the tragic dilemma between autonomy and destiny. My discussion of Stevens, too, centers around his central poetic concern with evil, which he sought to free from its religious conception as moral evil. His account of a violent, warlike universe hearkens back in some ways to Greek tragic conceptions of a cosmos governed by strife. In his poem "Esthétique du Mal" Stevens presents a moving picture of autonomy as a kind of bereavement—a possible corrective to the political concept of autonomy, which, as often understood, comes to look like a form of licensed selfishness. "Evil" is one name for what prevents law from attaining the simplicity and the separability toward which it aspires. It challenges in sundry ways the great good

---

31. In Chapter 1, Section 3 I assess some recent attempts to use tragedy—in particular, the *Oresteia*—in discussions of political and legal philosophy.

constituted by a public realm of rational discourse. Ultimately, it challenges the goodness of this good, and affords a more nuanced sense of law's aspirations toward simplicity.

The real fruitfulness of thinking about law through imaginative works is that it affords a way of thinking critically and skeptically about law, but in a way that avoids a flattening nihilism. Realist attacks on the claims of law to objectivity and neutrality have been a powerful stimulus in legal theory and practice, but have tended to reduce law to little more than force and coercion. It is one thing to charge the objectivity and neutrality of law with being fictions. If this is to be a truly productive insight, however, we must explore in greater depth what a fiction is; whether it is the sort of thing possible or even desirable to avoid; and how we might incorporate such a view into our thinking about our institutions. Legitimacy is not something factual about a legal system, but an ideal—a fiction that exerts a gravitational pull on it. Imaginative works help us to take fictions seriously for, as self-conscious fictions, they illuminate the role of fiction more generally in human society and its institutions.

Law's Interior, then, is addressed to those interested in legal theory. I hope, however, that it will expand that audience to include humanists as well. I have tried to show what I take to be an important dimension of literature—its continued pertinence when we undertake to think about the law. Literary works have their own inherent fascination, but they also have important social ramifications (this is especially the case with Aeschylus' *Oresteia* and Augustine's *Confessions*). They are, moreover, shaped by the same broad social currents that influence the practice of law (this is especially true of Stevens's poetry). I hope to have shown that law has light to shed on at least some literary works, and vice versa. The point of this book is that law is better thought of as a human practice—not an autonomous system—and that, as such, it should be situated alongside other and kindred human pursuits. Another point is that the theory of law and its legitimacy is an inherent part of law, not a dispensable supplement to it. To take an interest in legal theory, then, is to participate in the law and in the democratic work of constructing society.

CHAPTER 1

The Quest for Autonomy:
Modern Jurisprudence and the Oresteia

To speak of "law and literature" is to make the controversial claim that law is a vital and encompassing human practice—one that poses the kind of human issues addressed by the writers of literary fiction. At first blush, this doesn't sound terribly controversial, and at one level it isn't: what harm could be there be, after all, in casting an occasional side-long glance at the dramatic potential of legal disputes?

But "law and literature" is not simply a dispensable extra—a diversion from the hard work of law. Rather, it makes the serious assertion that literature is essential to our understanding of law. At the theoretical level, it denies that law is an autonomous system—a body of rules that works more or less on its own in accordance with its own internal principles. This claim—which is explicit or implicit in much of the best writing from the "law and literature" school—is controversial because what it denies is such a powerful and in many ways attractive model of the law. For to picture law as an autonomous system is, among other things, to think of it as a way of working out differences in a pluralist society where there are no comprehensive beliefs that are shared by all and that can serve as a basis for consensus. It is important that law not be tied to any particular belief, so that all citizens can respect it, regardless of their other allegiances. The claim that law is autonomous, then, is tied up with some deep and important conceptions about what constitutes a just state in a pluralist society.

But how incomplete this picture of society is, and how much it omits! In sealing law off as an entity in its own right, this approach threatens to make law irrelevant to the broad currents of life swirling around it. To put it paradoxically, the same conditions of dissensus make it both imperative and implausible to think of law as a kind of "safe harbor"—a realm that hovers safely above the fray. Certainly, this insular view of law seems—when you think about it—a highly idealized picture, out of touch with the divisiveness that characterizes some of the most important judicial decisions and insensitive to the disorientation and bewilderment such decisions sometimes provoke.

How to strike the balance between these two intuitions about law—law as removed from, and immersed in, the society it structures? Each picture is to a degree inevitable, and yet the two are to a troubling extent incompatible. If law is an autonomous system (a rational body of coherent rules), it is not the sort of thing that can be much illuminated by literature—the imaginative treatment of vital and conflicting human purposes. That is because the gist of law-as-system is the availability of strictly legal criteria for resolving conflicts in a ready and relatively uncontroversial way: the focus is not on the conflicts but on the power to end them. Conversely, to say that literature truly illuminates the study of law is to present law as something that does not, after all, achieve the well-bounded autonomy, the uncontroversial dispute-resolution that legal theory claims. Law, on this view, is a human practice, susceptible to all the flaws, failures, and conflicts that disturb other such practices.

In this chapter, I try to sort out the claims that each of these models of law has on us. In Section 1, I look at recent American jurisprudence, which presents a picture of law as autonomous—a picture that has achieved considerable subtlety and persuasive force in the hands of Ronald Dworkin and John Rawls but still seems to suffer some important blind spots. Rawls's model of law and "political liberalism" bears a surprising and fruitful resemblance to the account of the origins of the jury and the legal system in Aeschylus' *Oresteia*, and I devote Section 2 to a close reading of that play. The affinities between the *Oresteia* and Rawls's picture of law point to what I think are flaws in the latter—in particular, his insistence on the strict autonomy of law. In Section 3, I survey several writings from the law-and-literature school, and here too the *Oresteia* helps articulate what I think are shortcomings in them—in particular, their stress on the role of the emotions and empathy in adjudication. In Section 4, finally, I offer a statement of what I take to be the genuine theoretical importance of law and literature studies. Here, the challenge is to take seriously the imperfections and tensions troubling law, but at the same time to show why it continues to engage us and to command our (sometimes grudging) respect.

1. Autonomy as an Aspiration

Modern jurisprudence makes the fundamental assertion that law is separate from morals—that law is an autonomous practice, and, in particular, that it is distorted when ultimate values, beliefs, and commitments are invoked to reach legal conclusions. The idea is that only distinctively legal reasons should play a role in determining the outcome of cases at law. Hart's *Concept of Law* is one of the best-known and most influential formulations of this idea.[1] Hart argues that a legal system is a combination of primary rules (commands about what citizens must do or avoid doing in any case) and secondary rules. These latter are rules about *which* commands have the authority of law. One very important secondary rule, for example, is what Hart calls the "rule of recognition"—a rule that spells out what procedural steps are necessary for a command to have the force of law. These secondary rules are not addressed to primary conduct, but set down procedures for making and applying the law: they are *meta*rules, rules about rules. In effect, Hart sees as the distinguishing characteristic of a legal system that it is self-reflexive: not just a body of "transitive" commands (commands directed outward onto those obliged to obey it), but primary commands supplemented by rules about the commands. A valid command, on this view, evinces a certain ruled-ness: it cannot validly claim others' obedience unless it observes the secondary rules itself.

This notion of secondary rules distinguishes Hart's account of law from that of Austin, who famously treated law as "commands backed by threats"—a formulation that posited a difference between law and morals, but made it difficult to distinguish law from, say, a mugger's threat.[2] Hart deepens law's claim on its subjects: when citizens obey the law, they are responding not simply to the threat of punishment, but to the law's acknowledged validity. On the other hand, Hart does not deepen law's claim too much; he does not assert that law is entitled to obedience because it is *just*. Rather, he indicates, it has only the shallower claim of validity: a law is truly a law if it complies with the procedures laid

1. H. L. A. Hart, *The Concept of Law* (Oxford: Oxford University Press, 1961), esp. 97–119. See also Hart, "Positivism and the Separation of Law and Morals," *Harvard Law Review* 71 (1958): 593. For a brief and interesting history of the backgrounds of legal positivism in continental European thought, see Theodore Ziolkowski, *The Mirror of Justice* (Princeton, N.J.: Princeton University Press, 1997), 215–40, and esp. 215–24.

2. John Austin, Lecture I, in *The Province of Jurisprudence Determined* (New York: Noonday Press, 1954), 13. See also Thomas Hobbes, *Leviathan*, Part II chapter 26 ("Of Civil Laws"): "Civil Law is to every subject those rules which the commonwealth hath commanded him by word, writing, or other sufficient sign of the will, to make use of for the distinction of right and wrong—that is to say, of what is contrary and what is not contrary to the rule."

down in law for generating legal commands. The shallowness of this genuine claim, properly understood, discourages citizens from blindly or uncritically obeying the law. It is one of the very considerable merits of Hart's concept that it does not overestimate law's authority.

The elegant self-reflexivity Hart makes a defining characteristic of law serves to make it autonomous and to bound it off from other pursuits and disciplines: as a combination of laws and laws about the laws, it is to a degree self-referential. We can give an account of it in its own terms: legal questions are not parasitic on other—specifically moral—kinds of questions. A legal system is by and large capable of generating valid outcomes solely on the basis of law.

The separateness of law Hart posits has a powerful resonance in a liberal society, one that emerges, for example, in John Rawls's *Political Liberalism*.[3] Rawls begins from the proposition that our pluralist society is marked by disagreement about fundamental, ultimate beliefs, and the existence, side by side, of reasonable but incompatible pictures of the world, the individual, and society.[4] The state, if it is to be stable in a pluralist society, must not implicate any fundamental belief to the exclusion of others, but must be compatible with any reasonable belief. The liberal state, Rawls argues, is a kind of "module" that can be fit into any number of beliefs. A tolerant state that does not coerce on fundamental beliefs is a powerful good, but its goodness can be appreciated from within the perspective of any of a number of belief systems; it is not confined to any specific belief system to the exclusion of others. Rawls's "political liberalism" differs from other kinds of liberalism in that it expressly refrains from basing its account of the state on a picture of what human beings are ultimately like.[5] The liberal state does not claim to mirror any feature supposedly intrinsic or universal in the person. It is confessedly a contin-

3. John Rawls, *Political Liberalism* (New York: Columbia University Press, 1993).

4. Ibid., xxiv: "This pluralism is not seen as disaster but rather as the natural outcome of the activities of human reason under enduring free institutions." See also ibid., 54–58, on the "burdens of judgment"—aspects of judging that naturally tend to cause disagreement among rational persons. Charles Larmore, *Patterns of Ethical Complexity* (Cambridge: Cambridge University Press, 1987), xii-xiii, traces back to John Locke's *Letter Concerning Toleration* the idea that reason does not tend toward single solutions and unanimity of opinion.

5. This differs from Rawls's position in *A Theory of Justice* (Cambridge: Harvard University Press, 1971), part III, where he arguably presented the liberal state as the reflection of a particular view of the self. Larmore, *Patterns of Moral Complexity*, 118–30, criticizes Rawls's discussion in *A Theory of Justice* for failing to make clear that the conception of man articulated in part III of that work is intended solely as a political conception, not a comprehensive moral doctrine. Rawls has accepted Larmore's criticism, and sought to make the distinction clear. See Rawls, *Political Liberalism*, 176–77, n. 3.

gent arrangement that answers to the specific historical conditions of dissensus that characterize modern societies.

Law, for Rawls, is the "public reason" of the "module" state: it is a way of reasoning about the political community—who we are, what direction we want to go—without committing to a specific moral vision. Law works in terms of reasons other reasonable persons could be expected to find persuasive.[6] The separateness that characterized law in Hart returns in Rawls, now enriched. Social conditions of pluralism and dissensus now require that citizens argue and reflect in specifically legal terms—at least for public purposes—because law is not tied to any particular moral vision, and therefore is compatible with any reasonable belief about ultimate matters.

Ronald Dworkin's well-known legal theory is closely related to that of Rawls, and supplements and corrects the picture Hart gives.[7] Dworkin presents law as, in important part, a form of discourse, an ongoing debate about the principles informing our legal institutions. Of course, the majority of cases can be settled more or less without controversy under the authority of existing rules and precedents. In unsettled, rapidly developing times, however, courts are increasingly faced with situations in which the rules give out: they do not clearly indicate a determinate legal outcome. Dworkin's jurisprudence focuses especially on these "hard cases." They are no longer the exception to the rule (as they tended to appear in Hart), but are crucial for an understanding of what a legal system is. Dworkin's point is that hard cases are not decided by the judge's individual moral predilections. Even where the rules do not unambiguously dictate a particular outcome, cases are decided in distinctly legal terms. But Dworkin broadens the scope of what counts as a legal argument: a legal system does not consist simply in primary and secondary rules, but also in principles that inform the institutions that generate the rules. In a case where no existing rule conclusively determines the outcome, courts have recourse to the principles underlying the rules and to precedents that are relevant, but not dispositive.

Judgment in a hard case consists in projecting these informing principles into the present, to see what they require in novel and unprecedented situations. A correct judgment in a hard case is the one that gives the best account of the precedents—the reading that encompasses the greatest amount of existing relevant law, and presents the most com-

6. See Rawls, *Political Liberalism*, 212–54. For example, he writes, "[O]ur exercise of public power is proper and hence legitimate only when it is exercised in accordance with a constitution the essentials of which all citizens may reasonably be expected to endorse in the light of principles and ideals acceptable to them as reasonable and rational" (217).

7. Ronald Dworkin, *Law's Empire* (Cambridge: Harvard University Press, 1986).

pelling, plausible account of the principles underlying it. Dworkin invents a mythical judge, Hercules, who is ideally capable of encompassing the law and seeing down through the countless rules and precedents to the principles animating them, and then extrapolating an outcome from those principles. That they are controversial does not undermine the authority of Hercules' judgments in hard cases, for it is a mark of vitality when an institution continues to generate debate about what it stands for, and what it requires in a given situation. Hard cases show that law is ultimately an ongoing discourse about what law is—what are the principles underlying the legal system.

By expanding law's "empire" to include principles as well as rules, Dworkin mitigates some of the harsh amorality of Hart's account. He assumes, with Rawls, that there is a morality implicit in our institutions. This does not wipe out the boundary between law and morals, however, because this public morality is different from moral questions that are relevant to private life or that entail fundamental questions about how to live and what to do. Partly for this reason, Dworkin does not assert that our institutions are just. He makes the more modest claim that they have "integrity":[8] one may not agree with every legal outcome, but it should be possible to see that the outcomes are at least consistent and principled. This notion of integrity, even though it is something less than justice, nonetheless deepens law's claim on citizens. No longer does the authority of law consist, as it did for Hart, in the rather thin concept of "validity" (adherence to certain procedural norms); rather, it is based on the legal system's commitment to standing by its precedents and to seeing what the principles informing those precedents require in any given situation. We might say that Dworkin aims to show that law's claim on its citizens is not merely valid, but *legitimate;* that is, the legal system demonstrably possesses a quality (integrity) that gives the system a moral authority: it is truly entitled to citizens' obedience, and its use of coercion is morally unobjectionable.

The boundedness of law—its autonomy and separation from morals—has proved a constant in this line of thinking, from Austin through Rawls and Dworkin. At the same time, the way law's autonomy is conceived has become more and more sophisticated. Instead of Austin's rather crude notion of a command backed by a threat, the boundary has come to express in Dworkin and Rawls an affirmative picture of law as central to the democratic process. It is the way citizens try to articulate the community's scheme of principles and values.[9] Law is our clearly demarcated forum of principle—the activity

8. Ibid., 188.
9. Ibid., 190.

in which citizens return again and again to the moral sources of their polity and institutions, and debate about the best way to make these principles felt in concrete cases. Law is the primary means of making public life ever more consistent with the political community's foundational principles. That is the source of its claim to citizens' obedience.

This is an attractive picture of law—indeed, as I want to show in this chapter, it is *too* attractive, for it ignores or de-emphasizes features of the law that are an important part of our intuitive sense of it. For example, the coerciveness of law inevitably presents problems for theoretical attempts to justify it. Coercion cannot fully reflect our dignity, and shows that law— whatever else it may be—is a burden imposed on us, something we must perforce obey. Dworkin and Rawls portray law as reflecting our capacity for freedom, our dignity as beings capable of legislating rules of general import. They obscure law, however, by taking too sublime a view of it and of human conduct. They do not justify the state's actual exercise of force, emphasizing instead the state's restraint in exercising it. Dworkin's operating assumption is that if you can offer a reason for the use of force—which is essentially what courts do—then you have rendered that use uncontroversial. He can then argue that the state's use of coercion is legitimate partly because of its integrity: force is unleashed only in accordance with rules and precedents. Dworkin concludes that law is something different from force, and that law has the moral authority to use coercion. But that conclusion was implicit already in his initial assumption that law can be described coherently without reference to force. If you set force aside provisionally, then you can demonstrate that law has an independent, moral claim to our allegiance. Dworkin ignores the fact that, without force backing it up, the justice (or the integrity) of a decision would scarcely suffice to make it authoritative. In short, Dworkin's apologia for law does not quite tame the disturbing, and delegitimizing, role of coercion in our legal arrangements.

What we may want to say, in Dworkin's behalf, is that coercion is just a fact of social life, a necessity. The most we can hope to do is to see that it is not unjust. This, indeed, is one of the tasks modern liberalism arguably sets itself: to ensure that matters that lie partly outside our control are nonetheless rendered not unjust to the extent possible.[10] But this is a rather less ambitious program than Dworkin apparently undertakes: he wishes to establish that a thriving legal system has some affirmative moral

---

10. Bernard Williams, *Shame and Necessity*, Sather Classical Lectures (Berkeley: University of California, 1993), 128–29, writes:

[Modern liberalism] has given itself the task of constructing a framework of social justice to control necessity and chance, in the sense both of mitigating their effects on the

claim on us, not merely that it is "not unjust." In trying to establish that stronger claim, however, he supposes that coercion can be wholly subsumed within a theory of justification, and that assumption, as I have suggested, distorts his discussion.

Rawls's arguments are also problematic. His account of the state and the separateness of law calls for a great deal of sophistication in citizens: they must in the first place be able to appreciate the reasonableness of other fundamental comprehensive world-visions incompatible with their own. They must also be willing to think and argue in terms that leave to one side their deepest beliefs, and to reason solely on grounds that others could reasonably be expected to accept. This, however, puts considerable stress on the individual's powers of cognitive dissonance. These requirements are sufficiently exacting that failures to achieve them must be expected, and they therefore need to find some reflection in theory. To be sure, Rawls asserts that such complications can be ignored at least preliminarily for theoretical purposes. But can they? The point is that ignoring them distorts the theory and makes it to that extent unpersuasive.

Below I set forth in more detail reasons why Rawls's and Dworkin's case is hobbled by their insistence on a supposed "bright-line" distinction between law and morality: briefly, I think their account is psychologically unpersuasive, and that it fails to do justice to the most wrenching legal issues courts have had to address in the last fifty years. I wish to present a different picture of the boundary between law and morals, one that presents it more dynamically as unstable and open to contest. On the view taken here, law is a selection or winnowing of the profuse and inconsistent meanings that confront us: it is a simplification, for social purposes, of what I shall call our "ethical complexity." This simplification makes possible a stable order by providing a common set of understandings that sideline, for public purposes, the commitments and values that constitute people's deepest sense of their identity. These commitments and values, however, continue to press on law, and call for it to incorporate more aspects of citizens' deeper sense of their identity. Law, on this view, is caught in a bind between two imperatives: to simplify (in the interests of efficiency, clarity, order), and to make more complex (in the interests of fairness, equity). The tension between these two imperatives is a force for change in the law, and, more deeply, for change in our sense of what law is and its role in a democratic society. It will be the task of this book to

---

individual and of showing that what cannot be mitigated is not unjust. It is a distinctively modern achievement to have set the problem. However, we shall not know how great our distance really is from the ancient world until we are in a position to claim, not merely that there is this task, but that we have some hope of carrying it out.

work out this model of law in more detail. I want, on the one hand, to correct for what I take to be the excessive optimism of Dworkin's and Rawls's pictures of law, and their assumption that a stable boundary can be maintained between citizens' sense of their public and private selves. On the other hand, I will also want to show, especially in Chapter 3, that this tension in law does not reduce it to incoherence, a charge that has been made against it.

I begin by sketching out what I mean by "ethical complexity." The portrait I offer is meant to reflect a psychologically more compelling account of ourselves as moral agents. To regain a sense of this complexity has been the point of a growing body of work. My sketch draws from a variety of sources,[11] expressing from different points of view a common conviction that the ethical life is not captured by a morality of duty, and does not consist simply in adhering to certain rule-like obligations. One problem with such a view is that it tends to make the ethical life look occasional, switching on and off depending on whether we are faced with the performance of a duty at any given time. This model of the ethical life can scarcely do justice to that aspect of ourselves that is constantly open to (re)assessing what constitutes a good life and judging how we ought to live and to act. Beyond that, value—evaluating our lives and options, determining how best to discover and bring about what we value—is far deeper and more pervasive in our lives than a model of "duty morality" can convey. Iris Murdoch suggests this pervasiveness and depth when she writes that "consciousness is a form of moral activity: what we attend to, how we attend, whether we attend."[12] "I want to say that the emergence of awareness, perception, judgment, knowledge, in consciousness is a process in which value (moral colour) is inherent."[13] Murdoch's point has a distinctive resonance in an era familiar with the Freudian notion of an unconscious—that is, a depth to the self that makes us not wholly avail-

---

11. (1) Aristotelian. See, e.g., Martha C. Nussbaum, *The Fragility of Goodness* (Cambridge: Cambridge University Press, 1986), 290–317; and the same author's "An Aristotelian Conception of Rationality," in *Love's Knowledge* (Oxford: Oxford University Press, 1990), 35–44, 54–105.

(2) Communitarian. See, e.g., Charles Taylor, *Philosophical Arguments* (Cambridge: Harvard University Press, 1995), esp. 165–80, 181–203; and the same author's *Sources of the Self* (Cambridge: Harvard University Press, 1989), esp. 495–521; Michael Sandel, *Liberalism and the Limits of Justice* (Cambridge: Cambridge University Press, 1982), 179–83; and Alastair MacIntyre, *After Virtue*, 2d ed. (Notre Dame, Ind.: University of Notre Dame Press, 1984), esp. 204–25.

(3) Liberal. See J. Donald Moon, *Constructing Community* (Princeton, N.J.: Princeton University Press, 1993), 20–26; and Larmore, *Moral Complexity*.

12. Iris Murdoch, *Metaphysics as a Guide to Morals* (London: Penguin, 1992), 167.

13. Ibid., 250.

able to ourselves. Values form us, without our necessarily being entirely aware of their significance in our lives.

Once the ethical life is understood in this way—as the life of assessing and valuing, as distinguished from a morality of duty—the relation between law and our moral or ethical lives takes on a new color. When morality is looked upon as something law-like (consisting of rules that should be obeyed), the relation of law and morality entails the comparison of two similar things (even though one might conclude that the two are separate). Once the ethical life is conceived as an inescapable element in our lives, however, the relation between law and morals becomes necessarily more complex. Relegating one aspect of ourselves to a strictly public zone begins to look problematic, and the claim that it can be done once and for all seems unduly optimistic and psychologically implausible.

Ethical complexity, then, arises in the first place from the deep and abiding power that certain commitments have for us—the allegiance we owe our families, for example, or the beliefs and communities in which we have been raised. We do not choose such commitments; rather, we grow up into them. Upon attaining adulthood, we recognize that by dint of the love and protection our parents have afforded us, no less than by the authority they have exercised over us, we have profound duties toward them, and that these duties have made us who we are. Such duties are not given as propositions or rules—at least not primarily—but are fundamentally affective in nature; the affects in question, moreover, have roots in our earliest childhood. As a result, the commitment to parents and the beliefs we have been raised in "constitute" us in a way not fully available to us. To reflect on familial duties is in an important way to discover what is already there, to retrieve a part of ourselves that had been perhaps partially obscured. Such duties are like a horizon orienting our lives; they partly provide us with our sense of identity. We might, upon reflection, refuse to honor such duties, but such refusal, even if justified, would nonetheless reflect a profound change in our sense of who we are.

Because we do not, in the first instance, rationally choose what we value, no guarantee exists that our antecedent commitments will be in all circumstances fully compatible with each other. Part of our ethical complexity, in other words, arises from the fact that no single metric exists whereby we can, when in doubt, determine which duties take precedence. Each commitment reflects a distinct value in its own right. While circumstances may force us to choose one value over another, we feel this as a truly agonizing decision—not a discovery that one commitment was in fact less valuable than we had previously thought, but the realization that, in these circumstances, we cannot be true to two values, both of which we cherish. In short, conflict between a plurality of genuine goods and commitments and the anguish such conflict gives rise to are an important part of our moral experience and contribute to the complexity of that experience.

Even where such a choice is forced on us, we may not be able to avoid a certain remorse for our failure to live out a commitment to a particular ideal or value. That is, we bear responsibility for those of our actions that violate one set of values, even in situations where we acted out of fidelity to another set of equally valid commitments. As Bernard Williams has recently put it, our actions possess a certain "authority" in our lives, whether or not they were fully intentional.[14] Thus, we remain in an important way responsible for our actions, even if we cannot be said to have exercised full dominion over them. Here, too, the world—understood now to include our own conduct—contains meanings we did not intend or fashion. Our ethical experience, then, is in part shaped by the existence of conflicts that make it difficult or impossible to speak of a simple "right" or "wrong" course of action, conflicts in which one may suffer deeply painful consequences, notwithstanding one's efforts to act as well as possible in difficult circumstances. In other words, part of the complexity of our ethical lives is the experience of situations beyond our ability to classify as good or evil.

This picture of ourselves and our ethical life is by now a familiar one: it is associated particularly with the "communitarians," who challenge the liberal vision of Rawls and Dworkin,[15] but it is by no means confined to them:[16] indeed, it plays an important role in the work of both Rawls and Dworkin.[17] The sketch above does not purport to pronounce on ultimate issues of the meaning of the person, or the relation between the self and the world, but rather to outline a psychologically more persuasive account of the ethical life. It points to a different model of law as a deliberate simplification of the ethical complexities I have sketched. Once situated within an account of intricate moral beings law emerges as a kind of "terminable analysis"; it makes possible an *arresting* of scrutiny at some predetermined point through the introduction of certain formal criteria

14. Williams, *Shame and Necessity*, 69.

15. See, e.g., Sandel, *Liberalism*, 179–83.

16. See Bernard Williams, *Ethics and the Limits of Philosophy* (Cambridge: Harvard University Press, 1985), 174–96; Thomas Nagel, "The Fragmentation of Value," in *Mortal Questions* (Cambridge: Cambridge University Press, 1979), 128–41; Lawrence A. Blum, *Friendship, Altruism and Morality* (London: Routledge, 1980).

17. See, e.g., Rawls, *Theory of Justice*, part III, and esp. 462–67, 486, 490; Dworkin, *Law's Empire*, 190–216.

for recognizing and assessing the validity of rules. It affords an artificial end to disputes: one that stops the dispute less because of its inherent wisdom—its ability truly to resolve the deepest issues posed by the case—but rather because it bears the hallmarks of authority; it adheres to those procedural steps generally recognized as securing validity and authority for an enactment or a decision. On the view proposed here, "validity" tacitly recognizes the impossibility of securing a sure and universally recognized justice. It incorporates, so to speak, a principle of modesty by eschewing any claim to be absolutely right and settling for being "good enough." Validity, in other words, reflects law's exclusion of endless analysis—its crying "halt" at some point before the analysis has truly exhausted itself.

Law does not stably "possess" the moral legitimacy Dworkin attributes to it. This is not to deny that law can lay some moral claim to citizens' obedience, but Dworkin conceives of it too simply, as a quality demonstrably inhering in the legal system. Rather, as I shall argue, law arises from the attempt to keep the intricacies of our moral life at a remove and to establish a more manageable realm or arena where we can control the meanings of our acts, and, in particular, where the intentional or voluntary character of an agent's acts is an important, indeed decisive, consideration. The purpose of this simplification is to make possible a life together in society: it provides a preset and knowable way to settle disputes. In its own domain, law tends to sideline moral reflection by providing, first, a readily ascertainable answer to the question of what we should do, and second, a powerful reason—threats of punishment—for doing what should be done. Laws tend to displace moral reasoning and to make it, to some extent, irrelevant.

While law is different from morality, however, it is nonetheless deeply implicated in it, since it arises by seeking actively to distinguish its ethically complex sources. The relation between law and its sources is unstable and dynamic: the boundaries are subject to constant challenge. The complexity law rejects continues to press upon it, and requires law to become more responsive to our full moral dimensions. Indeed, precisely because it uses force to back its commands, law must continually defend and justify itself, in order to distinguish itself from mere force.[18] In attempting to secure legitimacy, therefore, law must attempt to be responsive to our complex moral nature. In other words, it must seek to avoid those coercive simplifications that undermine its legitimacy, once they come to be felt as reductive and insulting. Rather than a quality inhering in law, then, legiti-

18. To be sure, we can conceive of an ideal, circumscribed community where laws are not backed by threats, and solely reflect the aspirations of the community, each of whom fully endorses and desires to live up to these aspirations. Such a vision seems utopian, however, not least in its assumption that a single value or single set of values exists that all

macy is more like a project, an ongoing effort to incorporate emerging conceptions of the self and society.

At the same time, however, law cannot reflect the full scope of our moral life without ceasing to be what it is—a means of avoiding the intractable conflicts our ethical complexity entails. In reducing the ethical life to a set of rules, the law necessarily obscures or silences some voices or considerations, or at least makes it more difficult for them to be heard. I will suggest that the law cannot be completely legitimized—that is, it cannot be brought to a degree of responsiveness to our ethical complexity that would make it universally approved or approvable. Theories that hope to secure legitimacy as something stably or demonstrably "possessed" by a legal system are too optimistic. This chapter is in part an attempt to offer a model of law that captures this paradoxical feature: law's need for moral authority if it is to function as law, and the impossibility of finally securing such authority.

Dworkin's account of the sources of legal obligation attempts to take into account the richer sense of the person and personal identity sketched above. In my view, however, he does not succeed, and the reasons for his failure are instructive. Theories of consent or unjust enrichment, Dworkin writes, fail to explain the genuine moral claim law has to citizens' obedience, because they keep the relation between the individual and the political community too much at arm's length. They assume that we exist apart from our obligations—so that they attach to us only if we voluntarily accept them, or affirmatively do things that commit us to them. The moral obligation of law seems to go deeper than that: not only are we raised in a world that is populated with obligations, but we come to know our environment partly through our growing sense of our existing obligations toward it. The family and our obligations to it offer the readiest example of the way duties indubitably attach to us, even though we have not "consented" to them. Dworkin, accordingly, assimilates the political community to the family, as a way of explaining the sources of our moral obligation toward the law.[19] We grow up within a political community, animated by certain vital principles. We have an obligation to that community, for reasons analogous to those underlying the duties of respect, concern, and love we owe our families.

---

members of a community—even a highly circumscribed and select one—would find at all times fulfilling and complete. In the absence of such rarefied conditions, law seems to have an ineradicable coercive character—one that inevitably makes its claims to legitimacy open to challenge.

19. Dworkin, *Law's Empire*, 204–5. See too Philip Soper, *A Theory of Law* (Cambridge: Harvard University Press, 1984), 77–80.

The problem, however, is that this deepens law's claims of moral authority too much. Assimilating it to the family distorts the quality and character of legal obligation. For example, the depth of the sources of one's duty toward the family makes such obligations overwhelming and irresistible. These duties are finally inextricable from the passions that nurture them, and these passions in turn are rooted in strong and even ambivalent feelings of love and aversion—the ambivalence Freud identified as "the family romance." In short, the duties we owe to our family are so much more emotionally charged than our ties to the political community that they belong to a different order altogether. In assimilating political obligation to a powerful source of moral feelings—the family—Dworkin risks losing what is distinctive about law: the family threatens to overwhelm the thinner, more "detachable" obligations one owes to the political community.

Dworkin attempts to overcome this problem by offering a highly unrealistic picture of family life, one that makes it look more like a political community. Thus, he writes, a daughter owes a duty to defer to her father's choice of a spouse for her *only* if the family is a "true community"— a question that turns in part on whether it "genuinely accept[s] that women are as important as men."[20] Supposing that the family does so, the daughter may nonetheless marry against her father's wishes, but she has to confront a genuine conflict of duties, and has cause to regret her failure to obey her father. Yet there seems little doubt that the daughter, as Dworkin conceives her, will marry as she pleases.

There are at least two objections to this account. First, Dworkin's description is too idealized, and obscures the coercion that is an inextricable part of one's family relations.[21] Dworkin ignores the crushing effect the family's condemnation of the recalcitrant daughter is likely to have. It is unlikely that any young woman—except the most educated and financially independent—would ever sort through her options in a way even remotely like the process Dworkin envisions. Such duties do not permit

20. Dworkin, *Law's Empire*, 204.
21. The same may be said of Rawls's account of the origins of obligation in part III of *A Theory of Justice*, 462–96, and especially 462–67, 486, 490. Rawls argues there that the child's sense of duty toward the family is the result and sign of the child's experience of being loved and loving. Rawls's account is one of the most stimulating and beautiful parts of his theory, but it too is highly idealized, and the idealizations have the effect of distorting the picture of the family. For it seems clear that ambivalence is a part of our attitude toward our families, and that our sense of legal duty shares this ambivalence. To the extent that the family provides a model for political obligation, then, it also presents a subversive element, and suggests that ambivalence about the law—as coercive, threatening, harsh—is part of our experience of it.

that critical distance—the space in which we can coolly assess them—that is an important aspect of our political obligations.

That, in fact, is the second flaw in Dworkin's account: that he makes family obligations too revocable, too subject to rational inquiry. A daughter might be aware that neither her family nor her society at large treats women as equals, and to that extent she might feel that her father's command is unjust and onerous. The injustice of the command, however, does not *extinguish* its compelling force, if only because of the powerful emotional ties binding daughter to family. Dworkin treats this conflict as merely "apparent," since in fact the woman is under no "real" obligation, and is morally free to marry whomever she likes. The distinction between real and merely apparent conflicts surely makes little difference to most young women actually contemplating resistance to their families' wishes in a vital matter. Dworkin misses or represses that painful ambivalence and conflict that seems a constituent part of one's experience of the family.[22] In sum, Dworkin has recourse to the family in order to make sense of legal obligation, but, once introduced, it threatens to overwhelm the very concept it was intended to explain. He is obliged to offer a highly idealized and unpersuasive description of the family—one that unduly simplifies it—in order to maintain the coherence of his account.

Rawls's account of the separation of public and private is similarly unpersuasive. In his chapter on "The Idea of Public Reason," Rawls emphasizes its circumscribed nature: public reason—even, or perhaps especially, in matters of the greatest public import—should not necessarily be addressed publicly in terms individuals believe to have the best grasp on truth; rather, they should confine themselves to "common-sense" methods of reasoning about public principles. A commitment to public reason, then, is a commitment to *not* getting at the whole truth, as the individual subscribing to particular belief might see it.[23]

Yet Rawls's insistence on a sharp line dividing the values admissible in public reason from those informing other types of reasoning poses considerable difficulties. He discusses the case of the abolitionists, who lacked the public reasons to condemn slavery—for example, the Thir-

---

22. A persistent problem with liberal theory seems to be that it cannot give an adequate account of the family, since family ties and the situation of individual members within the family are strikingly at odds with the individualistic, rational picture of the self congenial to liberal theory. See, for example, the unconvincing description of the family in John Locke, *Second Treatise of Government*, para. 55. Soper's description of the family as a model for political obligation seems to me to suffer from much the same kind of defects as I have sought to identity in Dworkin's account. See Soper, *Theory of Law*, 77–80.

23. Rawls, *Political Liberalism*, 212–54.

teenth and Fourteenth Amendments—that the civil rights movement of the 1950s and 1960s had at its disposal.[24] As a result, the abolitionists often invoked religious reasons for condemning slavery. Did they, Rawls asks, therefore violate the limits of public reason?

His answer is curiously fussy. He writes: "Surely [the abolitionists] hoped for [the destruction of the great evil and curse of slavery] and they could have seen their actions as the best way to bring about a well-ordered and just society in which the ideal of public reason could eventually be honored."[25] The abolitionists, Rawls suggests, did not go against the ideal of public reason—despite their use of religious imagery and religious arguments—if on reflection they believed that "the comprehensive reasons they appealed to were required to give sufficient strength to the political conception to be subsequently realized."[26] This seems a strangely tepid description of the abolitionists' moral fervor: Rawls tries to pierce a religious veil to get at something more acceptable underneath.

Moreover, even to pose the question of whether the abolitionists "went against" the ideal of public reason seems odd. Clearly, the abolitionists' condemnations of slavery added substantially to the public debate. If what the abolitionists said had *solely* to do with their own view of good—if what they said seemed merely unreasonable to others—their speeches would have been greeted with silence and indifference. The fact that they did excite public debate demonstrates that people knew what the abolitionists were talking about. The power of their message to move others shows its public nature.

"Public reason," in other words, cannot be confined to a particular self-existing ideal that individuals either conform to or violate. Rather, it is a concept that develops as the debate evolves; it is shaped in large part by the considerations people find relevant. As an ideal, it is to a substantial extent informed by actual practice. This is not to say that we cannot point to certain boundaries demarcating public reason; rather, it indicates that such boundaries are provisional at best, and will yield to accommodate new perceptions of the relevant considerations. Rawls gives the appearance at least of setting down the boundaries antecedently and only then determining whether a particular argument falls within or outside them. The quite strict boundary Rawls posits—between public and other forms of reason—distorts our understanding of the political community and the

24. Ibid., 249–51.
25. Ibid., 250.
26. Ibid., 251.

way it reasons.[27] Rawls offers little sense of the dynamism of public reason, its ability to respond to and incorporate novel considerations.

Another, potentially more serious problem with Rawls's approach is that the retreat to a public ground may itself seem illegitimate, obscuring what is truly at issue. Perhaps the most striking contemporary example of this is abortion, a subject Rawls treats only briefly in *Political Liberalism*.[28] Once posed in terms of public reason, the abortion issue inevitably presents the question of women's status as equal citizens, and, as Rawls states, any reasonable balance of the publicly relevant factors will give a woman a "duly qualified right to decide whether or not to end her pregnancy during the first trimester."[29] In other words, far from enabling the parties to continue the discussion on the basis of mutually agreeable values, posing the question in public terms of "rights" effectively *ends* the debate. To speak of "rights" conjures up a world view that privileges reason and individual autonomy. Those opposing the availability of abortion might wish to do so precisely on grounds that question the centrality of reason or the value of autonomy.[30] Thus, instead of sealing off public debate from intractable problems, the boundaries Rawls envisions may make the debate even more bitter and divisive, for these public terms seem to predetermine the result and to silence opposing voices before the fact.

To think through what a model avoiding these flaws might look like, I propose to look at Aeschylus' *Oresteia*—which is an account of the rise of

27. This is a surprising flaw, since Rawls's theory of justice was in substantial part formed by new and turbulent developments in American society—the civil rights movement in the early 1960s (which informed his treatment of civil disobedience in *A Theory of Justice*, 363–77, 382–91), and the student antiwar movement in the later 1960s (which prompted his theory of "conscientious refusal" in *Theory of Justice*, 377–82). Rawls's chapters on civil disobedience are among the most fruitful and interesting things he has had to say about law (far more interesting, for example, than the rather mechanical treatment in his chapter on the "Rule of Law," in *Theory of Justice*, 235–43). It is strange, then, that his theory of public reason should have little to say about change and development, and indeed tends rather to deny its possibility.

28. Rawls confines his comments on abortion to a single footnote. See *Political Liberalism*, 243 n. 32, in which Rawls essentially endorses the position taken by the Supreme Court in *Roe v. Wade*, 410 U.S. 113 (1973)—i.e., that a woman has a right (subject to some qualifications) to decide whether or not to terminate her pregnancy during the first trimester. On the difficulties of Rawls's argument on the abortion issue, see, e.g., Michael Sandel's review of *Political Liberalism* in *Harvard Law Review* 107 (1994): 1765, 1782–89; Richard A. Posner, *Overcoming Law* (Cambridge: Harvard University Press, 1995), 188–91.

29. Rawls, *Political Liberalism*, 243 n. 32.

30. See for example the attitudes of women active in the "pro-life" movement, as reported by Kristen Luker, *Abortion and the Politics of Motherhood* (Berkeley: University of

the state (more correctly, the *polis*) from a reign of violence occasioned by the characters' powerful, but incompatible, ideas of justice.[31] The *Oresteia* bears a surprising but suggestive resemblance to Rawls's account of the rise of the liberal state as an escape from sectarian violence: in both, the state offers a "thinning out" of meaning that makes life together in a stable society possible. Yet the *Oresteia* offers the more persuasive picture of law. Rawls wants to maintain a distance between the self and its institutions—a disparity between man as he most deeply is and the institutions he erects to curtail and control his native condition. "The most intractable struggles," he writes, ". . . are confessedly for the sake of the highest things: for religion, for philosophical views of the world, and for different moral conceptions of the good."[32] The liberal state is a historically contingent arrangement designed to avoid these intractable struggles. More specifically, Rawls traces the origins of the modern liberal state to the religious civil wars of the seventeenth century: it is, above all, a response to the disastrous attempts to enshrine a particular comprehensive doctrine in the state. The liberal state offers a deliberately thin view of the self, one designed *not* to express its full depth, its ethical complexity. Rawls treats the liberal state as though it were a solution, once and for all, to the problems posed by a plurality of comprehensive, mutually incompatible beliefs. But why suppose that the line remains stable and uncontested, or that it is objectively or demonstrably correct? As the controversy swirling around the abortion issue suggests, this boundary is itself something that gets hammered out in public debate. The type of dissensus Rawls treats is confined to a rather lofty kind of conflict among articulable doctrines. Conflicts based on race, sex, or money are too elementary for his far more intellectual brand of dissensus, and therefore fall outside the type of "rational comprehensive doctrines" he addresses. Yet it is conflicts of this basic and intractable sort that truly threaten the coherence of society and its ability to function.

The *Oresteia*, too, is an account of the emergence of law, but it explores—in a way Rawls does not—the depth of those incompatible convictions that are excluded once the legal system is instituted, and addresses the role of subrational conflicts (especially those of sex and gender) in law and the state. The *Oresteia* suggests how such excluded meanings continue to press upon the state, and to require it to redraw the line, to simplify less

---

California Press, 1984), 161–62; see also Posner, *Overcoming Law*, 190–91; Moon, *Constructing Community*, 78–80.

31. I discuss the *Oresteia* in Section 2, below.

32. Rawls, *Political Liberalism*, 4.

and to incorporate a more complex model of the self. Rawls's account of the origins of the liberal state and the division between self and state seem to me to tend in this direction, without however carrying the point all the way through. The *Oresteia* provides a model that captures, as against Rawls and Dworkin, the *instability* of the boundary between the public and private. Aeschylus' trilogy has often been read as celebrating the triumph of reason and law over passion and vengeance. On that view, the optimism of the *Oresteia* parallels Rawls's model of the liberal state as a successful solution to incompatible religious beliefs. The dramatic structure of the *Oresteia,* on the other hand, is sufficiently flexible to accommodate another reading: one that questions the success of the state or *polis* in curing the deep conflicts it has so powerfully dramatized.

It was Aeschylus' splendid idea that the age-old, bloodcurdling tale of the House of Atreus was essentially a story about people's search for justice. Just by virtue of its dramatic, narrative modality, the *Oresteia* approaches the origins of the state from a perspective different from that of philosophy. It presents the state as emerging from individual human purposes for which we feel some sympathy, even though we see that they are limited and partial. One of the distinguishing features of the old Greek tragedies was that they turned the grandiose and remote figures of the mythic past into identifiable human beings, with fears, anxieties, projects, and limitations. The actors performing the *Oresteia,* for example, "impersonated" Agamemnon, Clytaemnestra, and Orestes not only in the straightforward sense that they pretended to be them, but in the deeper sense, too, that they made "persons" of them—agents with histories and hopes, who deliberated about their acts and took responsibility for them.

The devastation brought about by the individual characters' search for justice shows the imperative need for some workable, stable form of justice—a state-run legal system that achieves a good enough justice through procedural regularity. At the same time, however, the depth of these characters' passion for justice, and the multifarious motives underlying it, must call into question the stability of the final resolution. The *Oresteia,* then, helps loosen up some of the rigidity of the separation of law and morals—the division between public and private—that makes the legal theory of Rawls and Dworkin seem overly simplified and unpersuasive. It suggests that such a distinction exists, but that it can be challenged, and that the disparity between self and state is a destabilizing element that a legal system must somehow accommodate.

The *Oresteia* is pertinent not only because of its suggestive parallel to Rawls's account of the rise of the liberal state, but, more generally, because as tragedy performed in Athens it was, in an important way, a city's reflection on itself. Tragedy was a thoroughly civic genre, to an extent difficult to appreciate today. The *Oresteia* was performed as an official part of a state-run religious festival. It was selected for performance by state officials and judged by representatives from each of the ten tribes constituting the Athenian citizen body. Aeschylus was an Athenian who had fought the Persians in the famous and fateful battles of Salamis and Plataea. He not only wrote the three plays making up the *Oresteia,* but apparently acted in them at their performance at the City Dionysia in 458 B.C.

The *Oresteia* resonates with contemporary efforts to make Athens more deeply democratic, and to loosen the grip of the old aristocracy. For example, the democratic leader Ephialtes had recently redirected Athenian foreign policy away from Sparta, by entering into a treaty with Argos—an event Aeschylus almost certainly alludes to at the conclusion of the *Oresteia,* when Orestes promises eternal friendship between Argos and Athens. The establishment of the Areopagus as a court to address homicide cases—the central event in the last play of the *Oresteia*—unmistakably alludes to Ephialtes' democratic reforms of the Areopagus three years previously. Ephialtes had stripped this once powerful aristocratic body of most of its powers, effectively reducing it to a court with jurisdiction over homicide cases—the feature of it that Aeschylus celebrates. It is difficult to discern Aeschylus' attitude toward the reforms: did he see them as restoring the Areopagus to its original democratic function? The important point for my purposes, however, is that the *Oresteia* bristled with references to contemporary Athenian politics.[33]

Greek tragedy, then, was through and through a phenomenon of the *polis* and of the distinctive modes of organization and thinking characteristic of the city. Indeed, as Jean-Pierre Vernant writes, "Tragedy was one of the forms through which the new democratic city established its identity."[34] In the *polis,* man began to experiment with a sense of autonomy, of his ability to make his own world. Through the public dramatic festivals at which the tragedies were staged, the city considered the old heroic myths in light of its own ideals. Greek tragedy took place on two planes: the con-

33. On references in the *Oresteia* to contemporary political events, see, e.g., Alan H. Sommerstein, *Aeschylus: Eumenides* (Cambridge: Cambridge University Press, 1989), 25–32. See also C. W. MacLeod, "Politics and the *Oresteia,*" in *Journal of Hellenic Studies* 102 (1982): 124–44; Anthony J. Podlecki, *The Political Background of Aeschylean Tragedy* (Ann Arbor: University of Michigan Press, 1966); K. J. Dover, "The Political Aspect of Aeschylus's Eumenides," *Journal of Hellenic Studies* 77 (1957): 230–37.

34. Jean-Pierre Vernant, "Aeschylus, the Past and the Present," in Jean-Pierre Vernant and Pierre Vidal-Naquet, *Myth and Tragedy in Ancient Greece,* trans. by Janet Lloyd (New York: Zone, 1988), 257.

temporary and the mythic past; the civic and the heroic. Thus, in the
Oresteia, Aeschylus took the transgressive myths of old, with their strange
tales of parricide and incest, and subjected them to a new, distinctively
legal scrutiny: he treated Orestes' matricide as though it were conduct ad-
dressable in Athenian courts. The "ambiguity and tension" that characterize Greek tragedy arise from the inherent power of myth that resists the
city's efforts to tame it. So, the legal concepts of responsibility that climax
the *Oresteia* partly "trump" the searing tragic vision of justice that pre-
ceded, but that vision is so powerful and runs so deep that it cannot help
but call into question the stability of the final resolution—its ability truly
to conclude the turbulent quest for justice.

What the city arguably discovered about itself in the *Oresteia* is that its
ideals (consensus, argument, reason) derived their significance in part
from the heroic ideals they rejected (self-sufficiency, spectacular action,
emotion). These heroic ideals in turn exposed the limits of the democratic ideology. As I suggest in this chapter, the city aimed at a rational, legal
ideal that was more susceptible to human control, more predictable and
more stable than the hero's. But the hero and his sufferings inevitably
showed what was lost in attaining this ideal. More fundamentally, the
Oresteia suggests the instability in human attempts to create a fully deliberate institution—the city and its laws. In one of the most famous choral
odes from Greek tragedy, Sophocles celebrated man as *deinos*—a word
that simultaneously means "marvelous" and "terrible."[35] The chorus cata-
logues man's resourcefulness at subjugating nature and its harsh conditions to make the world a more prosperous and comfortable place. Only
his own nature—and in particular, his mortality—is beyond man's ability
to cure.

Law itself—like language—is one of the grand inventions humanity has
cleverly contrived.[36] As such, it is an optimistic institution: it speaks authoritatively, and seeks to ensure that even the unknown and the unforeseeable will be subject to rules. But unlike navigation, farming, or
hunting (other arts celebrated in the ode), law is directed inward, onto
humanity itself: it is an attempt to colonize our own nature, to domesticate ourselves to intelligibility. One point implicit in the ode is that, in
spite of his resourcefulness, man the clever, the terrible (*deinos*) will al-

---

35. See Sophocles, *Antigone,* 332–75. On this ode, see, e.g., Nussbaum, *Fragility of Goodness,* 72–75; Charles Segal, *Tragedy and Civilization: An Interpretation of Sophocles* (Cambridge:
Harvard University Press, 1981), 152–57; and the same author's "Sophocles' Praise of Man
and the Conflicts of the *Antigone,*" *Arion* 3 (1964): 46–66, reprinted in T. Woodard, ed.,
Sophocles: A Collection of Critical Essays (Englewood Cliffs, N.J.: Prentice-Hall, 1966), 62–85.
36. Sophocles, *Antigone,* 355–56.

ways be a mystery to himself: the human is that part of the world that can never be wholly mastered.

This suggests that law is just the point where human resourcefulness inevitably fails. It is a liminal institution, in that it occupies that space where our attempts to subjugate nature to human governance must bend back and warp. No wonder, then, that law was a central concern of the Athenian tragedians. Law, with its protocols, procedures, and rules, was an antitragic institution: it purported to keep at bay precisely that ambiguity and moral indeterminacy that constituted mortals' native condition. Tragedy showed the pressure constantly exerted on law by the necessities of human nature; it claimed that even this institution, *especially* this institution, exemplified at once the canniness and terror—the *deinos* quality—of human life.

2. The *Oresteia* and the Drama of Autonomy

As many have argued, law traces its origins to vengeance, and began as a mode of channeling and controlling the urge to return violence for violence. In his lectures on *The Common Law*, for example, Oliver Wendell Holmes argued that "the various forms of liability known to modern law spring from the common ground of revenge."[37] More recently, Richard Posner has elaborated extensively on the origins of law in revenge.[38] Such discussions are not of merely antiquarian interest, for, as Holmes wrote, "The history of what the law has been is necessary to the knowledge of what the law is."[39] Thus, Holmes hearkened back to the origins of law to demonstrate that, far from institutionalizing our moral beliefs, law is concerned with social control and is directed by public policy. In this section I want to explore the *Oresteia*—a dramatic treatment of the origins of law in vengeance—to show that law does indeed attempt to keep moral beliefs at bay, but that these beliefs continue to press on it and bring about change within the law.

The *Oresteia*—first performed in Athens in 458 B.C. and the only trilogy that has survived in its entirety from ancient Greece—shows the bleak and powerful demand for vengeance in the House of Atreus, which drives Agamemnon to kill his daughter, Clytaemnestra to murder her husband, and finally Orestes to slay his mother. The trilogy ends, surprisingly, with the

37. Oliver Wendell Holmes, *The Common Law*, ed. Mark DeWolfe Howe (Boston: Little, Brown, 1963), 33.

38. Richard A. Posner, *Law and Literature*, rev. ed. (Cambridge: Harvard University Press, 1998), 49–92. See also the same author's *The Economics of Justice* (Cambridge: Harvard University Press, 1981), 208–27.

39. Holmes, *Common Law*, 33.

inauguration of a jury whose split vote results in the acquittal of Orestes for the premeditated murder of Clytaemnestra. The purpose of enacting these painful and extreme episodes from Greek myth is to explore the idea of justice—particularly as this structures and informs the life of the *polis*, or city.[40]

A recent commentator on the trilogy identifies four "principles" that govern acts of justice / punishment in the first play: (1) such acts consist in the taking of violent revenge by the injured party or his / her representative; (2) notwithstanding their violence, they are nonetheless performed under the auspices of Zeus; (3) justice is inexorable, not to be turned aside or mitigated by prayer, sacrifice, or repentance; and (4) justice strikes at the innocent as much as at the guilty (for example, Greeks as well as Trojans die in the war to punish Paris for his adultery with Helen).[41]

These features, taken together, suggest that revenge is a highly inefficient mode of keeping the peace, for the costs it exacts threaten to outweigh the benefits it provides. Posner has discussed the extreme clumsiness of vengeance as a means of maintaining order. As he points out, for example, vengeance makes large-scale cooperation impossible, not only by putting a premium on ideals of individual honor, but by creating highly intense loyalties within small groups, especially the family. This points to yet another inefficiency—that vengeance might not be visited on the "right" person, since family members too may be punished for the wrongdoing of one of their kin. Revenge, moreover, fails to achieve an equal requital, one that matches the punishment to the

40. "The primary issue in the *Oresteia* is, of course, justice." Froma I. Zeitlin, "The Dynamics of Misogyny: Myth and Mythmaking in the *Oresteia*," *Arethusa* 11 (1978): 149, 161; "It is plain to the most casual reader that *dikê* (justice) is a central notion of the trilogy," MacLeod, "Politics and the *Oresteia*," *Journal of Hellenic Studies* 102 (1982): 133. See also Christopher Rocco, "Democracy and Discipline in Aeschylus's *Oresteia*," in *Tragedy and Enlightenment* (Berkeley: University of California Press, 1998), 136–70; J. Peter Euben, *The Tragedy of Political Theory* (Princeton, N.J.: Princeton University Press, 1990), 67–95 (chapter on "Justice and the Oresteia"); Richard Kuhns, *The House, the City and the Judge* (Indianapolis: Bobbs-Merrill, 1962). Euben's argument is similar to that found in Thomas Gould, *The Ancient Quarrel between Poetry and Philosophy* (Princeton, N.J.: Princeton University Press, 1990), 104–16. I discuss Euben and Rocco in greater detail in Section 3 of this chapter. The significance of the *Oresteia* for contemporary jurisprudence has been developed in many writings of the "law-and-literature" school. See, e.g., Ziolkowski, *The Mirror of Justice*, 20–41; Paul Gewirtz, "Aeschylus' Law," *Harvard Law Review* 101 (1988): 1043; David Luban, "Some Greek Trials: Order and Justice in Homer, Hesiod, Aeschylus and Plato," *Tennessee Law Review* 54 (1987): 279–325, reprinted in revised form in David Luban, *Legal Modernism* (Ann Arbor: University of Michigan Press, 1994), 283–334.

41. See Sommerstein, *Aeschylus: Eumenides*, 19. See also E. R. Dodds, "Morals and Politics in the *Oresteia*," in Dodds, *The Ancient Concept of Progress* (Oxford: Oxford University Press, 1973), 55–56 (discussing features of guilt as portrayed in the *Agamemnon*).

crime. First, because the one seeking vengeance is a party to the dispute, he or she is likely to misjudge the balance of right. Then again, vengeance tends to start feuds, which can prove to be far bloodier than the original aggression. Revenge can foment intergenerational conflicts; it does not point to any sure closure. For all these reasons, vengeance may result in an excess of punishment. As Posner points out, however, vengeance may also result in too little punishment, since it depends on the anger of the aggrieved. Because anger tends to fade rapidly, Posner writes, revenge may not provide sufficient motivation to track down and punish the aggressor.[42]

If we look upon vengeance essentially as a highly inefficient system of justice, the structure of the *Oresteia* as a whole looks like a move toward a more enlightened (and certainly less costly) way of satisfying the demand for justice. The progress from family-based vengeance to a city-administered legal institution represents a distinct advance. No small part of this progress is that the advent of law makes large-scale cooperation—specifically, that of the *polis*—possible at last. The *Oresteia*, then, is about not simply the advent of law, but the rise of the democratic *polis*.[43] To be sure, the order inaugurated at the conclusion of the trilogy may have its repressive aspects. As feminist interpretations in particular have pointed out, for example, the order envisioned for Athens is markedly patriarchal. Notwithstanding the important, indeed indispensable role it suggests for the female in the life of the *polis,* the trilogy makes abundantly clear that this role must be a strictly subordinate one.[44] Perhaps even more fundamental to this democratic order than its sexual politics is its dependence on the people's fear of the punishments to be visited

42. See Posner, *Law and Literature,* rev. ed., 49–60.

43. On tragedy as a democratic genre, see, e.g., Mark Griffith, "Brilliant Dynasts: Power and Politics in the *Oresteia,*" *Classical Antiquity* 14 (1995): 62–129; A. M. Bowie, "Religion and Politics in the *Oresteia,*" *Classical Quarterly,* n.s. 43 (1993): 10–31; Jean-Pierre Vernant, "Tensions and Ambiguities in Greek Tragedy," in Vernant and Vidal-Naquet, *Myth and Tragedy,* 29–48; Christian Meier, *The Political Art of Greek Tragedy,* trans. Andrew Webber (Baltimore: The Johns Hopkins University Press, 1993); Peter W. Rose, *Sons of the Gods, Children of the Earth* (Ithaca: Cornell University Press, 1992), chapter 4 ("Aeschylus' *Oresteia:* Dialectical Inheritance"); Euben, *Tragedy of Political Theory,* and the essays in J. Peter Euben, ed., *Greek Tragedy and Political Theory* (Berkeley: University of California Press, 1986); Froma I. Zeitlin, "Performing the Other," in *Nothing to Do with Dionysos?* ed. John J. Winkler and Froma I. Zeitlin (Princeton, N.J.: Princeton University Press, 1990), 63–96.

44. See Zeitlin, "Dynamics of Misogyny," *Arethusa* 11 (1978): 149–84. Simon Goldhill, *Language, Sexuality, Narrative: The Oresteia* (Cambridge: Cambridge University Press, 1984), 279–83, argues that the sexual ambiguity of Athena implicitly subverts the boundary between male and female upon which the order of the *polis* rests.

on those who transgress the city's laws.[45] As Paul Gewirtz has pointed out, the *Oresteia* is a powerful reminder that law entails violence and threats of violence.[46] Nonetheless, despite any crudity or inherent limitations in the Aeschylean concept of order, the predominant view has traditionally been that the trilogy concludes with a "ringing endorsement of Athens and its political system."[47]

To speak of the unacceptable costs of revenge as a system of justice, however, is to adopt a resolutely objective, third-person point of view— that of the social scientist or the anthropologist. The contradictions in *dikê* run much deeper than "inefficiencies" and raise troubling questions about the nature and even the possibility of justice. The rifts and tensions in justice that emerge in the first two dramas inevitably cast doubt on the ability of gods or mortals to cure them. For example, a justice that exacts its toll from the innocent and guilty alike is not simply a system that re- quires reengineering; it seems the very opposite of justice. That justice even conceivably entails its own antithesis, however, raises questions about the adequacy or attainability of our human notions of justice.

Again, it might seem to be a fundamental tenet of justice that the party actually responsible for violence or injury be required to give satisfaction, whether by accepting punishment or by offering compensation. As Aeschylus' trilogy repeatedly makes clear, however, it is impossible finally to "pin" responsibility on any one agent. So, for example, Agamemnon killed his own daughter in order that the Greeks might sail against Troy, but whether he had any genuine choice—and therefore whether he can properly be held responsible—proves to be unexpectedly complex and knotty, as reflected in the extensive scholarly discussion the question has

45. See *Eumenides*, 490–565, 681–710. On this "good fear" and its connections with de- mocratic theory, see Rose, *Sons of the Gods*, 253–54.

46. Gewirtz, *"Aeschylus' Law,"* 1043. Hugh Lloyd-Jones, *The Justice of Zeus*, Sather Classi- cal Lectures, vol. 41 (Berkeley: University of California Press, 1971), 94–95, provoca- tively—if not altogether persuasively—writes: "The cliché we have heard repeated all our lives, that the *Eumenides* depicts the transition from the vendetta to the rule of law, is ut- terly misleading. . . . When the Erinyes become Eumenides there is not the least question of their giving up their function; we have been assured that if they did the government both of the state and of the universe would collapse. . . . If . . . Athene chooses to institute a new court of justice, this court is not to replace, but to assist the Erinyes."

47. Griffith, *"Briliant Dynasts,"* 64, describing the "prevailing view of the *Oresteia*." See Kuhns, *The House, the City and the Judge*, for an eloquent example of the traditional view. Goldhill, *Language, Sexuality, Narrative*, is an important exception to the prevailing view, for he tries to show the unmanageable linguistic and moral ambiguities that persist throughout the trilogy. I believe Goldhill overstates his case, however, by suggesting that the language of the *Eumenides* is fully as opaque and ambiguous as that of the *Agamemnon*.

raised.[48] As Bernard Williams has recently remarked, a major difficulty in understanding this passage has been ethical in nature. "The critics," he writes, "could not understand how someone might have to choose between two courses of action both of which involve a grave wrong, so that whatever he does will be bad. . . ."[49] Agamemnon's dilemma, in other words, is structured in a way that confounds our sense of freedom, will, and responsibility, and thus challenges some of the fundamental bases of our sense of justice.

To treat these contradictions as curable flaws, then, is to underestimate their depth. Moreover, as Thomas Rosenmeyer has remarked, there is reason to believe that the system of justice was never strictly confined to vengeance: the Homeric poems, for example, contain several references to financial compensation and other surrogates for the blood of the guilty. On Rosenmeyer's reading, therefore, the "near-automatic perpetuation of guilt and punishment" was a poetic construct.[50] "Precisely because a 'life for a life' was an atavistic fantasy," he writes, "a literary sanctification of what could no longer be enacted without suicidal harm to society, it gripped the imagination in a way that everyday reality could not."[51] Tragedy, as a vivid enactment of events, invites us to identify with the characters on stage: to adopt a sympathetic view, one that experiences the enacted events firsthand, viscerally.

48. Denys Page and Hugh Lloyd-Jones, for example, argued that Agamemnon had no freedom since he could not have given up the expedition against Troy. See J. D. Denniston and D. Page, eds., *Aeschylus, Agamemnon* (Oxford: Oxford University Press, 1957), xxiii–xxix; Hugh Lloyd-Jones, "The Guilt of Agamemnon," *Classical Quarterly*, n.s. 12 (1962): 187–99. E. R. Dodds has argued that events are typically overdetermined in archaic Greek literature, and in particular that an agent may at once be fulfilling Zeus's will and acting on his own volition. See E. R. Dodds, "Agamemnon's Apology," in *Greeks and the Irrational* (Berkeley: University of California Press, 1951). See also Albin Lesky, "Decision and Responsibility in the Tragedy of Aeschylus," *Journal of Hellenic Studies* 86 (1966): 78–85. See more recently the discussion by Martha C. Nussbaum, "Aeschylus and Practical Conflict," in *The Fragility of Goodness* (Cambridge: Cambridge University Press, 1986), 25–50. Nussbaum rightly stresses the existence of irresolvable conflict as a part of moral experience. Williams, *Shame and Necessity*, 134–35 offers some necessary adjustments to Nussbaum's treatment.

Other discussions include K. J. Dover, "Some Neglected Aspects of Agamemnon's Dilemma," *Journal of Hellenic Studies* 93 (1973): 58–69; Mark Edwards, "Agamemnon's Decision: Freedom and Folly in Aeschylus," *California Studies in Classical Antiquity* 19 (1977): 17–38; N.G.L. Hammond, "Personal Freedom and its Limitations in the *Oresteia*," *Journal of Hellenic Studies* 85 (1965): 42–55. The scholarly discussion is usefully summarized in D. J. Conacher, *Aeschylus' "Oresteia": A Literary Commentary* (Toronto: University of Toronto Press, 1987), 85–92.

49. Williams, *Shame and Necessity*, 133.

50. Thomas G. Rosenmeyer, *The Art of Aeschylus* (Berkeley: University of California Press, 1982), 294.

51. Ibid., 294–95.

What appear as "inefficiencies" at one level, then, at another level evince a powerful resonance; the contradictions embedded in vengeance come to feel like persisting and ineliminable paradoxes informing our existence.

As Dodds has commented, no distinction between morals and politics had yet been drawn when Aeschylus wrote.[52] Accordingly, the manifold perplexities of the ethical life as explored in the *Agamemnon* and the *Libation-Bearers* exert a powerful influence on the view of law, justice, and the *polis* ultimately presented in the trilogy. As the *Oresteia* makes piercingly clear, the demand for justice goes very deep and entails some of people's most passionate longings. The origins of law in vengeance—the story told in the *Oresteia*—suggest that law deals with matters about which people may be expected to have the deepest and most passionate feelings, yet does so in a way that is intended to avoid such passions. Law thus seems to be in substantial part a liminal entity: it touches on the most elemental matters—matters calling forth the person's most powerful emotional resources—yet seeks to keep the passionate at arm's length, disposing of such matters with procedures and rules intended to limit the scope of the injured's wrath.

To appreciate the significance of the *Oresteia* for an understanding of law we must first grasp the complexity of justice, or *dikê*, as presented in the trilogy. I begin by elaborating on the way justice looks to the characters before Athena bestows her gift of the jury in the final play. In brief, I reinterpret those four "principles" of justice described above along more subjective lines, to account for the way they are experienced by the characters in the drama. On the view taken here, the regime of revenge is not merely a primitive stage in society to be transcended, but one that partly expresses the depths and complexity of our ethical life. Concomitantly, the inauguration of law reflects the attempt to cut this complexity down to size—to confine ourselves, for at least certain purposes, within an arena in which questions of responsibility and response can be more easily managed.

A. Justice as Vengeance

The interminable character of revenge is a fundamental structuring device in the *Oresteia*. The violence that sends the plot hurtling forward is unstoppable because on the one hand every act of violence is backed by a powerful claim of justice, while on the other hand no such claim can win unanimous assent. Grounds will always exist for condemning the antecedent violence and for concluding that a further act of

52. Dodds, "Morals and Politics," in *Ancient Concept of Progress*, p. 45.

vengeance is called for. The unstoppability of revenge rests partly on the plurality of commitments the characters in the *Oresteia* have: Agamemnon, for example, is trapped between his commitment to avenge his brother Menelaus (as well as by his indebtedness to the warriors he has amassed for his campaign against Troy) and by his father–love for Iphigeneia. Clytaemnestra, in turn, claims to avenge Iphigeneia's murder, but in so doing treacherously violates the loyalty she owes her husband and the father of her children. Inevitably, Orestes avenges his father, and murders his mother, doing so under what appear to be the most urgent moral demands—yet he is in turn faced with the wrath of the Furies for the heinous crime of matricide.

Revenge, for these characters, is an irresistible demand. While the characters actively plot out and execute the murders, in an important sense what they do "befalls" them: they cannot *not* kill the person who has blood on his hands. To be sure, the characters deliberate and fully will to do the abhorrent acts they commit; yet the very depths of their desire, as well as the extreme circumstances in which they conceive their desire, weigh against a straightforward culpability on their part.

This feature of the characters' motivations emerges perhaps most forcefully in the *Libation-Bearers,* where Orestes lists the fearful punishments Apollo has threatened unless he avenges his father: "diseases that creep upon the body with gnashing jaws, ulcers to devour my former self, leprosy at my temples" (*Libation-Bearers,* 279–82). At one level, this listing of punishments might seem to diminish Orestes' responsibility for the matricide in a straightforward, readily comprehensible way: he is doing what a god has expressly ordered him to do, and the god has backed his commands with the most terrifying threats. Yet matters are not so simple, since Orestes himself plainly desires to do the deed. "Even if I did not obey the god, the deed would still have to be done," Orestes says. "Many yearnings conspire to this one end: the gods' commands, my own grief for my father. Besides, my poverty presses hard, and the thought that citizens of the greatest renown—those who by their courage conquered Troy—are now made subject to these women" (*Libation-Bearers,* 301–4).

Orestes is constrained to do what he does, but at the same time deeply wishes it; his whole sense of himself is implicated. The fearsome punishments Apollo threatens have their ultimate source in the anger of Agamemnon, Orestes' father, should his son not respect his father's pleas for revenge (ibid., 286–90). Orestes' "duty" to kill his mother is not a universalizable one, but is imbued with his own particular circumstances: Agamemnon has become Orestes' suppliant (287), and this "supplication" calls for *this* son in particular to avenge his father: because Agamemnon was murdered "in the family" (*en genei*) he must be avenged "in the family" as well (287). Orestes' sense of himself as his father's son is the deep source of his sense of obligation; his identity and his duty can scarcely be distinguished from each other.

What is true of Orestes holds as well for Clytaemnestra (who was led to a basely treacherous act by grief for her slain daughter) and for Agamemnon (who killed his daughter to ensure that the assembled warriors would not die of starvation). The inexorability of revenge—at one level, one of its "inefficiencies"—has a continuing resonance at a "first-person" level, since it not only calls upon the individual's deepest passions, but suggests that the engagement of such depths is bound to be catastrophic. This resonance is crystallized in a phrase that threads its way through the entire trilogy in various forms: "the doer suffers" (*pathein ton erxanta, Agamemnon,* 1564). On the one hand, this seems to state a founding proposition of justice—namely, that the one who does or acts criminally shall suffer for it. But the expression supports another, more unsettling sense: that the one who thinks she is acting may in fact be enveloped by powers and drives outside her control; that her action is more deeply a "suffering", an undergoing of external forces. Tragedy uses legal concepts ("the doer shall suffer"), but by showing the ambiguities and stresses in such concepts makes them problematic.

This is not to wipe out the characters' responsibility, however. Agamemnon is not simply ordered to kill his daughter; he is given a choice either to kill her or to see his army starve to death. Orestes too must make his own choice, notwithstanding Apollo's threat-backed commands; and certainly he is on his own in finding the courage and resolve to do what must be done. Because they must actually choose, the characters cannot evade responsibility, or hope to be exonerated. That would be to render their situation fundamentally untragic by enabling the characters to argue that they were merely obeying orders that were plainly entitled to obedience, despite their harshness.[53]

Moral responsibility seems constitutive of the tragic dilemma: the agent has no "other"—more powerful, more knowledgeable—to which he can, with indubitable justice, defer. Nor can the tragic hero avail himself of an objective standard he can neutrally apply to a situation: if such a standard were available, the hero would cease to be tragic, for the responsibility

---

53. Orestes, of course, makes this argument with some force during the trial in the final play, and it partly explains why he is ultimately "acquitted." But to the extent that Orestes can evade responsibility by claiming that Apollo was more truly the cause, he is scarcely a tragic hero. On the transformation of Orestes into *homo legalis* in the *Eumenides,* see below, Section 2.B.

would lie less with him than with the standard that plainly required this or that particular outcome. His responsibility is a mark of what we might call his radical loneliness—a sense that no beneficent authority exists to help evade the agent's own accountability.

Justice, or *dikê*, as invoked by the avengers in the *Oresteia*, is in large part the name they give their hunger to do "what must be done." This sense of "must" is not confined to a destiny imposed externally (as though the person must bow to some fate essentially unrelated to him or her). It encompasses a sense of the avenger's own character: what people "must" do is a part of their identity. The irresistible sense of obligation that drives Clytaemnestra and Orestes reflects the intensity of the blood bonds between them and the one they seek to avenge: it grabs them at a deeper level of identity than any particular ideals they may subscribe to. The relation of the avenger to this duty is far more intense than it would be to some maxim or general principle (e.g., "Justice requires that one's father be avenged"). As a duty, it is at once the "right" thing to do (which the agent should therefore undertake), and necessary—scarcely within the avenger's will. At this level, it is hardly possible to distinguish between coercion and a sense of moral rightness.

The overwhelming sense of obligation that compels the person to act whatever the cost is strangely at odds with the cunning schemes of both Clytaemnestra and Orestes. They act efficiently and coldbloodedly, but in the interest of carrying out an emotional imperative that simply defies calculation. Justice, then, in these first two plays is inexorably linked to treachery. This feature arises in part from the disparity in power between the avenger and the one on whom she seeks to take vengeance—the wife must wreak justice on the warrior husband; the child must effect justice on a mother now entrenched in royal power. Beyond that, Aeschylus regularly underscores the persistence and vividness of his characters' memory, their unswerving intent to rectify past wrongs. As the chorus of old men in *Agamemnon* say, "There awaits the fearsome, inexorable, abiding and treacherous—the Wrath of long memory who avenges the child" (*Aga.*, 155). This interiority makes even one's nearest and dearest secret and threatening. One of the curious features of the *Agamemnon,* in particular, is the air of dread and foreboding that attends the chorus's belief in a cosmic justice that punishes evil deeds. That belief *should* support a sense of moral confidence—a shared assurance that the world works in edifying ways. Instead, however, the atmosphere of the *Agamemnon* is thick with menace. Its characters are notably furtive and speak deceitfully, or in deliberate enigmas and double meanings. Clytaemnestra's speech welcoming Agamemnon home, while the king treads the red carpet leading into the house (*Aga.*, 958–74), is a masterpiece of duplicity, in which a palpable menace lurks just beneath the apparently benign surface of the words:

> Let a path strewn with dark red be spread at once,
> So that Justice [*Dikê*] may lead him to a home he had not hoped for.
> My concern, never succumbing to sleep, will dispose
> Justly [*dikaiôs*] everything fated by the gods.
>
> (*Aga.*, 910–13)

Clytaemnestra hopes to persuade Agamemnon, and so purports to praise his victory as just, and calls for a red carpet to be spread in celebration of his success. Her speech, however, cannot completely disguise her menacing intent. The "path strewn with dark red" is the blood Agamemnon will shed, and the "home he had not hoped for" is his imminent death. "Justice," in turn, refers not to the supposed justice of his victory over Troy, but the punishment to be exacted for his murder of Iphigeneia. The profuse significance inherent in language subverts the purported simplicity of Clytaemnestra's false praise.[54]

The chorus's sense of dread arises from their uncertainty about where or when retribution will come. More deeply, however, it grows from the felt impossibility of controlling the meaning of events, and, concomitantly—as Clytaemnestra's deceitful speech of welcome brilliantly shows—of controlling the meaning of the language we use to discuss events. In such a world, justice becomes a source of anxiety: it is a necessary framework for making sense of the world, but actual events seem always to outstrip it, to baffle and frustrate it. The clear distinctions justice draws between right and wrong are at odds with concrete acts, in which the praiseworthy and the culpable, the voluntary and the destined seem indissolubly united.

Because of the treachery of justice and of those who seek to bring it about, *dikê* tends to be a defensive claim: the avenger asserts that a murder was "right" and "just" notwithstanding the fact that what he or she did entailed an outrageous breach of trust.[55] What the claim of *dikê* is intended to justify, in other words, is in large part the deceitfulness of the revenge. Justice is not only the name the avenger gives his hunger for revenge, then; it is the claim with which he hopes to break out of the circle

---

54. The most notable recent exposition of the multiple layers of meaning in the *Oresteia's* diction is in Goldhill, *Language, Sexuality, Narrative.* See also Ann Lebeck, *The Oresteia: A Study in Language and Structure* (Cambridge: Harvard University Press, 1971).

55. Both the herald and Agamemnon himself assert the justice of the Trojan war. See *Agamemnon,* 524–37; 813–17. Clytaemnestra repeatedly insists on the justice of murdering Agamemnon. See *Agamemnon,* 1396, 1406, 1432, 1527. Orestes too is at pains to show the justice of his matricide. See *Libation-Bearers,* 973–1006, 1026–33.

of vengeance. *Dikê*, in short, represents the avenger's attempt to control the meaning of what he or she has done. It picks out just those features that should win others' approval, and seeks to suppress other features as irrelevant. The very defensiveness of the claim, however, suggests that the meaning of one's acts falls outside the individual's powers. We have become familiar with the idea that in some sense language speaks us (rather than the reverse), and that its resources of meaningfulness cannot be channeled to suit an individual speaker's conscious intention. Language, on this view, is elusive, both requiring and accommodating endless interpretation, and defying efforts to hitch it to a particular purpose. In the *Oresteia*, action is like language: it is, in some powerful way, something that befalls the doer, who can never command others' reading of it. Justice, then, as a defensive claim is intended to narrow the significance of events to one particular meaning—to draw attention to the edifying fact that a transgressor has been punished, and to sidestep questions of the costs (lives lost, innocent blood shed in order to bring the wrongdoer to book). I will suggest below that law enables the characters finally to achieve this narrowing of meaning, and to establish authoritatively a single and agreed-upon significance for an event.

Before we can understand what is entailed in that achievement—and, in particular, its deeply ambiguous nature—we need to consider a quite different, indeed contradictory use of the word *dikê* to capture the profuse significance of events, and the difficulties involved in "doing justice to" their full complexity. For example, the chorus of old men try to assess Agamemnon accurately, with neither excess nor deficit. Only in this way will their praise be just. Thus, as Agamemnon returns from Troy, the chorus says:

> My king, destroyer of Troy,
> Child of Atreus,
> How to name you, how to honor you,
> Neither over-shooting, nor falling short of
> The exact measure of grace?
> Most men transgress justice (*dikên*),
> Preferring appearance to reality.

> (*Aga.*, 783–89)

The chorus's predicament is this: how to capture in public speech a complex reality? For to praise Agamemnon as a victor and as an unquestionable champion of justice goes too far: it ignores the terrible costs of the war—not only the lives of the Greek soldiers, but the life of Iphigeneia at her father's hands. To concentrate on those deaths, on the other hand, and to ignore the victory—and the fact that Paris and Troy have now paid for their transgression—would be to fall short. Justice consists in capturing the complex reality precisely, as though it were an especially challenging target: how, in other words, is the chorus to "do justice to" Agamemnon's victory in Troy?

Justice, on this view, signifies honoring the complexity of persons and events, their resistance to easy intelligibility. Along these lines, the chorus reflect on the surprising richness of unsuspected meanings a word or a name can harbor. "Who ever named her so truly—Helen?" the chorus reflect on the woman they blame for their misery: "Hell for the ships; hell for the men; hell for the city" (*Aga.*, 681–82, 690).[56] Later, the seer Cassandra will unearth a new significance in the name of Apollo, which bears a strong resemblance to *apollunai*—the Greek word for destruction.[57] These words, so to speak, do justice to those they name, by capturing their ambiguity, their rich significance that overflows our usual categories.

In contrast, the claim by the avenger that his or her act was "just" is an attempt to simplify events, to reduce the surfeit of meaning to a single denotation. So, in responding to the chorus of old men, Agamemnon insists on the unequivocal justice of what he has done. His speech harps almost obsessively on the word *dikê* and its various forms:

> First, it is just (*dikê*) to address Argos
> And its gods, rightly judging (*dikaiôn*) them to be
> Joint causes of my return home and of what I exacted from
> Priam's city. For when the gods heard the claims (*dikas*)—
> From no man's tongue—they placed their votes
> Unswervingly for men's death and Troy's destruction in the
> Urn of blood.
>
> (*Aga.*, 810–16)

Agamemnon offers a picture of the gods unanimously casting their vote in condemnation of Troy (and, by implication, in approval of his campaign against Troy, and in particular the sacrifice of Iphigeneia). Clearly, this is special pleading; Aeschylus has been at pains throughout to show the deeply ambiguous nature of the victory at Troy. Agamemnon's words anticipate the conclusion of the trilogy, when a jury of humans will acquit Orestes by a split vote. The comparison with the badly split jury in the *Eumenides* only underscores that Agamemnon's insistence on the unanimity of the gods' verdict was wishful thinking.

56. The pun in the original is untranslatable. "Helen" sounds like the Greek word for "capture" or "seize." Like Richmond Lattimore and Robert Fagles in their translations, I indicate the pun by playing on the acoustic similarity between "Helen" and "hell."

57. *Aga.*, 1073, 1080–82.

Dikê, then, in one way consists in honoring the fullness of meaning, and *not* suppressing darker elements. In another way, however, it is precisely the opposite: a defensive insistence on the single and unambiguous meaning of an act or event. It is important to understand for the emergence of law, however, that the wish to limit events to a single meaning runs far deeper than the self-serving desire to escape blame and punishment. The very profusion of significance calls forth the attempt to reduce it to something more manageable. To appreciate this, we need to consider one of the best-known passages in the trilogy, the so-called "Hymn to Zeus" from the *Agamemnon:*

> Zeus, whoever he be,
> If he is pleased to be so called,
> I will call him Zeus.
> I have nothing to which to liken him. . .
> [Zeus], who set mortals on the path to wisdom,
> Who set it down that learning comes by suffering.
>
> *(Aga.,* 160–66, 176–78)

"Zeus, whoever he be" crystallizes the unnameable, and all that eludes the chorus's attempts to assess and characterize the world. He resists naming partly because he is unique: he has vanquished all those gods with whom he might once have been compared. "The one who once was great and bursting to fight in every battle shall not be reckoned—he's a thing of the past. The one who existed before has been overthrown and is gone."[58] Zeus is above all the *victorious* god, and as such the mysterious fashioner of human existence, who holds an unquestionable and almost ineffable authority over mortals. Indeed, to grasp this—and to sing "victory songs" (*epinikia*) to him—is the path to understanding.[59] The chorus's point is not simply that Zeus is now entrenched in power, but that he oversees and exemplifies a world structured by strife, or *eris.* In other words, Zeus is the god of victory in the deep sense that he reveals the fundamental role of strife in human existence. The impossibility of finding words equal to Zeus, or capable of truly naming him, is the same as the impossibility of truly naming or assessing events. By showing the strife at the heart of existence, Zeus's victory reveals the deepest reason why human language seems unequal to the complexity of the world.

---

58. *Aga.,* 168–70.

59. *Aga.,* 174–75 ("But the man who cries out victory songs to Zeus will hit full upon the target of understanding.") My translation of these lines is based on that by Eduard Fraenkel, *Aeschylus: "Agamemnon"* (Oxford: Oxford University Press, 1951), 1.100.

Human wisdom itself evinces a structure of strife and victory, for, as presented by the chorus, understanding comes as something that gets the upper hand over us: "Soundness of mind comes even to the unwilling—a kind of grace from the gods who sit in force upon their sacred bench."[60] The Greek deliberately juxtaposes *kharis* ("grace") and *biaiôs* ("violently," "forcefully") to bring out the paradoxical nature of understanding, as something visited or imposed upon us perforce, rather than as something we attain through our own powers. This, too, is the sense of the chorus's difficult but powerfully suggestive phrase *pathei mathos:* "[Zeus,] who set mortals on the road to wisdom by laying it down that learning shall come through suffering (*pathei mathos*)."[61] The point is not the pedestrian one that "we learn from experience," but the far more troubling thought that insight and understanding are possible only by being overwhelmed. This can have an optimistic sense, when applied to wrongdoers: the apprehended criminal learns that wrongdoing will inevitably be punished. But the phrase inevitably bears the sense that ultimately we cannot plan in advance, using what we know to provide against the future, for wisdom must always come as an incursion, a *pathos* or suffering.[62] Wisdom is therefore never settled or final, for it consists precisely in appreciating that it is something borne in upon us from without, as a kind of violent grace from the gods.[63] Singing victory songs to Zeus is the path to wisdom because it impresses on the singer that, in the world ruled by victorious Zeus, understanding itself is essentially a victor in a struggle with us.[64]

The "law" that Zeus sets down—"learning through suffering"—is a kind of anti-law: because a mortal can attain learning only through being overcome, the future is ultimately beyond calculation, prediction, or rational arrangements. The "natural law," in other words, is: you can't learn anything before you suffer it. But this "wisdom" seems to undercut the very

60. *Aga.,* 180–83.

61. *Aga.,* 176–78.

62. To be sure, it is also a part of Zeus's law that suffering (*pathos*) does lead somewhere—to "learning" (*mathos*): it is not as though mortals are like dumb beasts who are uncomprehendingly struck down by obscure powers. See Fraenkel, *Aeschylus "Agamemnon,"* 2.112. The relevant point for my purposes, however, is that little if any public use can be made of such *mathos,* for it remains liable to an unpredictable and upsetting *pathos.* See Rosenmeyer, *Art of Aeschylus,* 277–80. For a review of scholarly opinion on the significance of *pathei mathos,* see Conacher, *Aeschylus' "Oresteia": A Literary Commentary,* 83–85. Lebeck, *Oresteia,* 25–29, offers a useful survey of references to *pathos* and *mathos* in the *Agamemnon.*

63. This is the point too of *Aga.,* 179–80 ("Not sleep, but the pain from remembering griefs drips before the heart.") As Fraenkel, *Aeschylus "Agamemnon",* 1.106 suggests, the image Aeschylus uses here for wisdom or understanding is that of a wound whose pain is the theme of persisting remembrance.

64. See *Aga.,* 174–75.

possibility of law, since there apparently exists no way to conform to the dictates of wisdom in advance. Zeus's law, moreover, places a burden on action itself. A man must act somehow, but what he does exposes him to a train of consequences he could not have foreseen. This is the very opposite of the principle of law that Holmes, for example, identified—that only intentional acts should be subject to liability: "As action cannot be avoided, and tends to the public good, there is obviously no policy in throwing the hazard on what is at once desirable and inevitable upon the actor."[65] Holmes concluded that liability should be confined to intentional acts, since only such acts can be avoided. The thrust of Zeus's "anti-law," however, is just the opposite: that responsibility is visited on the agent solely in virtue of the fact that he did it.

What Aeschylus captures in the Hymn to Zeus and, more generally in the *Agamemnon* and *Libation-Bearers,* is a sense of the strife, or *eris,* that lies at the heart of human existence. The violence of revenge is not simply an unfortunate "event"—difficult to stop, once started. Rather, it is an abiding truth about the human condition. The connection between the generations, as presented in the *Oresteia,* is inherently one of bitter conflict. Agamemnon kills his daughter; Agamemnon's father, Atreus, had earlier murdered his brother's children. In the second of the plays, the children in turn rise up against the mother. Pervading the first two plays in the *Oresteia,* then, is a sense of the generations preying on each other, and in particular of parents brutalizing the young. This predation cannot be reduced to individual malice, but is in a deep sense inescapable: the generations are caught up in an eternal, internecine struggle.

We notice how the inexorability of strife at once cries out for law—a means of channeling and containing violence—and, at the same time, how improbable it is that law could ever successfully address such rooted and inexorable conflicts. What the inauguration of the jury finally permits is an authoritative means for settling on "the" meaning of an event, a meaning that can then be generally acknowledged and condoned. The attainment of an agreed-upon sense of things represents a distinct advance: it makes communal life possible by providing a shared store of meanings. Yet it also represents a truncation, a violence to the fruitfulness of possible meanings. As Robert Cover has argued, law, as administered by the state, is coercive not least in its attempts to squelch meaning, and to enforce an unequivocal consistency.[66] I will ultimately want to suggest

65. Holmes, *Common Law,* 77.

66. Robert Cover, "Nomos and Narrative," *Harvard Law Review* 97 (1983): 4, 40–44; reprinted in Robert Cover, *Narrative, Violence and the Law* (Ann Arbor: University of Michigan Press, 1992), 109–13.

that this disparity in the senses of *dikê* captures our ambivalence about law—whose simplification of meaning seems at once an advance and a loss. This ambivalence surfaces in modern jurisprudence. It also underlies the inauguration of the jury in the final play of the trilogy, the *Eumenides,* to which I turn in the next section.

B. Justice as Procedure

Philip Soper has compared law to one of those optical illusions where the figure is now a duck, and now a rabbit, or oscillates between being a young girl and an old woman. Law, Soper writes, "is a concept that balances precariously between the view that it is nothing but, and the view that it is something more than, force."[67] Like Dworkin and Rawls, Soper holds that law exerts a morally obligating force on its subjects, and that it is something more than a "command backed by threats." The *Oresteia* too reflects a view of law as something more than force, but relates force and morality in a distinctive and interesting way. Not only does Aeschylus make evident the deep sources of the demand for justice—a demand law must certainly respect—but Orestes in effect *pleads for* the inauguration of law, as a way at least of obtaining an authoritative decision about his morally complex and bewildering act.

This is a view of law not quite like anything to be found in modern legal theory.[68] As presented in the *Oresteia,* law is not a set of commands handed down from on high by a powerful sovereign, nor again a social contract voluntarily entered into by individuals equally situated. Rather, law is a means by which those tormented and confused by their own acts seek relief from those in power. I want to propose that this "model" of law's origins—which at first blush might seem merely archaic—in fact offers a potentially fruitful way of thinking about the law. Law is a kind of safe harbor (peaceful solutions, agreed-upon meanings, limited liability) constructed within a besetting condition of strife, fear, and endlessly profuse significance. This safe harbor represents a distinct advance, in that it makes possible society as a cooperative system. Yet it also entails a certain impoverishment in terms of the self and moral responsibility inherent in the tragic vision.

67. Soper, *Theory of Law,* 14.

68. This statement requires some qualification. H. J. Wolff, "The Origin of Judicial Litigation," *Traditio* 4 (1946): 31–87, proposed that litigation owed its origins to supplication. Wolff suggested that when the injured party (the plaintiff) sought through self-help to obtain redress, the other party (the defendant) fled to a public officer, and asked for protection. The officer then extended temporary protection and called a court into session to adjudicate the dispute. This is much the same as what happens in the *Eumenides.* For a more recent account of the possible origins of litigation in supplication, see Raphael Sealey, *The Justice of the Greeks* (Ann Arbor: University of Michigan Press, 1994), 107–11.

Law, then, begins in an act of supplication, and makes its appearance literally as an answer to a prayer. Both Apollo[69] and Athena[70] look upon Orestes as their suppliant, and both undertake to respond to his earnest entreaties for relief. The jury is the means Athena devises to decide Orestes' case, and, in the event of a vote acquitting him, to free him forever from the Furies' wrath. Law, in short, emerges as a kind of *deus ex machina*, a happy conclusion more or less imposed externally on a conflict that does not admit of resolution in the purely human terms in which the drama, up to this point, has been worked out. Law constitutes a kind of wish fulfillment: it affords just that stable conclusion that the characters have striven for in vain, and that has come to seem unattainable. As Athena remarks, the resolution of such a case is beyond the power of mere mortals (*Eum.*, 470–71), and apparently can only be tendered from above and outside.[71] Aeschylus contrives to make law (that pragmatic, workaday institution) seem unreal and fantastical—simply too good to be true. The gods now do just what the mortal characters would have them do. Apollo is no longer the mysterious and destructive force he was for Cassandra, but a reliable advocate and champion.[72]

Against the austere and terrifying tragic vision of the first two plays, the benevolence and dependability of the gods in the *Eumenides* appears all the more unreal—a child's vision of a world responsive to its wishes.[73] The implication seems to be not, surely, that law is an illusion, but rather that it is highly artificial, and sits uneasily on the mortal condition. Although a reliable method of dispute resolution is a vital necessity to society, it does not emerge or grow naturally from our own resources. As something imposed from on high, law does not truly "cinch" or conclude human strife (*eris*), which is, on this view, perennial and inexorable. Legal decisions simply "stop" the conflict, in the sense of imposing an end—which is the most one could expect from a *deus ex machina*, after all.

69. See, e.g., *Eumenides*, 40–45, 92, 151, 176, 232–34, 577.

70. See *Eumenides*, 474.

71. Of course, as Athena says, it is not right (*themis*) for her to decide the case by herself, either. *Eumenides* 470–71. For this reason, she inaugurates a human jury, in which she participates. The relevant point for now, however, is that without Athena's intervention the jury would not have been possible: the human jury is a divine gift.

72. See, e.g., *Eumenides*, 64, 232–34.

73. Sommerstein, *Aeschylus: "Eumenides,"* 25–26 collects instances of the extraordinary deference the gods show mortals in the *Eumenides*. For example, the Erinyes at the conclusion tell the Athenians that Zeus "reveres you" (1002). Such expressions, Sommerstein notes, are more characteristic of comedy and its fantasias than of tragedy. See, in addition, Rosenmeyer, *Art of Aeschylus*, 348. For this reason I disagree with Sommerstein's point (24) that the gods "develop" over the trilogy, if he means to suggest some organic development in their attitude toward mortals. It seems better to admit the striking discontinuity

Thus, the *Eumenides* does not offer anything like the wisdom of Solomon, nor do we find there a judgment that "solves" or "resolves" the conflicts. Athena does not pronounce judgment at all, but merely states her own reason for casting her vote. The vote by the human jurors, furthermore, is badly divided: at least half of them find that Orestes' matricide cannot be justified on the grounds he has asserted.[74] The jury's decision, therefore, does not stop the dispute because of its inherent wisdom.

Rather, the jury's decision is final in large part because, once the Furies decide to cooperate, it is generally recognized to be the jury's particular business to issue authoritative decisions. A decision is final, in other words, because a duly constituted jury has issued it. Validity (an adherence to certain stipulated procedures) thus serves a kind of "default" function, given the impossibility of attaining a stable and universally satisfying substantive justice. What the jury offers is a "good enough" decision that people will settle for, if only because it comports with standards of fairness that are open for all to see.

This change in the way justice is conceived leaves its trace in the way *dikê* is used. "You do not wish to be just, but only to seem just," Athena tells the Furies in the *Eumenides*, when they seem unwilling to let Orestes' advocate have his say.[75] "Justice," in other words, now conveys an essentially procedural notion of fair play, in which each contestant has the opportunity to be heard—a far different kind of *dikê* from that substantive and passionate demand for another's death that drove the characters in the first two plays. At one level, this procedural insistence on hearing all sides "corrects" the characters' tendency in the earlier plays to suppress the unpleasant or sinister aspects of events or deeds. Yet this procedure is also intended to ensure that hearing all sides does not result in simple incoherence or indecision. The procedure devised by Athena abstracts from the inextricable node of blood ties, commitments, hungers, and fear that have so far motivated the characters, and distills from these cer-

---

between the *Eumenides*' portrayal of the gods and that found in the first two plays. On the discontinuities between *Eumenides* and the first two dramas, see Rosenmeyer, *Art of Aeschylus*, chapter 12 ("Trilogy, Trial, Resolution"), esp. 341–42, 345.

74. Scholars have long disputed whether Athena's vote breaks a tie between the human jurors (i.e., whether there is an even number of human jurors), or whether her vote in fact creates a tie (i.e., whether the number of human jurors is odd). Sommerstein, *Aeschylus: Eumenides*, 222–26 offers a useful survey of the scholarly debate. The different sides of the debate seem to me about evenly balanced, but I don't think much depends on it for purposes of my argument. It seems significant that the vote for acquittal results from a deeply split vote, however that split might be more precisely defined.

75. *Eumenides*, 430.

tain discrete "issues"—all far removed from the particulars of Orestes' murder of his mother. So, for instance, the Furies—representatives of the older gods—debate with Apollo, a younger god associated with Zeus's reign, over the relative merits and faults of each regime (*Eum.*, 614–73). Athena casts her vote partly on the basis of her beliefs about the relative importance of the sexes in the generation of offspring (735–41). The dispositive issues in the trial may arise from the tragic events, but have become detached from them and taken on a quasi-autonomous life of their own. The transformation of *dikê* over the course of the trilogy could be described as a change from strife to contest, from *eris* to *agôn*. It is a movement from a boundless and unfixable wrangling to a pre-established format for dispute and decision. Rather than a substantively satisfying, wise decision, then, the jury offers a "valid" one. On this view, validity is a kind of disappointed justice: it is what *dikê* becomes after its disruptive effects have finally become unendurable.

So far, I have stressed the importance of procedure as the means of putting a stop to the bloodshed. It would be a mistake, though, to suppose that it is a matter of indifference—from a legal standpoint—whether the jury decided on conviction or acquittal. For the jury, as presented in the *Oresteia*, is not a value-free mechanism that happens to issue a verdict acquitting Orestes. The jury stands, more generally, for the *polis*, whose spirit of rationality and practicality it reflects and embodies. The acquittal of Orestes expresses just these qualities.

The *Eumenides* richly conveys the new spirit of the *polis*. Athena's decision to use a body of jurors suggests the importance of achieving consensus: not only will the decision be based on a variety of opinions, but it will be selected on the basis of a neutral principle—majority rule. The play and the trilogy climax with a demonstration of the importance placed on consensus-formation in the *polis*, when Athena uses her powers of persuasion to bring the Furies around to a more cooperative attitude. Indeed, forces that had been notably dangerous and prone to violence in the earlier plays are now reinterpreted as capable of forming community. Persuasion, for example, had been presented in the earlier plays as a kind of seduction—most strikingly in the menacing way Clytaemnestra persuaded Agamemnon to tread upon the red carpet.[76] Only in the *Eumenides* do we see its potential for building consensus, and the model of the person implicit in persuasion—as one capable of looking beyond the immediate appetite for revenge and able to reckon long-term effects and benefits. *Eros*, too, had been presented individualistically in the earlier

76. *Agamemnon*, 931–94; see also 385–86 ("Wretched Persuasion, the irresistible child of cunning Destruction, uses force.")

plays as a hunger or painful memory, and, as such, capable of catastrophic effects. Menelaus' erotic longing for Helen, for example, resulted ultimately in the deaths of many Greeks.[77] In the *Eumenides* it is recast as the basis for solidarity and community—the cement of marriage, now understood as a public promise between a man and woman.[78]

The opening of the *Eumenides* already sounds a new spirit. There the Delphic priestess recalls the succession of power at Delphi—an account that unmistakably emphasizes the peace and harmony with which power passed from generation to generation. The struggle between Zeus and the earlier generations of the gods, too, is strikingly different in the *Eumenides*. In the *Agamemnon* Zeus's victory made him singular, incomparable, and therefore mysterious. In the context of the *polis* and the lawsuit at Athens, however, the victory is considerably demystified, and Zeus appears in part as a litigant allied with Apollo against the Furies, representatives of the older generation of the gods. The violent myths of Zeus's accession to power are now stripped of their oracular suggestiveness and become grist for the parties' arguments in court: the Furies use Zeus's violence toward his father Kronos to refute Apollo's contention that Orestes properly honored his father's claims over his mother's.[79] This disenchanted view of Zeus is especially expressive of the new spirit of the *polis:* as a litigant, Zeus still crystallizes the struggle at the heart of the world, but this struggle is now conceived less as "strife" (*eris*) and more as "contest" (*agôn*).

The acquittal of Orestes signifies that under this new regime, characterized by procedural fairness, exoneration is a possibility in situations where it had been unthinkable before. In purporting to absolve Orestes of any guilt in the murder of his mother, the jury (and by extension the *polis*) in effect assert their authority over one of the basic tenets of natural law: they lay claim to the power effectively to undo a breach of the child's natural duties of loyalty and trust toward the parent. What the law claims for itself in the *Eumenides*—the authority to acquit—is as momentous in its way as the law's claim of authority to kill. The acquittal makes clear, in a way that a guilty verdict could not, the claim by the *polis* and the law to supersede or transcend the natural law condemning matricide.

The jury decision gains authority and legitimacy, therefore, because it flows from and reflects the underlying morality of the institution itself—law, and ultimately the *polis*. The jury's verdict is a self-definition by the city, for it embodies those ideals of reason, compromise, and consensus that are the hallmark of the *polis* and distinguish it from the family (or

---

77. *Agamemnon*, 404–55.
78. *Eumenides*, 213–18.
79. *Eumenides*, 640–56.

oikos). This aspect of the jury decision both assimilates it to and differentiates it from Agamemnon's fateful decision at Aulis. For there too Agamemnon chose public values over those of the family: in choosing to sacrifice Iphigeneia for the sake of the military expedition against Troy, Agamemnon proved loyal to those values of honor and renown that constitute the "heroic ethic" informing the warrior society portrayed in the *Iliad*. The jury is faced with a similarly impossible decision:[80] whether the son should prove more loyal to the father or to the mother. While the split vote expresses just how deep the ambivalence goes, the jury's ultimate verdict reflects public values, but this time the more communitarian values of the *polis*, rather than the individualistic heroic ethos.

One very important *polis*-centered value is the reconciling of opposites, the incorporating of what had previously been marginalized into a new totality. Thus, the male is now construed as that which safeguards and makes possible the values of the household, and to that extent as embracing or comprehending those values and the female principle that embodies them. Apollo argues on behalf of the male that it is only through the marital promise that "the things dearest to mortals"—for example, our blood relatives—come about (*Eumenides*, 216). Athena too casts her vote on the grounds that the man is the guardian (*episkopos*) of the household (740). The male does so, however, because he stands for that spirit of rationality and consensus (crystallized in the marriage promise) that ultimately makes the household possible.

The decision for Orestes, then, is a victory for the male, but a victory of a distinctive kind: the male, by virtue of its associations here with rationality (and compromise and consensus), now represents the rejection of the heroic ethic that puts a premium on individual supremacy. The "victory" of the male, in other words, is presented as a victory over the ethos of victory.[81]

Aeschylus' resolution of the *Oresteia* is ingenious and moving, but the new *polis*-centered order he contemplates is not without its flaws. For despite the reconciling thrust of the finale, the element of victory—of one

---

80. Aeschylus seems to invite our comparison of the two scenes. Thus, Agamemnon reflects on the impossibility of the choice presented to him: "A heavy doom if I disobey; but a heavy doom, too, if I slay my child. . ." (*Agamemnon*, 206–8). In the *Eumenides*, when Orestes and the Furies lay their dispute at her feet, Athena similarly rehearses the unfeasibility of any choice available to her: "Nor is it right for me to distinguish the claims of angry murder, especially since you [Orestes] have come here unharmed as a purified suppliant to my house, while these [the Furies] have an office not to be despised." *Eumenides*, 471–76.

81. On the conclusion as the overcoming of heroism, see Rosenmeyer, *Art of Aeschylus*, 352. Another significant difference between Agamemnon's decision and the jury's is the

party "besting" another—cannot be eliminated. To be sure, the female is incorporated as a necessary element (the Furies are persuaded to act as the nurturing "Benevolent Ones" or Eumenides, who protect the Athenians). It is clear, nonetheless, that their place in the new order is ultimately subordinate. The conclusion of the trilogy is a victory, then, that tries to deny its nature as a victory by softening to the extent possible its "vanquishing" aspects and emphasizing the possibilities of rapprochement it leaves open.[82]

I pause for a moment to reflect on the pertinence of these expressive aspects of the jury's verdict to Dworkin's jurisprudence. For Dworkin locates legitimacy in the judgment's ability to reflect the principles that generally inform our political institutions. Thus, he argues that controversial decisions do not undermine law's claim to legitimacy; the controversies, after all, concern the kind of polity we are and what the principles underlying that polity require in this particular case.

The debate between Apollo and the Furies, however, suggests that law itself, and the political values underlying it, occupy a contested position. Law in the *Eumenides* is affiliated with agreement, contract, and consensus; but these very features are unacceptable to the Furies, to the extent that they allow for any result but the immediate punishment of a son who has murdered his mother in cold blood. Athena's preference for the male principle, on the basis of which she casts her decisive vote, only underscores that the political ideals legitimating the decision are themselves partisan. The fact that the acquittal is an expressive act—expressive, that

---

different type of responsibility each decision maker must shoulder. Agamemnon bears the full burden of responsibility for his murder of Iphigeneia. The jury, in contrast, seem largely immune to the consequences of their vote. Each member (except Athena) votes anonymously, and the final verdict is the result of a number count, over which no one individual exerts final control. On the elusiveness of official responsibility, see Thomas Nagel, *Mortal Questions* (Cambridge: Cambridge University Press, 1979), 75–90.

82. The scholarly discussion reflects this ambivalence in the conclusion to the trilogy. Michael Gagarin, *Aeschylean Drama* (Berkeley: University of California Press, 1976), 87–105, stresses the reconciliation of the male and female in the *Eumenides,* and denies that either sex "wins." Gagarin points to the split vote, and the reconciling properties of Athena's bisexuality, as well as the Furies' (now Eumenides') blessings. See also Sommerstein, *Aeschylus: "Eumenides,"* 230, who argues that Athena's vote contains no male prejudice. In contrast, D. J. Conacher, *Aeschylus' Oresteia,* 211–12, insists that a victory does indeed take place, and the decision is made that Agamemnon's murder is the greater wrong. See also Zeitlin, "Dynamics of Misogyny," 149–84, who writes that, notwithstanding the pacification of the Furies, the *Eumenides* reasserts male dominance in patriarchal marriage; and D. Cohen, "The Theodicy of Aeschylus: Justice and Tyranny in the *Oresteia,*" *Greece and Rome* 33 (1986): 129–41, who argues that the political order instituted in the trilogy has its foundations in force and fear.

is, of the life of the *polis*—cannot, in the context of the *Oresteia,* disguise the violence done to the complexity of meaning, the enforced simplifications that make it possible for the jury to bring the bloodshed to a halt.

Thus, the jury verdict only acquits Orestes; it does not offer an account of his responsibility that is in any way adequate to its complexities, nor does it parse the intricate mix of desire and compulsion that drove him to murder Clytaemnestra. Indeed, it scarcely occurs to us to subject Orestes to a searching ethical scrutiny in the *Eumenides,* since our entire interest is focused on whether he will be acquitted or not. Once acquitted, the action seems resolved; Orestes leaves the stage happy and victorious. Orestes, in short, has ceased to be a tragic hero, and has become instead a legal agent—a being who can be adequately construed within the terms of the law.

This metamorphosis of Orestes can perhaps best be appreciated if we first consider the transformation of the Furies in this final play. They have been present throughout the trilogy, but never physically until the *Eumenides;* rather, they have functioned as the mythical projection of men's and women's fears. The Furies are all the more powerful for being invisible; they are a part of the individual's emotional landscape, the unknown internalized. To personify them and give them a bodily shape—even a no doubt grotesque and frightening shape—is already to tame them. From being the mythical projections of dread and anxiety, they are hardened into individuals capable of argument and open to persuasion. Deep fears—which the Furies essentially incorporate—are transformed into legal adversaries. This may seem to be no more than a dramatic sleight-of-hand. Yet I believe the transformation is a suggestive one for the birth of law: for the personification of the Furies has the inevitable effect of simplifying the individual, whose unknowable interior life is purged and partly transformed into a public figure. Under the earlier conception of them, an acquittal by a public forum would be absolutely irrelevant to the Furies' power to torment and drive insane. As presented almost from the onset of the *Eumenides,* however, they are more like public executioners; to be acquitted is to escape them forever.

This transformation of the Furies entails a simplification of Orestes from someone vulnerable to madness and remorse into *homo legalis,* a being conceived largely in terms of public guilt or non-guilt. The deeper implications of his matricide and the ghastly circumstances that led him to it are reshaped into discussable (although perhaps not finally decidable) "issues" concerning the relative importance of male and female. In the *Eumenides* Aeschylus deliberately eschews tragedy; the characters are simplified so that their conflicts are capable of resolution. Law makes possible an end to otherwise irresolvable conflicts, but it does so at the cost of a certain shallowness in the conception of the person.

The law and the jury thus considerably simplify the way responsibility is conceived. This conclusion may seem misleading, for at one level law introduces a host of new distinctions that are felt to entail quite distinct consequences; in other words, the law may seem to introduce a new complexity to our ways of thinking about responsibility. When, for example, the Furies explain to Athena that Orestes is a matricide, they are shocked and bewildered by her response, which is to ask whether he committed the deed "from necessity, or fearing someone's anger" (*Eumenides* 426). The Furies fail to see what conceivable relevance the circumstances might have to such an appalling deed: no situation could possibly justify killing one's own mother (427). In the legal regime Athena's question adumbrates, however, such circumstances carry an important weight, and may even excuse a deed as apparently heinous as matricide. In the seventh century B.C.E., Dracon apparently instituted a system of courts to judge crimes of bloodshed, and covering different grades of seriousness, "arranged in descending order according to the strength of the collective feeling regarding the excusability of the crime."[83] Thus, for example, the Areopagus (the court whose establishment is dramatized in the *Eumenides*) was competent to judge murders calling for the full penalty. Another court, the Palladion, handled *phonoi akousioi,* or "excusable murders," while a third court, the Delphinion, addressed *phonoi dikaioi,* murders traditionally looked upon as justified (e.g., killing an adulterer, or accidental homicide in the course of public games).[84]

This divergence in degrees of culpability may seem to make our moral life more complex, since it recognizes the variety of ways agents may stand in relation to their acts. In particular, it seems far more complex and nuanced than the rather insensitive mechanism of vengeance. As Vernant insists, however, it would be wrong to see these legal distinctions as the fruit of moral thought on the sources of action; rather, we should understand them as reflecting rough and ready categories imposed by law.[85] These categories reflect a wish for consistency in judgment, and for assurance that a certain parity exists between the crime and the punishment. This parity is essential if the punishment is to be generally condoned as just and appropriate. More important, these distinctions, in the words of Thomas Rosenmeyer, "shift the dramatic focus from the personal to the legal, from the play of

83. Vernant, "Intimations of the Will in Greek Tragedy," in Vernant and Vidal-Naquet, *Myth and Tragedy,* 61.
84. See ibid.
85. See ibid.

forces in which the agent is automatically caught up to the fiction that a person is to be defined in terms of what he has done."[86] As Rosenmeyer suggests, this is a fundamentally untragic conception of the person.[87]

The verdict apparently enables Orestes to feel no remorse, and seems to afford him the sense that, in fact, he has done nothing wrong—because the father's right plainly trumps the mother's. Law ultimately enables the characters to do what they have wanted to do throughout the trilogy—to make the world consistent and predictable. Rather than permitting a deep conflict to continue, law "prioritizes" duties. The precedence of one duty over the other means, in effect, that no conflict exists. So in the *Oresteia*, the jury vote, albeit deeply split, means that the duty to one's father outweighs any duty that might be owed to one's mother. The jury resolves the conflict by sorting through the claims and awarding the palm to one or the other. What the *Oresteia* as a whole suggests, however, is that this absence of conflict—the consonance of values and duties—is purchased at the cost of a certain narrowing of the ethical life.

I conclude this section by looking at force, which plays an important role in the simplifications wrought by the law. The *Eumenides* concludes with Athena's successful recruitment of the Furies—now transformed to the Benevolent Ones (Eumenides)—to apply violence solely in order to punish the unjust, and, by doing so, to ensure the continued stability of Athenian law. The Furies remain objects of mortal dread, but these fears are now so formed and channeled by law as to be socially constructive; they promote a peaceful state. As the Furies say, "There is a place where the fearsome is a good thing" (*Eum.*, 517). Athena concurs: in founding the jury, she says that it will be a place where "the citizens' reverence and innate fear will prevent them from unjust acts both day and night" (690–92).[88]

We note at once that fear plays a much more forthright role in Aeschylus' conception of the polity than it does or possibly could in Dworkin or Rawls. For Aeschylus, law grows from a sense of mortal beings as deeply fallible, misled by passion, and tending easily to excess and injustice. (The Furies grimly claim that without their threatening presence, children would rise up as one to kill their parents.)[89] Law and its use of force is to this extent an unproblematically good thing: only because it uses force can law make people behave better than they otherwise would and

86. Rosenmeyer, *Art of Aeschylus*, 356.

87. See ibid.

88. On the positive role of fear as presented in the *Eumenides*, and more generally in early fifth-century political thinking, see Rose, *Sons of the Gods*, 253–54.

89. *Eumenides*, 490–98.

thus make society possible. Law, then, purports to create a boundary between "good" violence and "bad." "Good" violence keeps people in line, and enables a society to function.

Aeschylus may be making a still deeper point about the law's use of coercion. For it is not simply that people perversely choose the worse course of action over the better, or viciously decide to be unjust. Rather, mortals find themselves in situations where the distinction between good and evil seems irrelevant. This was precisely Agamemnon's dilemma: it did not much matter whether killing Iphigeneia was a good thing (since that would not prevent Clytaemnestra from plotting revenge) or a bad thing (since in any event it could scarcely be avoided). The existence of law tends to prevent situations from presenting these morally bewildering questions: it offers an authoritative answer, and if one does not already exist, it will generate one. Law, on this view, seeks to root out the tragic aspects of existence, or at least to push them back as far as possible. It is a deliberately "antitragic" institution; its use of force serves in part to keep tragic conflicts at bay. It simplifies ethical deliberation by providing one very powerful reason to follow one course of action rather than another.

As the *Oresteia* suggests, the strife, or *eris,* between the generations is a fixed condition in which mortals, to their hopeless confusion, are situated. The fear-backed law excludes certain dreadful possibilities to which the strife innate in mortal existence gives rise; it prevents our natural disorder from playing itself out. In other words, it is not simply that law happens to entail a thinning of our ethical life; rather, it is *intended* to do so. Law uses fear to ensure that its subjects keep far away from those passionately desired things—things that represent an authentic, if deeply flawed, good—in order to avoid the uncharted ethical depths that plague the Atreids. Here, too, law purports to distill what is constructive about force and to use that for its own purposes.

The Furies and Athena, in their claims about the law, present force as a tool: people are induced to toe the line because the threat of reprisal is there to ward them off from behaving unjustly. This means-end relation is drastically different from the *Libation-Bearers,* where justice and violence seem inextricably related and indeed difficult to distinguish. It is not as though Orestes and Electra are in the unfortunate position of having only violence available to them to bring about justice. Rather, the justice they desire consists precisely in the violent death of Clytaemnestra. Indeed, the vehemence of their desire for justice is itself a kind of violence. The *Agamemnon* and *Libation-Bearers* strongly suggest that justice is a kind of violence, an aggressive instinct whose source is in mourning for the loss of one beloved. Law redefines the relation between justice and violence: the latter is now a carefully controlled tool for effectuating a reasonable facsimile of the former. But this redefinition cannot hope to make justice and force two completely different things, for the two are deeply and inextricably joined.

By showing the deep sources of justice, and its near merging with violence at that depth, the *Oresteia* inevitably shows the shallowness of law. As the *Oresteia* suggests, it is a saving shallowness, for it enables mortals—now conceived as citizens—to avoid the terrors of life without the law. Law erects boundaries for itself to simplify the world and keep at bay inscrutable moral complexities. Yet these boundaries can only be tentative, provisional. The complexity of the world exerts a pressure against these boundaries, and requires that they be continually renegotiated.

3. LAW AND THE POLITICS OF RECOGNITION

The *Oresteia* is a tragic treatment of the boundary between law (reason, consensus, persuasion) and morals (justice as a compelling desire and an irresistible imperative). It is quite different from the picture of this boundary presented by Rawls and Dworkin, and to some degree more persuasive. The *Oresteia* and Rawls share the premises that there exists in society a surfeit of meaning (several incompatible visions of the good) and that these must somehow be winnowed or pared down in order for a stable and manageable order to exist. Rawls presents law as, at least ideally, a successful solution to the potential for deadly conflict in a pluralist society: he assumes that the state can more or less unproblematically surmount its background and relegate fundamental controversies to a strictly private zone. The *Oresteia,* in contrast, seems more realistic: the moral depths that threaten to tear apart public life cannot be clearly or unambiguously separated off, for the very simplifications that such boundaries make possible can become a part of political conflicts.

To be sure, law is clearly a step up from vengeance. Not only does it make possible social cooperation of a far more complex kind than was previously conceivable; it also affords its subjects a far greater degree of mastery over their lives. However, law represents a deliberately blinkered view that looks away from those dimensions of a conflict that threaten to make it truly irresolvable. Aeschylus presents law, then, as a deeply paradoxical kind of progress, in which a greater clarity is achieved, but only at the price of a narrowed vision.

This suggests, in turn, that legal systems never "possess" justice, or integrity, or any other quality that could plainly entitle them, once and for all, to citizens' obedience. For at least one of the purposes law serves—to create a forum in which citizens can set aside ultimate questions—at once legitimates it (since it is the source of the very great good of a stable order), and inevitably delegitimizes it (since it cannot express the totality of its citizens; since it "thins out" the individual). In other words, because law has an ineradicable simplifying element, it inevitably does some violence to the integrity—the moral complexity—of the persons it rules, and therefore can never achieve complete legitimacy. Rather than a stable body that acts within the legitimate boundaries laid down, law is better understood as a practice that moves continually back and forth between reducing communal life to a set of easily understood and administered rules, and attempting to capture more of the ethical complexity of citizens, with a view to becoming more fair, less unjustifiably coercive. This splintered or conflicted quality at the heart of law serves to drive it forward: the order law secures is a provisional and precarious one that is constantly revisited. The values that legitimate a legal system are not characteristics inhering in it, but ideals that are conceived within a specific historic situation and that a system must then strive to incorporate if it is to be felt as legitimate. For this reason, law is bound to be unstable, because the boundaries it erects to simplify situations will be continually contested, and subject to renegotiation. This sense of instability and impermanence should inform our theorization about the law.

To clarify the point I want to make about law, it will help to distinguish the conclusions for legal and political theory that others have recently drawn from the *Oresteia*. Aeschylus' trilogy has been an important text for writers seeking to challenge some basic assumptions of liberal theory, but it seems to me that they, too, err in drawing too optimistic a picture of law, one that fails to do justice to its complex, conflicted character. For example, J. Peter Euben, in his study of political justice in the *Oresteia*,[90] captures something like the ambiguity I have tried to show here. He writes that justice "represents both a gain in clarity *and* a loss of meaning. . . . For order requires the vivid potential of disorder; the relative abstractness of political discourse requires both distance from and dependence on the primal passions and compact poetry of the earlier plays and world."[91] The *Eumenides,* he writes, does not offer hope for an escape from contingency, so long as "men are both doers and victims, actors and analysts of action, free and constrained—that is, as long as they live human lives."[92] Political justice, as envisioned in the *Oresteia,* then, is never a stable, transcendent

90. J. Peter Euben, "Justice in the *Oresteia*," in *Tragedy of Political Theory*, 67–95.
91. Ibid., 88 (emphasis in original).
92. Ibid., 85.

institution. Part of what makes it justice is that it does not claim too much for itself; it does not purport to "conquer" or vanquish what is intractable.

The *Oresteia,* then, provides a program for the kind of justice to which states should aspire. For Euben, political justice as it emerges from Aeschylus' trilogy is essentially a matter of recognizing diversity. By this Euben means not simply a passive tolerance of difference, but an active incorporation of it in decision making, so that authority is genuinely shared. This more active recognition of diversity "involves the capacity to see things from another's point of view and so accept the human condition of plurality—and to practice what Hannah Arendt calls representative or political thinking."[93] This is the vision Euben finds enacted onstage in the finale of the *Eumenides:* "men and women as partners in sustaining a whole that gives identity and dignity to each. . . .Similarly young and old are not warring factions but mutual participants in a collectivity that communalizes the burdens of action while providing object and limit for passion."[94]

More recently, Christopher Rocco has offered a reading of the *Oresteia* and drawn conclusions from it for political theory.[95] He is perhaps even more sensitive than Euben to the rich ambiguities that suffuse Aeschylus' trilogy, for he shows how it simultaneously celebrates the inauguration of law and questions the hierarchies that prop up the new order. "Despite the celebratory and triumphant ending," he writes, "the *Oresteia* constructs the meaning of the democratic founding, and so of democracy itself, as open to further contest, struggle and renegotiation."[96] To be sure, the *Oresteia* is a celebration of the *polis* and the law that structures and animates it, for it "institutes and legitimates a democratically constituted hierarchy of values, establishes norms of inclusion and exclusion, and creates bonds of membership by drawing boundaries." At the same time, however, the *Oresteia* is realistic about the hierarchies and norms structuring law and the city. For it shows "how such boundaries are constituted, that they are ultimately political, and that such limits are transgressed the very moment they are established." In fact, then, the "problem of *dikê* [justice] is not solved in the *Eumenides,* but the trilogy as a whole shows us that we cannot live without such (temporary) solutions."[97]

The *Oresteia's* simultaneous celebration and deconstruction of legal

93. See ibid., 81–82. Euben refers to Hannah Arendt, "Truth and Politics," in *Between Past and Future* (New York: The Viking Press, 1968), 241–43.

94. Euben, *Tragedy of Political Theory,* 85.

95. Christopher Rocco, *Tragedy and Enlightenment: Athenian Political Thought and the Dilemmas of Modernity* (Berkeley: University of California Press, 1997), 136–70.

96. Ibid., 169.

97. Ibid., 167.

norms, Rocco argues, resonates with the contemporary contest over the meaning of democracy. This contest, crystallized in the work of Jürgen Habermas and Michel Foucault,[98] "vacillates between the quest to instantiate norms of consensus, and the suspicion that such rationally achieved agreement is . . . one more strategy that effectively masks the mechanism of power." In other words, the simplifying definitions law introduces tend to produce "normalized and disciplined selves and citizens for the effective functioning of the order."[99] The awareness that law exerts this normalizing tendency undermines the legitimacy of the norms and categories introduced to promote the possibility of consensus. Aeschylus' *Oresteia,* Rocco concludes, illuminates a politics of identity *and* difference: it yields a "democratic politics of disturbance that maintains a commitment to the ideals of democratic consensus even as it disrupts democracy's normalizing effects."[100]

Rocco emphasizes more than Euben does the disruption of received categories that is necessary if society is genuinely to accommodate differences. For Euben, the *Eumenides* shows how the city incorporates the female element, and thereby how the just city avoids the struggle between the sexes for mastery. Rocco, in contrast, better brings out the intricacies of sexual politics in the trilogy. The democratic reason embodied in the law court is "masculine in gender and founded squarely on women's exclusion from, and subordination to, the male-ordered polis."[101] The *Oresteia* does not merely expose the male bias of the legal system it dramatizes, then, but suggests that even this most basic difference can be recognized and renegotiated.

Despite their different emphases, Euben and Rocco share a common view of justice as requiring a genuine recognition of difference and an embodiment of it in making, administering, and adjudicating the laws. They converge on a rich body of thought, generally called "communitarian," that resists what it sees as the tendency in liberalism to impose a model of "rational autonomy" as an inherent feature in all persons, and thus to abstract too much from the specific differences that partly constitute anyone's sense of his or her identity. For liberalism the source of our dignity—and the basis for each one's entitlement to equal concern and respect—is the general capacity to have a conception of the good and to take responsibility for one's ends.[102] But this tends to sideline what is dis-

98. I address the "contest" of Habermas and Foucault below in Chapter 2, Section 1. I deal with Habermas in greater detail in Chapter 3, particularly Sections 1 and 3.

99. Rocco, *Tragedy and Enlightenment,* 168.

100. Ibid., 168.

101. Ibid., 169.

102. See, e.g., Rawls, *Political Liberalism,* 30–33.

tinctive in the individual as being less relevant for political purposes than what is shared. This tendency to homogenize—to assimilate all persons to a common model—can be subtly oppressive and demeaning in its own right.

Euben's and Rocco's readings of the *Oresteia,* then, seem to reflect what Charles Taylor has called the "politics of recognition," whereby a just political unity consists in the recognition of differences—i.e., those specific traits that make the individual who she or he is.[103] As Taylor points out, we tend to experience our identity in terms of what is individual and distinctive about us. Taylor calls this an "*individualized* identity, one that is particular to me and that I discover in myself."[104] It carries with it an ideal of being true to what is distinctively oneself—the ideal of authenticity. The idea is not, as in Rawls, simply to set off or "bracket" those differences, but to make them an integral part of public life and reason. For, as Taylor asserts, recognition by others is a crucial part of the individual's sense of his or her distinctive identity. That is because "[w]e define our identity always in dialogue with, sometimes in struggle against, the things our significant others want to see in us."[105] Taylor refers, then, to the "dialogical character" of human life.[106] We become full human agents by developing richly expressive languages, but we can develop these languages only with and through others. To discover one's identity, therefore, does not mean that one works it out in isolation, but rather that one "negotiates" it through dialogue with others. This "dialogic" character of human identity thus places added importance on others' recognition of me, which, on Taylor's view, is deeply a part of my own self-understanding.[107]

A society that aspires to neutrality and to ignoring differences may be subtly but deeply discriminatory. Assimilating everyone to a common model (e.g., a moral agent capable of endorsing a good) may obscure whatever is specific or idiosyncratic in the individual, and suggests that anyone is worthy of respect only to the extent that she or he is like everyone else. This not only sins against the ideal of authenticity, but risks silencing those who in fact are different.

103. Charles Taylor, "The Politics of Recognition," in Taylor, *Philosophical Arguments* (Cambridge: Harvard University Press, 1995), 225–56. The same essay also appears in Amy Gutmann, ed., *Multiculturalism and "The Politics of Recognition"* (Princeton, N.J.: Princeton University Press, 1992).

104. Taylor, "Politics of Recognition," 227 (emphasis in original).

105. Ibid., 230. See also Sandel, *Liberalism and the Limits of Justice,* 149–50, 152–54.

106. Taylor's use of the term "dialogic" is indebted to Mikhail Bakhtin, and especially his *Problems of Dostoyevsky's Poetics,* trans. Caryl Emerson (Minneapolis: University of Minnesota Press, 1984).

107. Taylor, "Politics of Recognition," 231.

I pause to note that the "politics of recognition" rests on a view of the self suggestively close to that found in Greek tragedy: specifically, the sense that the individual is immersed in values and meanings that constitute who she is, but which she has not willed or specifically endorsed.[108] For Taylor—as in Greek tragedy, as well—self-knowledge takes the form of discovering what was already true about oneself, a kind of retrieval of depths forgotten or obscured by daily life.[109] The name Aristotle used for the tragic hero's coming to grips with himself—*anagnorisis*, or "recognition"—is appropriate, too, for the process by which the Taylorian self attains self-knowledge: a cognizing or re-cognizing of its own thickness.

Taylor's "dialogic" account of the experience of breaking with one's family (as one deep source of our sense of identity) is more plausible than Dworkin's,[110] and in a way that strongly suggests the pertinence of Greek tragedy. Thus, Taylor writes: "Even after we outgrow some of these others—our parents, for instance—and they disappear from our lives, the conversation with them continues within us as long as we live."[111] Taylor's account conveys, as Dworkin's does not, the depth of one's ties to the family, and the way these ties strongly constitute one's identity, even where the relations are markedly unjust.

Thus, the politics of recognition is better able to do justice to that ethical complexity the *Oresteia* explores, because it grants an important role in ethical experience to the possibility of conflict among genuine values. That is partly because values are not confined to those that are universalizable, but also include those "particularistic" values we cherish just because they are distinctive to us. These goods are strongly invested with emotional energies, and indeed are difficult to distinguish finally from the passions that attend them. Such particularistic goods are a rich source of moral conflict, if only because no guarantee can exist that they will all be perfectly congruent with each other on all occasions.

Because it is highly sensitive to the possibility of conflict among values, the politics of recognition is less sanguine than Rawls, for example, about

108. Michael Sandel's communitarian description of the self at times recalls Orestes' predicament in *Libation-Bearers:* "Crowded by the claims and pressures of various possible purposes and ends," Sandel writes, "all impinging indiscriminately on my identity, I am unable to sort them out, unable to mark out the limits or the boundaries of my self, incapable of saying where my identity ends and the world of attributes, aims and desires begins . . . Too much is too essential to my identity." *Liberalism and the Limits of Justice*, 57.

109. Taylor makes this point powerfully in his *Sources of the Self* (Cambridge: Harvard University Press, 1989), esp. 502–13. See also Sandel, *Liberalism and the Limits of Justice*, 58–59, 62–63, 152–61, 179–83.

110. See above, Section 1.

111. Taylor, "Politics of Recognition," 230.

the possibility of creating a neutral state that simply avoids disputed areas. That is a strength in Taylor's account: he can explain better than Rawls can the possibility of fundamental conflicts about the state and a just public order. Thus, under the banner of the politics of recognition, one might attack a supposedly fair and difference-blind society on the grounds that it is "not only inhuman (because suppressing identities) but also, in a subtle and unconscious way, itself highly discriminatory."[112] Taylor's account does not purport to lock out fundamental disagreements, and appreciates that neutrality itself is a contested value.

Martha Minow has dealt in a specifically jurisprudential context with the problems identified by the politics of recognition.[113] Minow points to the deep connection between law and prejudice, by stressing the tendency of law to classify and thereby entrench social hierarchies. For Minow, the problem of law is its inherent tendency to harden prejudices through its very modality of classifying. This is not to say that law does not try to be fair to minorities. But, as she writes, difference presents a dilemma: how can we acknowledge difference without thereby perpetuating the exclusions that define the difference?

The answer to this dilemma is to raise to consciousness the reality and relativity of individual perspectives. Thus, a litigation model informed by a politics of recognition (and the view of self presupposed by it) would challenge the ideal of neutral objectivity as silencing those who have been traditionally marginalized. Because we are "situated" within milieus that deeply characterize our thinking, litigation should be a discourse in which we overcome what is narrowing in our individual perspectives and attain through sympathy and reflection some sense of another's point of view. On this view, litigants confront and challenge the state's temptation to coerce a single authoritative version of society and the political community. What they offer, in part, is a perspective on officialdom, one that challenges the court's sense of itself as neutral and impartial and invites the

112. Ibid., 237. I should add that Taylor is not necessarily endorsing this critique, but only articulating one mode in the politics of recognition. Taylor himself finds that a liberalism that insists on uniform application of rules and is suspicious of collective goals is "guilty as charged by the proponents of a politics of difference." Ibid., 248. Taylor goes on, however, to describe a different form of liberalism that, while refusing to tamper with fundamental rights, is nonetheless "willing to weigh the importance of certain forms of uniform treatment against the importance of cultural survival, and opt sometimes in favor of the latter." Ibid., 248. Such a liberalism is better able to cope with multiculturalism; it is the version Taylor himself endorses. See ibid.

113. See Martha Minow, "Foreword: Justice Engendered," *Harvard Law Review* 101 (1987): 10. See also the same author's *Making All the Difference: Inclusion, Exclusion and American Law* (Ithaca, N.Y.: Cornell University Press, 1990).

judge to appreciate the partialness of his own perspective—as, for example, male, white, educated, and belonging to a powerful elite. The litigant offers a view of the law that makes the world safe for difference, that allows a variety of perspectives to thrive. A good judgment, on this view, is precisely one that avoids silencing people and that fosters difference—one that broadens the official perspective, so that it incorporates points of view other than its own. In doing so, the judge makes the law more just.[114]

Seyla Benhabib's discussion of discourse as a "moral-transformative process" is relevant here.[115] In such discourse, participants not only debate issues within the terms of a controlling norm or ideal, but subject the ideals themselves to critical scrutiny. Benhabib offers a picture of discourse undertaken in relation to a "concrete other," in which we view "each and every rational being as an individual with a concrete history, identity, and affective-emotional constitution."[116] She advocates a critical discourse that seeks to reveal the "partiality and ideological biases of interests claimed to be universal or general." Through "moral-transformative" discourse, participants "come to realize a certain truth about their needs and interests and change their previously held beliefs about them."[117]

While litigation will never attain to being a moral-transformative discourse, Benhabib's work provides, together with the work of Taylor, Sandel, and others, an ideal model that functions as a kind of background to Minow's communitarian account. Minow's model of litigation differs in several particulars from that offered in Dworkin's liberal jurisprudence, and specifically in the importance it assigns to advocacy, narrative, persuasion, and judgment. I treat each of these four differences below. My point is that this model describes litigation and legal practice in a way that seeks to do justice to our complexity, and so to make law

114. Minow, *Harvard Law Review* 101 (1987): 73–95. Judith N. Shklar, in *The Faces of Injustice* (New Haven: Yale University Press, 1990), 81–82, offers a view of public discourse similar to Minow's:

> The voices of victims must always be heard first, not only to find out whether officially recognized social expectations have been denied, but also to attend to their interpretations of the situation. Are changes in the order of publicly accepted claims called for? Are the rules such that the victim could have consented to them had she been asked?

115. See Seyla Benhabib, *Critique, Norm and Utopia* (New York: Columbia University Press, 1986), 313–16. The process Benhabib has in mind contrasts to Rawls's "original position," wherein individuals choose the governing norms under conditions ensuring impartiality. This "generalized" discourse establishes "a lowest common denominator, while leaving the substantive conflict of interest untouched." Ibid., 314. For a model of discourse concerning moral commitments similar to Benhabib's, see Charles Taylor, "Explanation and Practical Reason," in *Philosophical Arguments*, 34–60.

116. Benhabib, *Critique, Norm and Utopia*, 341.

117. Ibid., 312.

more just. In some ways it more accurately reflects our practices and affords a better justification of them. I will conclude, however, that ultimately this model distorts our notion of law, precisely in its attempt to make it more just.

A. *Advocacy*

Minow's model of litigation presupposes a central role for the litigant and her advocate. It is just Minow's point that the judge cannot appreciate unaided the litigant's position, for judge and litigant may be divided by a host of subtle but fundamental differences in outlook and values. The advocate's role, then, is to bring these differences to the surface, to ensure that the final judgment in the case has taken them into account. The lawyer, in other words, seeks to make eloquent those whom society has tended to silence. She does so by translating the client's case into the language of the law—that is, by offering a public account of the broadest significance of what has happened.[118] To do so, however, the lawyer must first discover the relevant public considerations, which need not be confined to those that have been deemed relevant in the past. The client's story, inventively and sympathetically understood, can invest with public and legal significance considerations that may not have been properly appreciated before. The advocate is, then, a fashioner—an inventor—of relevant arguments, the one who guides where and how the issue will be joined.

Nowhere in *Law's Empire* does Dworkin discuss the role of the advocate; advocacy is apparently regarded as lacking any theoretical importance for understanding litigation. Rather, the central figure in Dworkin's jurisprudence is the judge, who is most clearly seen in the apotheosized form of Hercules, a supreme jurist. Hercules has no particular need for advocates, since he is able to build his own political theory of our institutions based on his own knowledge of the institutions and case precedent. Hercules resolutely faces backwards as he reads and rereads the universals generating the law. Minow's model, in contrast, presupposes the importance of facts as exerting a gravitational pull in creating the law. Law, on this view, is not principally an ongoing interpretation of the past, because it is informed in substantial part by the purposes and situations of those who are actually invoking it in the present. Law responds to concrete par-

---

118. See James Boyd White, *Justice as Translation* (Chicago: University of Chicago Press, 1990), 257–69, which explores this metaphor, and offers the salutary warning that something might well be lost in translation. I would add, however, that the translation from private experience to public narrative might also clarify the client's story, by showing its widest significance.

ticulars, and looks for the right way to respond to events and situations that were unforeseen and unforeseeable.

B. Narrative

The significance of the advocate's role allows us in turn to appreciate the importance of *narrative* in the law. Far from applying a preexisting rule to a body of neutral facts, the lawyer in the first instance sifts through the facts to pick out the pertinent details, and configures them in a variety of ways, the better to explore the reasons why the client's demand is of public importance. Narrative captures the notion that "facts" do not exist in some neutral, wholly objective way, but emerge from and reflect a particular set of values, a particular perspective. The story an advocate or judge tells consists of events related and arranged in such a way as to evince irresistibly a distinctive vision.[119] To invoke Aristotle, the narrative not only tells "what happened," but persuasively conveys "the kind of thing that happens."[120] The advocate attempts to present the client's situation as crystallizing one aspect of our lives together in society. Narratives are, then, the way an advocate vividly conveys the client's own perspective. They are also the means through which the judge may ponder the difficult case, becoming convinced as to the proper result by weighing the different narratives expressed or implicit in the parties' claims or defenses.

These are, to some extent, practice tips: any litigator appreciates the importance of vivid, particularized storytelling in advocacy. More deeply, however, the undoubted importance of storytelling reflects a distinct view of the individual as inevitably situated within an encompassing milieu.[121] The art of narrative partly consists in making sense of desire and decision by showing how they occur against a thickly detailed background. Thus,

---

119. See the Introduction for references to recent "law and literature" studies. On the importance of storytelling for adjudication in particular, see for example Martha C. Nussbaum, *Poetic Justice: The Literary Imagination and Public Life* (Boston: Beacon, 1995). That judges offer persuasive narratives is argued or explored in, e.g., Richard A. Posner, *Law and Literature*, rev. ed. (Cambridge: Harvard University Press, 1998), 255–304; L. H. LaRue, *Constitutional Law as Fiction* (University Park: Pennsylvania State University Press, 1995). On the filiations between law and narrative, see for instance James Boyd White, *When Words Lose Their Meaning* (Chicago: University of Chicago Press, 1984), and *Heracles' Bow* (Madison: University of Wisconsin Press, 1985); Richard H. Weisberg, *The Failure of the Word* (New Haven, Conn.: Yale University Press, 1984); Robin West, *Narrative, Authority and Law* (Ann Arbor: University Of Michigan Press, 1993); Kim Lane Scheppele, "Foreword: Telling Stories," *Michigan Law Review* 87 (1989): 2073.

120. Aristotle, *Poetics*, 1451b5–b12.

121. On narrative as reflecting a model of the self as deeply situated, see Taylor, *Sources of the Self*, 41–52; MacIntyre, *After Virtue*, 204–25.

narrative conveys a view of the individual different from a Kantian model, which construes the self as capable of transcending its circumstances and engaging in free acts of will unconditioned by the agent's immediate circumstances or particularized needs or desires. The Kantian model offers a law-like view of freedom and morality, for freedom consists precisely in acting upon maxims that are perfectly general and law-like, and therefore not contingent on the agent's idiosyncratic circumstances.[122]

In arguing their cases, however, lawyers have adhered to the virtues of storytelling. Our practice implicitly corrects the idealistic, transcendental features of the Kantian model. One of the strengths of the communitarian model of litigation is that it captures the central role narrative plays in advocacy and judging. Common to Taylor, Benhabib, and Minow is a view of the individual as deeply abiding in a thickly settled world. Narrative takes on a significant theoretical role because it is a medium peculiarly adapted to understanding the actions of the individual so construed.

C. Persuasion

The central significance of the advocate and narrative points in turn to a central role for persuasion. For it is now a defining characteristic of the judge's impartiality that the judge is open to being acted upon—is, so to speak, vulnerable to persuasion—and is willing to question her operating assumptions. (The Dworkinian Hercules, in contrast, need never question the basic political theory he brings to bear on particular cases.) Impartiality, on this view, is compatible with the judge's feeling emotions, to the extent these enable him to experience the parties' perspectives, and thereby truly to hear them.[123] Thus, persuasion implies a more complex, more internal and personally intricate model of adjudication than Dworkin allows.

The theoretical significance of persuasion, like that of narrative, suggests a view of law as something not fully autonomous. Persuasion is a dispensable side-phenomenon, if law, as Dworkin believes, has verifiably correct answers. To be sure, we can suppose, if we like, that judges may arrive at a correct answer because they have been persuaded by an advocate's argument. But, for theoretical purposes, we can dispense with the judge's particular route to

122. See I. Kant, *Foundations of the Metaphysics of Morals,* trans. Lewis White Beck (Indianapolis: Bobbs-Merrill, 1959). Kantian ethics, however, may accommodate a more flexible and virtue-based view. See Barbara Herman, *The Practice of Moral Judgment* (Cambridge: Harvard University Press, 1993).

123. Minow, "Foreword," 89–91; on the role of the emotions in ethical deliberation, see Martha C. Nussbaum, *Love's Knowledge: Essays on Philosophy and Literature* (Oxford: Oxford University Press, 1990), 40–43, 75–82.

the correct decision, and concentrate on the legal criteria that show the decision's correctness. The essential account is why the answer is correct, not the particular rhetorical means used in arriving at the correct answer.

If, on the other hand, hard cases do not have verifiably correct results, then persuasion becomes indispensable to an account of law and adjudication. Persuasive rhetoric is not merely a means to get the judge to the independently correct answer, but itself constitutes the reasoning that justifies the result. In other words, the legal opinion is in significant part a piece of rhetoric that attempts to offer a compelling vision of what the law should be. Law, on this view, does not truly transcend us, by having answers whose correctness exists outside us; rather, it is what we construct out of the materials we find most persuasive. More broadly, who we are as a community is partly constituted by rhetoric and persuasion. Community is not a given fact about us, but must continually be rearticulated, and indeed exists only to the extent that we are able to express it in compelling, persuasive speech.

D. Judging

On any view of adjudication, the judge's role cannot be confined to applying rules to concrete cases, for it is clear that at some point the rules give out. Problems have arisen, however, in describing what judges do in the absence of a clearly applicable rule: it may seem that what they do reduces to a fundamentally unprincipled exercise of discretion. That is obviously unsatisfactory, and suggests that judging must entail something more than the application of rules. One response is to assimilate legal judging to the ethical experience of situations where rules either do not exist, or fail to determine how we should act. In such cases, judgment or practical reasoning—what Aristotle called *phronêsis*—becomes central.[124] Good judgment, in this Aristotelian sense, is a matter of construing a situation in all its concrete particulars, discerning its pertinent features, and seeing the most appropriate course of action.[125] The past may inform such a decision, but cannot completely determine it. For this reason, good judgment is a practical skill, a question of "knowing how" rather than "knowing that." It is partly a skill at seeing the applicable principles abiding in a situation. Aristotle draws the analogy of perceiving a triangle or other geometric figure in a group of lines. This perception, in other words, is a construing—an active process of seeing what a situation amounts to, and what it requires.

124. Aristotle, *Nicomachean Ethics*, 6.5, 6.7–8; see also 2.9, 5.10.
125. For discussions of *phronêsis*, see Nussbaum, *Love's Knowledge*, 54–105, and *Fragility of Goodness*, chapter 10; Larmore, *Moral Complexity*, 1–21; MacIntyre, *After Virtue*, 146–64.

But if judgment is a skill, it is not one that can be taught, since, being addressed to concrete situations, it is not an activity governed by general rules. Because by its very nature it resists formulation, good judgment is deeply puzzling.[126] Legal judgment is a theme in mythology and folklore, partly no doubt because it has the potential (however seldom realized in actual practice) for uncanny insight—for seeing a situation in a surprising but trenchant way that all acknowledge as compellingly right. Benjamin Cardozo was being strikingly Aristotelian when he emphasized the variety of considerations that enter into adjudication and the crucial significance of experience:

> My analysis of the judicial process comes then to this, and little more: logic, and history, and custom, and utility, and the accepted standards of right conduct, are the forces which singly or in combination shape the progress of the law. . . . If you ask how he is to know when one interest outweighs another, I can only answer that he must get his knowledge just as the legislator gets it, from experience and study and reflection; in brief, from life itself.[127]

Given the centrality of judgment in ethical deliberation, what effect might this have on our view of adjudication? The puzzling quality of judging—its resistance to exact formulation—is a troubling feature in a legal context, since the Rule of Law is felt to require that expectations not be subject to unfair surprise. Legal judging, therefore, is not to be assimilated entirely to moral judgment, but must be governed by rules to the extent possible.[128]

The point remains, however, that when the rules do give out, we are not left with a vacuum, in which the judge simply foists his own personal opinion on others. Rather, the good judge sees what the rules re-

126.   See Larmore, *Moral Complexity*, 14–19, on the puzzling nature of judgment.

127.   Benjamin N. Cardozo, *The Nature of the Judicial Process* (New Haven: Yale University Press, 1921), 112–13.

Cardozo's analysis of *Riggs v. Palmer*, 115 N.Y. 506, 22 N.E. 188 (1889) contrasts interestingly with Dworkin's central treatment of it in *Law's Empire*. For Cardozo, the *Riggs* decision exemplifies that indescribable quality of judgment as a seeking to do justice in the particular case. "History or custom or social utility or some compelling sentiment of justice or sometimes perhaps a semi-intuitive apprehension of the pervading spirit of our law must come to the rescue of the anxious judge, and tell him where to go." *Nature of the Judicial Process*, 43. This is quite different in letter and spirit from Dworkin's reading of *Riggs* as essentially an interpretation of the principles underlying the case law. Dworkin, *Law's Empire*, 15–20. Dworkin's Hercules is never "anxious," as Cardozo's judge may well be.

128.   Aristotle recognized the distinction between judgment in legal contexts and in other contexts. In his treatise on rhetoric, he lists the reasons why as little as possible should be left to the judge's judgment. See *Rhetoric*, 1.7–8.

quire, given the particulars of this case. Good judgment negotiates the gap between the rule and its application—a gap that may require a high degree of insight and understanding.[129] Aristotle writes that the judge needs something analogous to a "Lesbian rule"—a builder's tool that adapts itself to the shape of the stone.[130] Where the facts fall outside those contemplated by the legislators, judges are to apply their practical judgment—their knack of seeing how a rule is to make its force felt in these particular circumstances. This is a skill requiring a certain sympathy—that is, an ability to enter imaginatively into the given situation.[131]

This capacity for sympathetic judgment is at the heart of the model of adjudication I am sketching. Unlike Dworkin's account, this model stresses the importance of facts as exerting a gravitational pull in creating the law. Law emerges as far more open-ended, in that it is not only responsive to the complaints and defenses before it, but actually takes its shape in part from the specific purposes and desires of those who have recourse to it. This is to emphasize the nature of law as an ongoing practice (as distinct from a static "body" of commands, rules, and principles). It lays stress on the gap between the rule and its application in any given situation—a distance to be negotiated by persuasive narrative and skill in practical judgment. It assimilates both advocacy and adjudication to a fact-intensive mode of ethical scrutiny. It also allows for the influence of actual practice on the rules: the concrete situations in which the rule is invoked and debated help shape the rule's meaning and scope.[132]

So far, I have been describing a model of litigation that seeks to "do justice to" our complexity, and that avoids the falsifying simplifications I have tried to point out in Dworkin and Rawls. The model builds on several features that Euben and Rocco identified as part of the *Oresteia*'s teachings about a just society. The communitarian model, in short, could be read as a theoretical projection of that view of the self and society that finds expression in Greek tragedy.

I think that in many particulars the proposed model describes our actual practice more accurately than Dworkin does, partly because it rejects (or at least tempers) the view that law is an autonomous discipline, marked off from the surrounding political, social, and economic currents. I think, too, that it offers a better justification of our practice. It suggests that law is not antecedently entitled to our respect, but, as David

129. Taylor, "To Follow a Rule," in *Philosophical Arguments*, 177.
130. See Aristotle, *Nicomachean Ethics*, 5.10.
131. See ibid., 6.11.
132. See Taylor, "To Follow A Rule," in *Philosophical Arguments*, 165–80.

Lyons has remarked, must earn it.[133] Law requires a constant effort to discern as acutely and sympathetically as possible the facts—and, more fundamentally, the varying perspectives—that come before it. Law does not have its legitimacy built into it. Failure to articulate a principled view of law and the political community compromises the law and weakens the community that, on Dworkin's view, is the source of its legitimacy. The legitimacy of law, then, is to some extent tentative, a work in progress, and partly consists in the very modesty of the claims it makes for itself.

Yet the very strengths of this model are, paradoxically, also its flaws. In making law more like ethical deliberation, we can make it seem more legitimate—more intuitively appealing. At the same time, however, we risk losing sight of what makes the law distinctive. Law is official, in a way that moral deliberation is not, and uses coercion to enforce its authority. It is, to an important extent, imposed on us from the top down. The force that seems an inherent part of our experience of the law is always there to undermine efforts to legitimize our legal institutions.

Consider, for example, the judge's role as presented in Minow's model. In responding as fully as possible to the perspectives and values of each of the litigants, the judge may feel pulled in two directions. Good judging, on Minow's view, rests upon the judge's fully appreciating the values at stake, and upon her acknowledgment that a decision privileging one value over the other is a tragic decision in that it results in the loss of something truly valuable. This awareness of the tragic dimensions of the decision contributes to its legitimacy, by conceding that it imposes a considerable cost.[134]

This model, in other words, tends to frame law as itself a tragic institution, presenting judges with profound ethical questions and exacting much the same misery that hard decisions cause. This stands in marked contrast to Rawls, who presented law as an institution intended to avoid such tragic dilemmas. The strict boundary Rawls drew marking law off from intractable disagreements seemed implausible and unnecessary. On the other hand, as I now suggest, to dissolve this boundary altogether distorts our sense of what it is judges do. For it is the distinguishing mark of the judge that he stands outside the conflict; he is a judge—an umpire— only because he will *not* suffer the consequences of his choice. The judge's disengagement from the case is fully as important as his engagement.

Moreover, the subject's agonizing may be a constitutive element of any ethical deliberation that addresses a conflict in authentic values. Indeed,

133. David Lyons, *Ethics and the Rule of Law* (Cambridge: Cambridge University Press, 1984), 214.

134. Minow, *Harvard Law Review* 101 (1987): 92–95.

it is doubtful whether the person has really grasped the conflict and addressed it in an ethically responsible way unless he has felt some genuine anguish. Such emotional turbulence, in contrast, seems strictly irrelevant to the judge's task. This is not to deny that judges wrack themselves over an opinion. Rather, the point is that once the decision is issued, we assess it in terms of its competence as a piece of legal craftsmanship. The judge's moral virtue is dispensable when we analyze her opinions; we are interested instead in how skillfully she has construed the facts and how persuasively she has interpreted the relevant law.

The difference between ethical deliberation and adjudication recalls the distinction Aristotle draws between virtue and the arts.[135] In ethical deliberations about what one should do, an involuntary mistake is more excusable than a deliberate one. In the arts, however, we blame ignorance and incompetence quite as much as we do deliberate error. Our response to legal judgments suggests that they are less like ethical deliberations and more like examples of legal craftsmanship. When we criticize them, we do so because of what we take to be the judge's ignorance of the law, or his incompetence in construing it.

More deeply, one purpose of law is to make moral deliberation unnecessary and irrelevant. A command backed by a threat takes the guesswork out of how we are to behave. But in removing the guesswork, law also vitiates the puzzlement—that questioning attitude—that characterizes any genuinely ethical scrutiny. Given the existence of a legally enforced speed limit, no motorist need ask whether a moral duty to drive safely exists, and, if so, what it requires. The authority of law provides a powerful reason for doing what we ought on other grounds to do. Indeed, so potent is law's incentive that it tends to displace whatever other reasons we might have. I do not in fact really worry about what the moral duty to drive safely requires, because the traffic laws have already done all the thinking for me (indeed, they have made any thoughts I might have on the subject irrelevant for all practical purposes).

Beyond that, one of the most disturbing features of a legal system is that it contemplates leaving injustice in place, where doing so secures peace and quiet. As Judith Shklar writes, for example, "A decent society requires a bundle of positive conditions, among which peace and a general spirit of tolerance are certainly not insignificant."[136] It is not an unreasonable position, therefore, to accept a certain amount of injustice in the interest of

---

135. This is the distinction between ethical action and the productive arts, as discussed by Aristotle, *Nicomachean Ethics*, 2.4.3., 6.5.7.

136. Shklar, *Faces of Injustice*, 45.

maintaining public order. This, indeed, is the way the *Oresteia* concludes: harmony is restored by the decision *not* to avenge Clytaemnestra.

Let me conclude, then, by returning to my reading of the *Oresteia*. I agree in particular with Christopher Rocco that Aeschylus simultaneously celebrates and deconstructs the hierarchies (especially the sexual ones) structuring the city. Rocco projects this reading, however, into a bracing political program, in which citizens both endorse the ideals of democratic consensus and disrupt democracy's normalizing effects. Applying this program to litigation yields a model like that sketched above—the courts not only express ideals like fairness, freedom, equality, but are the sites in which these ideals are made to open up to the realities of diversity, plurality, difference.

The coherence of this program, however, seems to me to ignore the depth of the dilemmas explored in the *Oresteia*. The communitarian account of litigation affords too optimistic a reading of law and its possibilities, for it seems to suggest that an increase in sensitivity, an alert responsiveness to difference and the claims of the other, would make law (at least for theoretical purposes) fully legitimate. But that is just what the *Oresteia*, properly understood, seems to deny: law arises in the first instance by erecting limits—by refusing to engage in a full-blown ethical scrutiny of a case. Law is law, not morality, partly because it rejects consideration of arguably relevant particulars. Indeed, its purpose is partly to silence just that "sense of injustice" Judith Shklar has described so provocatively—the victim's anguished demand for vengeance and satisfaction.[137]

The "communitarian" view of law sketched above aims at being more adequate to that ethical complexity explored in the earlier parts of the *Oresteia*. In doing so, however, it introduces a distortion by making legal judgment *too much* like ethical deliberation. The simplifications effected by law's boundaries seem to be a constitutive part of what law is. Law, in other words, is destined to be inadequate to our moral complexity; it will always distort us, and to that extent it will always feel somewhat coercive and unjust. Its imperfections, however, are partly its point, for without these distorting simplifications we would lack the efficiencies that simplification makes possible. Law is something we can never be taught to love completely.

We could understand this communitarian model of law as seeking to "learn through suffering" how to construct a model of law and litigation more adequate to our complexity. Yet the more pessimistic reading of "learning through suffering" is also pertinent to our experience of law. Because wise planning can never foreclose the possibility of suffering,

137. Ibid., 1–14, 37–38.

tragedy does not offer us a recipe for evading our condition; it reflects on and illuminates the contours of that condition. It may well be that rapprochement between antagonists is possible at some deep level of mutual understanding (Benhabib's "moral-transformative discourse"), but that is distinctly *not* the province of law. When the possibility of such "bridge-building" dialogue is articulated, we at once appreciate its attractiveness and force as an account of one possibility in our ethical lives. We also appreciate that law can never attain to that finally satisfying ethical state that would secure its legitimacy. It is destined always to simplify, and, in doing so, to distort and oppress.

This does not mean that all attempts to improve the law might as well be abandoned. Indeed, it could not possibly mean this, since law, to be of any use, must be felt to be legitimate, and it can only seem legitimate if it responds to criticism. This returns me to my earlier point about the instability of law. Because law arises, in the first instance, from the arresting of analysis at some artificial point, its authority—the regard in which it is held; its prestige—may then depend on how natural this pause or resting place in the analysis is felt to be. Law is authoritative to the extent that its validity does not seem to require scrutiny of its effects, its efficiency, its moral claims, since these are simply assumed, for whatever reason, to be unproblematic. Without a broad social consensus concerning the essential justice of the system, however, the boundaries demarcating the Hartian "concept" of law are bound to wobble and become unsettled. The *Oresteia* offers a model of law for unsettled times: the seriousness of the conflicts portrayed in it necessarily casts doubt on any claim to repair them through essentially procedural means. The *Oresteia* is a drama about *homo simplificans*—man the simplifier, who seeks to domesticate his own ethical complexity into something more fathomable and more easily managed. I have rejected the suggestion that law is itself a tragic institution: it distorts law to see it as posing those radical conflicts of values we may confront in our extralegal lives. A qualification is necessary, however, for law can never quite root out the complexities that made it necessary in the first place. By presenting law at its moment of inception, the *Oresteia* suggests that law is in a perpetual state of emergence, of always being partly rooted in those passions and appetites it seeks to exclude.

4. ON LAW AND LITERATURE

The complex relation between vengeance and law in the *Oresteia* throws light on the connections, more generally, between law and literature. Law's aspiration is in significant part to simplify situations to intelligibility and predictability. Legal rules provide a kind of medium of exchange—a standard likening us to others. The justice law metes out, therefore, is objective: it deliberately ignores the specifics of the subjective and the irreducibly individual. Indeed, its impersonality—its blindness, its disregard of persons—is largely its point. Law could be seen as an extension of an innate disposition in individuals to simplify complex wholes to more easily manipulated contours. What we call "discrimination" (against a race, a sex, a religion) is often rather a *refusal* to discriminate (among individuals)—a denial of the specific. The "blindness" of prejudice and of law alike applies general categories to individuals and assimilates the specific to the norm. Law and discrimination tend to bleach out particulars.

Literature, in contrast, draws our attention once again to the complex individual.[138] The "uselessness" of art is in no small measure linked to its concern with the irreducible detail. Of course, art too simplifies the world, but it does so in the interest of enabling an appreciation of the complex and opaque. Literature suggests the instability of law even conceptually. For if it counts as a gain to find a common medium of exchange, an objective "realm" in which we can play certain predictable roles, this very simplification of ourselves—to the extent that it is imposed on us—is also a distinct loss: a violation of one very important sense we have of ourselves. Law, then, is caught in a constant oscillation between the wish for predictability and the wish for the intricately detailed. The sense of self may be sufficiently complex that it can be pared off, and distributed among various roles (one of these roles being the legal person); but this very complexity demands that it not be ignored by confining the person to his various roles. The self seeks transcendence in different ways: on the one hand, it seeks to transcend its immersion in particulars, to live rationally and in accordance with universal concepts. That "conceptual" world, on the other hand, is itself something the self wishes to escape: the person's sense of her own irreducible uniqueness represents one form of transcendence.

The instability of law on this view arises from its status as an institution that serves crucial human ends, and that therefore entails all the irresolutions in people's most deep-seated desires. Literature reflects these irresolutions, and in so doing shows the complexity of the ties between persons and their institutions. It corrects the tendency in modern jurisprudence

138. I have stated the point baldly. It has been elaborated with great beauty and vigor by Martha Nussbaum, in *Poetic Justice* and *Love's Knowledge.* See also Kathy Eden, *Poetic and Legal Fiction in the Aristotelian Tradition* (Princeton, N.J.: Princeton University Press, 1986), 32–54.

to direct attention away from the emotional sources of law, and toward the legal system and its claims to be a coherent and distinct entity. Put differently, it implicitly criticizes law's pretensions to well-bounded autonomy, by situating it within an ongoing drama, one in which the law is shown to serve or frustrate the purposes of particular agents, and which takes its meaning in significant part from the fears and ambitions of those who invoke it on any given occasion.

It is perhaps more the theory than the practice of law that treats it as an entity describable in its own terms, apart from the way it functions in individual lives. The foundational question of jurisprudence—"What is law?"—has buried within itself the powerful assumption that law is indeed a separable thing with its own "quiddity" or "whatness," a coherent entity in its own right. Literary depictions of law, on the other hand, do not labor under the assumption that law is a thing apart; instead they construe it within a milieu of multifarious and inconsistent human purposes. The *Oresteia* depicts what is special and distinctive about law, while leaving it essentially tethered to human life.

More specifically, literature points to the theoretical importance of certain aspects of the practice of law—advocacy (in the sense of creatively conveying the significance of the client's case) and judging (in the sense of skillfully discerning what is to be done in situations not fully determined by rules). At the heart of the poetic text, for example, is the vivid description of a character's plight so that the audience may enter into it imaginatively. That is what advocates, too, try to do in court. Moreover, in order to hold our interest, the characters in fictive narratives must face choices that are not determined by rules, and so oblige them to judge what they ought to do in a given circumstance. Our own judgments as readers, too, are important, and these judgments include as essential elements sympathetic identification, flexibility, and nuance. Kathy Eden writes of the parallel between the effect a tragedy, say, has on its audience and the effect advocates seek to elicit in court:

> The audience's reaction to the tragic action. . .corresponds to the psychological response of the judge or jury leading up to an equitable judgment. When a reasonably good man like ourselves commits a tragic error, the completed play demonstrates, much as the forensic speech tries to do, that the protagonist deserves a milder judgment: not the rigid justice of the law, but pity, equity, and pardon.[139]

139. Eden, *Poetic and Legal Fiction*, 59. On equity in Aristotle's thought, see Ziolkowski, *Mirror of Justice*, 144–62, and esp. 159–62; Max Hamburger, *Morals and Law: The Growth of Aristotle's Legal Theory* (New Haven: Yale University Press, 1951).

These qualities, because they are central to literature, suggest the importance of their analogues in legal practice, and the relevance of these features to an adequate understanding of the law. Legal theory, however, in seeking to identify what makes law distinctively itself, has tended to overlook the importance of precisely those features of law that literature tends to make central—the disparity between the rule and the world, the importance of advocacy and equity.

On the other hand, it would distort law to suppose that advocacy and equity could even ideally make of it a perfectly responsive institution. That was the flaw in the communitarian arguments explored in Section 3. One point in having law is that it enables us to get past perplexity and irresolvable questions; it helps ensure that they do not paralyze society. The knotty ethical dilemmas explored in literature, and the emotional responses such works evoke, should indicate how different, after all, law is, and how disparate and inconsistent the purposes served by law and literature. This inconsistency is itself important as a driving force for change in law, and therefore should form part of our theorizing about it.

It may well be that reading literature is a way some people have of making their institutional judgments more tempered and humane, and thereby making the institutions themselves less unfair.[140] The real pertinence of literature to law, however, seems to me to lie elsewhere. In drawing attention to concrete particulars, works of literature implicitly question—or, more precisely, should lead us to question—the ability of any political institution fully to capture or reflect its members in all their intricacy. A gap or disparity between the self and its political institutions seems inescapable, and this gap affects the way institutions work. In particular, it affects how a legal system makes good on its claim to fairness or integrity. For law does indeed reflect a deep and powerful human need for order, predictability, closure. But it would be wrong to suppose that that need is fully consistent with others—for example, for judgments that are fully responsive to particulars, and that fully capture the complexity of the person or act being judged.

That jurisprudence and literature offer different models of the law illuminates one facet of the "ancient quarrel between poetry and philosophy" described by Plato in the *Republic*.[141] There Socrates famously banished the poets for displaying highly emotional scenes that afford spectators a noxious pleasure, one that distracts them from the im-

140. We might ask, however, why confine this property of humanizing judgments to literature. Many different kinds of experience can serve to awaken the sympathies and a keener awareness of the reality of others' suffering.

141. Plato, *Republic*, 10. 607 b 5, c 3.

mutable verities underlying the state and securing its justice. As we have seen, however, a tragedy like the *Oresteia* offered a powerful image of the origins of the law and the state. In banishing tragedy, then, Plato was not merely getting rid of frivolous and dangerous entertainments; he was also banning a rival view of the *polis* and its institutions. In particular, by banning tragedies like the *Oresteia*, Plato would have excluded a vision of legal institutions as emerging from the passions, and never quite leaving them behind—especially the passionate demand for justice, and the polysemous, thickly opaque language in which this demand finds expression. Tragedy, in other words, implicitly challenged the philosophical project of offering a rational, theoretical account of just institutions. What I have attempted to show in this chapter, in part, is the strength of the picture of law that literature offers as against the philosophical, jurisprudential model. Law is in a perpetual state of emergence; it is never wholly separated from those conditions that simultaneously necessitate and compromise it. These intimations of our mortal condition—obliged to make decisions that can never quite be fully adequate to our complexity and that therefore can never quite attain legitimacy—sharpen our sense of law and, in particular, its deepest sources in our most vital drives.

CHAPTER 2

Dilemmas of the Self: Law and Confession

Law can often look largely irrelevant to the self. On the conception that comes most easily to us, law consists of rules; by obeying these rules, we get the space we need to live our own lives. The self is essentially private, and *problems* of the self—"who am I?" "what good will I pursue in my life?" "how to live? what to do?"—are decidedly outside law's jurisdiction. This division of self and law is not just an unintended byproduct of a positivist conception of law; rather, it is crucial to the legitimacy of the legal system that it take a hands-off approach. To put it paradoxically, law is not just *unless* it is largely irrelevant to the most vital concerns of the individual.

But this cannot be right. Conceptions of the law have typically been premised on a view of the person—if only to explain why law must be kept apart from it. The very conception just sketched, for example, envisions a self that needs freedom to explore different ethical paths (the model articulated by John Stuart Mill). John Rawls has attempted to articulate a "political liberalism" that harbors no presuppositions about the person, and depends on an "overlapping consensus" of different beliefs. But even here it is clear that the state reflects lively conceptions of the self and the world. Rawls has not demonstrated that the state does not need some conception of the person; he has shown only that it is not linked to any particular model.

In a legal system premised on individual rights, it is especially difficult to disentangle law and ideas about the person. For rights are most readily thought of as inhering in the individual. To that extent, they tend to reflect a model of the person as an individual—reasonable, autonomous, deliberative. Such beings are not only the objects of law (the ones addressed by law's commands); they are also its authors, in a perhaps somewhat attenuated, but nonetheless significant way. This is not an unreasonable view to take of ourselves, but it is only one among many different models we have for thinking about ourselves. And indeed, this individualistic conception of the person has become in many ways implausible, even for the legal purposes it was supposed to serve. The simplifications it entails have come to seem increasingly distorted and distorting.

This chapter and the next will explore the relation between conceptions of the law and of the person. I begin by looking at the difficulties courts have had in addressing custodial confessions. Such confessions entail a fascinating, convoluted psychological element, and so run counter to the prevailing legal model of ourselves as straightforwardly rational and deliberative beings. The watershed decision here, of course, is *Miranda*. In that case, the court reached a sane result, but only by invoking a rationalist conception of the person that, especially in this context, looks unrealistic and implausible. As I will try to show, the equivocations of *Miranda* reflect a real split in modern perceptions of the self, as articulated above all by Jürgen Habermas and Michel Foucault.

In the second section of this chapter I turn to Augustine's *Confessions,* which in many ways marks the beginning of the intricate, interior self, and already shows the rifts apparent in the work of Habermas and Foucault. Augustine's view of the self was centered on the will; he was in fact one of the great pioneers in articulating the importance of the will. (Thus Augustine hovers in the background of legal decisions attempting to discern a "free act of the will" in custodial confession cases.) From Augustine there derive two powerful (but inconsistent) models of the self—a self that is free, autonomous, and responsible; and a darker, more fascinating self that is deeply conflicted and incapable of encompassing itself. These different streams are still with us today.

Augustine's considerable interest as a legal thinker has to do with the way this quite complex, nonreductive view of the person informs his ideas about law and the state. I address this feature of his legal thought in the third section of this chapter. Augustine was strikingly prescient in his model of a limited state that represents a "composition" (*compositio*) of different wills. For Augustine, the state secures the basic good of earthly peace—something everyone wants, whatever else they might want. Although Augustine held many beliefs and argued for some positions we find appalling today, there is a core to his mature political thought that is genuinely bracing and attractive.

My point will be that Augustine's sketch of a secular state grew from a complex and persuasive model of the person. He was able, in consequence, to offer a view of the state that is still of interest, if only because it exposes some of the shortcomings of modern legal theory. Augustine showed how legal systems do not and never can securely "possess" justice (or any other legitimizing virtue). He goes on to show how they nonetheless have a genuine claim to the respect and active cooperation of citizens. The idea of a legal "system," moreover, is incomplete and misleading, to the extent that it ignores the dimension of time in our understanding of law. It is crucial to the legitimacy of law that it is an ongoing practice, with deep roots in the past and an openness to the future. I address some of the implications of law–as–practice in the concluding section.

1. Confession in Law and Theory

Law is a kind of language. Austin, for example, famously characterized law as a command by a sovereign backed by a threat—envisioning law as a one-way speech act addressed to subjects who passively heeded it.[1] But an adequate theory of law cannot so limit its authoritative speakers. The ferment in Anglo-American jurisprudence over the last fifty years or so has loosened up our sense of law, so that it no longer seems sufficient to characterize it as a static or inert body of rules. Rawls now presents law as the public discourse of a democratic society.[2] Ronald Dworkin complements Rawls's argument: for him, judges participate in this public conversation when they decide how a rule or a principle applies in a given case.[3]

The arguments litigants present in courts have also taken on for some writers a theoretical significance as legal discourse: the law is a means of translating their private experience into arguments with public ramifications.[4] On this view, law is a means of communication endowing us with a distinctive eloquence—the ability to identify and articulate the foundational principles in our own lives, and to show the consequences for the way we think about society. It is a practice, a kind of rhetoric. As such, law

1. John Austin, *The Province of Jurisprudence Determined* (New York: Noonday Press, 1954), Lecture I, 13.

2. John Rawls, *Political Liberalism* (New York: Columbia University Press, 1992). The idea of community has become central to constitutional theory. See, e.g., Paul W. Kahn, *Legitimacy and History: Self-Government in American Constitutional History* (New Haven, Conn.: Yale University Press, 1992), 1–8.

3. Ronald Dworkin, *Law's Empire* (Cambridge: Harvard University Press, 1986), 254–58.

4. See the discussion in Chapter 1, Section 3, and the writers cited there.

may lack that completely objective precision that has sometimes seemed to be the source of its authority; but it compensates for this lack by making law a more general, argumentative activity with scope for imagination and vision. This ideal picture of law rests on its being an empowerment of the self. As a common language, law secures order, to be sure, but in a way that need not squelch or homogenize difference.

So far, law seems to consist in highly assertive speech acts—whether it is a question of a sovereign sternly laying down what must be done, or empowered litigants articulately demanding their rights. Jurisprudence builds on these highly assertive speech acts, and has increasingly recognized the theoretical significance of an ever more embracing set of assertive speakers. Law is a matter, apparently, of a state commanding that people behave in a certain manner, or the people demanding that the state recognize and incorporate a principle or point of view. The point is that speech has had to be in the imperative mode in order to be recognized as theoretically significant—that is, as speech that must play a role in any plausible theory of law.

Yet legal speech is not always so straightforward: it does not necessarily speak in terms of orders and demands. Consider the confession, in which the individual does not demand his rights, but admits that his own conduct has violated the law's commands. Confession does not appear to be a progressive force: it does not evidently challenge the law to broaden its perspectives or expand its vision. If anything, it further entrenches law: confession entails the acceptance—or at least the acknowledgment—of the law's authority. The confessing party accuses not the law, but *himself,* of being out of line. At least in the case of confessions born of remorse, the confessant speaks in order to restore a sense of personal coherence by addressing himself to an acknowledged moral authority. Rather than a means of empowering the self, confession entails a cleansing of it, by addressing oneself to an authority one recognizes as legitimately setting standards for conduct. Confession has to do in part with the way law forms the self, and in particular with that part of our identity—that sense of ourselves—that holds us to certain standards.

Confession, in short, is a mode of legal speech quite different from the way litigants address the courts when demanding their rights. Courts, in consequence, have had difficulty understanding just what motivates legal confessions. Apparently this has always been so. One ancient Roman rhetorician, for example, wrote that anyone giving information against himself might well seem to be out of his mind, for "he is impelled by madness: one man by drunkenness, another by error, another by sorrow, another by interrogation. No one speaks against himself, unless something drives him to do it."[5]

Police interrogation is the converse of confession and it, too, is very troubling: here the law speaks not in general terms, but to specific individuals; not in clear commands, but in subtle suggestions; not expecting silent obedience, but coaxing detainees to condemn themselves out of their own mouths. The speech of police interrogators (suggesting, cajoling, now threatening, now friendly), while certainly a part of the legal process,[6] is wholly unlike that assertive plain speaking which seems to be the law's usual mode, and with which the courts seem most at home. The law's imperative mode never leaves the public in doubt as to where it stands: they must obey the clear dictates of the law. Police interrogation methods, in contrast, aim partly at disorienting the detainee, throwing him off his stride and breaking any sense of confidence that he can "get away with it."

Confession and interrogation represent two forms of legal speech strikingly different from the more familiar "imperative" mode and, in many ways, in conflict with that mode. For it seems clear that our legal institutions by and large presuppose an arm's-length relationship between the law and its subjects. The criminal justice system is "accusatory" or "adversarial," rather than inquisitorial. Every legal subject has rights (including the right to remain silent), which he or she is expected to use rationally: this rational use may include waiving one's rights, of course, but only provided that the waiver was fully intended, and undertaken with sufficient knowledge of the facts.

Police interrogation with its wiles and cunning ways therefore faces courts with the question of whether the confessing defendant acted in an adequately arm's-length way—i.e., whether she acted *voluntarily*. Voluntariness has been, in the words of one court, the "ultimate test" for confessions, and "the only clearly established test in Anglo-American courts for two hundred years."[7] That is because, as the Supreme Court wrote in

---

5. Ps.-Quintilian, *Decl.* 314, quoted in James J. O'Donnell, *Augustine: Confessions* (Oxford: Clarendon Press, 1992), 2.3 (my translation).

6. That was in part the significance of the Supreme Court's watershed decision in *Miranda v. Arizona*, 384 U.S. 436 (1966): because the police investigation is a part of our accusatory system of justice—not just a prelude to a criminal case—the detainee must be apprised of her rights. See *Miranda* 384 U.S. at 460–67 (the Fifth Amendment privilege against self-incrimination applies to in-custody police interrogations). *Miranda* has been reaffirmed in *Dickerson v. U.S.,* 120 S.Ct. 2326 (2000).

7. *Culombe v. Connecticut,* 367 U.S. 568, 602 (1961). Even so, voluntariness has proved a difficult and elusive concept, partly because it represents a complex of values, including not only values of individual autonomy, but due process considerations posed by police

Bram v. United States, "the facts by which compulsion might manifest itself, whether physical or moral, would be necessarily ever different." As a result, "the measure by which the involuntary nature of the confession was to be ascertained [is] stated in the rule, not by the changing causes, but by their resultant effect upon the mind."[8] So, in *Bram,* voluntariness was understood as requiring that a confession be the result of a "purely voluntary mental action."[9]

The voluntariness of a confession is felt to make it an *authoritative* statement (the autonomous decision of a rational agent) and therefore *authentically legal,* rather like the imperative modes of speech described above. Only if a statement is voluntary can courts treat it as flowing from an acceptably arm's-length relation between state and citizen. Voluntariness is such a central conception because it ultimately implicates the legal system's legitimacy, which rests in significant part on its respect for citizens' autonomy.

---

misconduct or overreaching. For an attempt to summarize the jurisprudence of voluntariness as reflected in Supreme Court decisions, see *Dickerson v. U.S.,* 120 S.Ct. at 2330–31; *Schneckloth v. Bustamonte,* 412 U.S. 218, 223–27 (1973).

For pre-*Miranda* voluntariness determinations in custodial confession cases, see, e.g., *Ashcraft v. Tennessee,* 322 U.S. 143, 147–55 (1944), and J. Jackson's dissent at 159–63; *Haley v. Ohio,* 332 U.S. 596, 599–601 (1948), and J. Frankfurter's concurrence at 601–04; *Haynes v. Washington,* 373 U.S. 503 (1963). Since *Miranda,* see *Dickerson v. U.S.,* 120 S.Ct. 2326; *Arizona v. Fulminante,* 499 U.S. 279, 285–88 (1991); *Colorado v. Connelly,* 479 U.S. 157, 163–67 (1986).

Some commentators have sought to replace "voluntariness" with a more concrete test— e.g., whether the police interrogation was proper. See Yale Kamisar, "What Is an 'Involuntary' Confession?" in Kamisar, *Police Interrogation and Confession* (Ann Arbor: The University of Michigan Press, 1980), 1–25, esp. 14, and more recently, Yale Kamisar, "On the 'Fruits' of *Miranda* Violations, Coerced Confessions, and Compelled Testimony," *Michigan Law Review* 93 (1995): 929, 936–49. See also Richard Posner, *The Problems of Jurisprudence* (Cambridge: Harvard University Press, 1990), 179–84.

For an argument that more objective tests do not capture everything we mean by "voluntariness," see Alan Wertheimer, *Coercion* (Princeton, N.J.: Princeton University Press, 1987), 104–13. Wertheimer writes that voluntariness is meant to reflect certain core values—respect for personal integrity—that the law must honor (120–21).

See also the discussion in Joseph D. Grano, *Confessions, Truth and the Law* (Ann Arbor: The University of Michigan Press, 1993), esp. 59–83.

8. *Bram v. U.S.,* 168 U.S. 532, 548 (1897).

9. Ibid., 562. What constitutes "voluntariness" is controversial. Courts have sometimes spoken about it as an "unfettered exercise of [one's] own will." *Molloy v. Hogan,* 378 U.S. 1, 8 (1964); see also *Wan v. U.S.,* 266 U.S. 1, 14 (1924): "A confession is voluntary in law, if and only if, it was in fact voluntarily made." (Brandeis, J.), and the cases cited in *Connelly,* 479 U.S. at 177–78 n. 2. On the other hand, in *Connelly,* 479 U.S. at 163–67, the Supreme Court expressed the view that coercive police activity was necessary in order to a find a confession not "voluntary" within the due process clause.

The custodial context of confessions, however, points to a quite different—and far more troubling—model of the relations between the state and citizen, in which the state is an inescapable environment that actively shapes citizens and their expectations. How to locate a "purely voluntary mental act" in an environment where so much depends on suggestion, nuance, and psychological influence? The problem posed for courts by the confession cases is just their potential for undermining the model of rational autonomy that seems central to the legitimacy of our political and legal system. Confession points to a split between the rhetoric and the reality of our legal system. Habermas situates law "between fact and norm"—the practical work law does and the ideals it claims to embody and that entitle it to go about its work.[10] Confession, however, shows that a tension exists between these two: it is an indispensable tool for fighting crime, and yet it is difficult to square with the fundamental principles of our legal and political system. Confession poses a challenge to our "official" view of ourselves, as rational beings who reach articulate decisions. It has a powerful potential to debunk our institutions, and prompts us to ask what role legitimizing ideals play in a legal system.

The Supreme Court's watershed opinion *Miranda v. Arizona*[11] is an especially striking instance of this split between our legal system's factual needs (efficient police investigations of crime) and its normative needs (the ability to demonstrate its respect for individual autonomy). In *Miranda,* the Supreme Court held that the Fifth Amendment's guarantee against coerced self-incrimination obliged police interrogators to disclose the right to remain silent and the right to an attorney. The court's opinion is replete with references to the individual as possessing an innate human dignity. Custodial questioning techniques intended to bend the suspect's will to that of the police are found inconsistent with "dignity."[12] Similarly, the basis of the constitutional guarantees against compelled self-incrimination is the "dignity and integrity of its citizens."[13] Furthermore, "our accusatory system of criminal justice" is based on the "inviolability of the human personality."[14] In other words, *Miranda* found that voluntariness is essential because the ability to deliberate and make rational choices is central to the concept of the person presupposed by our government. Thus, in the last analysis, a confession must be voluntary be-

---

10. See Jürgen Habermas, *Between Facts and Norms: Contributions to a Discourse Theory of Law and Democracy,* trans. William Rehg (Cambridge: MIT Press, 1996).

11. 384 U.S. 436 (1966).

12. *Miranda,* 384 U.S. at 457.

13. Ibid., 460.

14. Ibid.

cause only in this way does the criminal justice system respect the individual's integrity, and maintain its own legitimacy.

Notwithstanding its emphatic insistence on voluntariness, however, *Miranda* paints a picture of custodial interrogations that makes the ideals of dignity and autonomy look implausible. *Miranda* is a fascinating decision. It did not involve police misconduct, or any methods (prolonged questioning, enforced sleeplessness, threats, deception) obviously intended to break the defendant's will. Rather, it was the circumstances of police custody itself and the sheer psychological skill of interrogation techniques that worried the Court. Police custody, the Court wrote, presents an overwhelming impression of authority—one that is entitled not only to get an answer but to use whatever means are necessary to obtain one. More, it plays on the susceptibilities of detainees, in particular their willingness to grant the implicit claims of authority and to subordinate themselves to it.

For example, the Court quoted from one police handbook, advising that the investigator question the subject

> steadily and without relent, leaving the subject no prospect of surcease. He must dominate his subject and overwhelm him with his inexorable will to obtain the truth. . . . In a serious case, the interrogation may continue for days, with the required intervals for food and sleep, but with no respite from the atmosphere of domination.[15]

These "How to Interrogate" handbooks were offensive in that they taught police how to play upon just those susceptibilities that persuade people to speak out against themselves. Such techniques had been developed in part to assure that police not have recourse to more brutal methods of extracting confessions. But it was their very subtlety that made the newer techniques disturbing. For the basic message of these handbooks was that the interrogator should convey an omniscient authority that already knows what the detainee has done. Quite apart from the specific techniques used by police interrogators, the *Miranda* court wrote, "the very fact of custodial interrogation exacts a heavy toll on individual liberty and trades on the weakness of individuals."[16] That is because "[a]n individual swept from familiar surroundings into police custody, surrounded

---

15. Ibid., 451, quoting from Charles E. O'Hara, *Fundamentals of Criminal Investigation* (Springfield, Ill.: Thomas, 1956).

16. The *Miranda* court summarized their message:

> To be alone with the subject is essential to prevent distraction and to deprive him of any outside support. The aura of confidence in his guilt undermines his will to resist. He

by antagonistic forces, and subjected to the techniques of persuasion described above cannot be otherwise than under compulsion to speak."[17]

Miranda seems to go in two directions at once—emphatically underscoring the liberal ideals of dignity and autonomy, while at the same time inevitably making them appear mere fictions, implausible and unreal.[18] *Miranda* makes clear the considerable disadvantages from which most detainees suffer—their youth, their indigence and lack of education, their pervasive sense of powerlessness.[19] Such unfortunates can scarcely be thought to have that sense of rational control over their lives and conduct that the legal model of the individual seems to presuppose. *Miranda's* view of voluntariness, when pressed, seems to be a projection of the wealthier and more educated classes onto a model of an innate human dignity. Economic and social privileges obviously promote and nurture the autonomy that is supposed to be inherent in us. More deeply, however, *Miranda* depicts persons as deeply suggestible and susceptible—not really rational or autonomous at all.

Notwithstanding the prominence it gave to this subversive view (or maybe just because of it), the *Miranda* court applied an exceedingly strong version of voluntariness as a kind of impermeability, or independence from one's circumstances. The privilege against self-incrimination, the Court wrote, was fulfilled "only when the person is guaranteed the right 'to remain silent unless he chooses to speak in the *unfettered exercise of his own will.'*"[20] The whole point of voluntariness, in other words, was to insure that the individual remain able to stand aloof from her circumstances, that she be permitted to decide independently whether and how to react to the custodial environment. Voluntariness was no longer an as-

---

merely confirms the preconceived story the police seek to have him describe. . . .It is important to keep the subject off balance, for example, by trading on his insecurity about himself or his surroundings. The police then persuade, trick, or cajole him out of exercising his constitutional rights.

Miranda, 384 U.S. at 455.

17. *Miranda*, 384 U.S. at 461.

18. See the discussions of *Miranda* in Louis Michael Seidman, "*Brown* and *Miranda*," *California Law Review* 80 (1992): 673, 718–47; and Robert Weisberg, "Criminal Law, Criminology and the Small World of Legal Scholars," *University of Colorado Law Review* 63 (1992): 521, 538–45. Seidman and Weisberg both show how confession challenges the liberal model of a freely willing, autonomous agent. See also George C. Thomas III and Marshall D. Bilder, "Aristotle's Paradox and the Self-Incrimination Puzzle," *Journal of Criminal Law & Criminology* 82 (1991): 243.

19. *Miranda*, 384 U.S. at 472–73.

20. *Miranda*, 384 U.S. at 460, quoting *Molloy v. Hogan*, 372 U.S. 1, 8 (1964), emphasis added.

pect of the give-and-take between the detainee and his circumstances (as it had been in the case law before *Miranda*).[21] Instead, it came to be the power to reflect rationally before acting, to reason objectively—as it were, from outside—about one's circumstances. As Justice Harlan wrote in his dissent: "[T]he thrust of the new rules is to negate all pressures, to reinforce the nervous or ignorant suspect, and ultimately to discourage any confession at all." This utopian vision, Justice Harlan wrote, was "voluntariness with a vengeance."[22]

The discrepancy between the marginalized people brought before the criminal justice system and the abstract model of a rational self (a model that presupposes a considerable degree of talent, education, and privilege) puts a palpable strain on the *Miranda* decision. The court required that detainees be advised of their right to remain silent and their right to an attorney. But the *Miranda* warnings can hardly achieve voluntariness in the strong sense the Court seemed to find constitutionally mandated: the power to reflect on one's circumstances and to choose the best course of action is not so easily bestowed on disadvantaged persons.[23] One possible reason why the *Miranda* court considered the right to counsel so important may be that the lawyer is the very paradigm of rational autonomy—educated, knowledgeable, capable of reflecting and reaching reasoned decisions. The lawyer's presence may be felt to supply otherwise disadvantaged suspects with all the marks of autonomy and voluntariness life has effectively denied them.

I believe the *Miranda* court reached the right result, although I think its reasoning was seriously flawed. *Miranda* may perhaps be best understood under a due process rationale: on this view it is a part of due process to advise citizens, when detained by the police, that what they confront is, indeed, a legal process. Reading detainees their *Miranda* rights effectively accomplishes this. The *Miranda* warnings thus secure a

21. See, e.g., *Haynes v. Washington*, 373 U.S. 503, 514 (1963), stating that the rule depended upon "a totality of circumstances evidencing an involuntary . . . admission of guilt." The *Haynes* court continued: "The line between proper and permissible police conduct and techniques and methods offensive to due process is, at best, a difficult one to draw, particularly in cases such as this where it is necessary to make fine judgments as to the effect of psychologically coercive pressures and inducements on the mind and will of an accused." Ibid., 515.

22. *Miranda*, 384 U.S. at 505 (Harlan, J., dissenting).

23. As one of the *Miranda* dissenters pointed out, why assume that an interrogator—whose questioning is inherently coercive—can cure the coercion by telling the detainee that he need not speak? See *Miranda*, 384 U.S. at 536 (White, J., dissenting). For an account of police questioning methods in the post-*Miranda* era, see, e.g., David Simon, *Homicide: A Year on the Killing Streets* (Boston: Houghton Mifflin, 1991), 194–207.

kind of rough fairness in the criminal investigation. By seeking to achieve this fairness, the warnings incidentally acknowledge the dignity of the individual. They do not, however, purport to ensure a fully autonomous, informed, and intelligent decision about the detainee's best interests. (The *Miranda* warnings also make it much easier for courts to determine whether a confession was voluntary or not.)[24]

Nonetheless, the tensions that trouble the *Miranda* opinion as actually written are significant and interesting in their own right. The emphasis laid upon voluntariness in *Miranda*—and, more generally, in the custodial confession cases—has even deeper roots than the need to demonstrate the legitimacy of the legal system. For, as the classicist Jean-Pierre Vernant writes, the will constitutes an essential dimension of the person for contemporary Western societies.[25] The will in some sense simply *is* the person, construed as an agent. Because of the will, our actions truly express who we are; they are a manifestation of our authentic self. The will secures a continuity across time for the self, and seems to ground a moral sense of responsibility for one's deeds. In other words, the *Miranda* court's conception of legitimacy was rooted in a powerful and persuasive picture we have of ourselves as endowed with a will, and therefore free.

At the same time, however, Vernant writes, there is a powerful countersense that this picture is false, and that the will, far from being a timeless category, an inherent part of being human, is an elaborate construct. On this view, the self-portrait of our personhood as centered on will is a myth—an idea that seems deeply true, even though it cannot be rationally demonstrated. This mythic "will" is in fact a historical phenomenon whose background is, in Vernant's words, "difficult, multiple and incomplete."[26] The *Miranda* decision evinces the tension between these two different ideas of the will. On the one hand, the will seems central to the idea of personhood (and therefore something the state must respect, if it is to be legitimate); on the other, the conditions of police custody cause this powerful, "mythic" conception of ourselves to fray and unravel. They threaten to expose it precisely as a myth.

24. See Seidman, *"Brown* and *Miranda,"* 745, pointing out that *Miranda* has enabled courts to collapse a voluntariness determination into a much easier examination of whether the accused was read his or her rights. In fact, *Miranda* appears not to have affected the percentage of incarcerated defendants who confess. See Stephen J. Schulhofer, "Reconsidering *Miranda," University of Chicago Law Review* 54 (1987): 435, 455–61.

25. Jean-Pierre Vernant, "Intimations of the Will in Greek Tragedy," in Jean-Pierre Vernant and Pierre Vidal-Naquet, *Myth and Tragedy in Ancient Greece,* trans. Janet Lloyd (New York: Zone, 1988), 49.

26. Ibid., 50.

Confession thus seems to be an especially evocative "site" in which opposed conceptions of the self are played out. Indeed, two of the most celebrated thinkers of the late twentieth century, Michel Foucault and Jürgen Habermas, have each used the idea of confession to crystallize their very different pictures of rationality and modernity. I believe the strain in the *Miranda* opinion ultimately reflects the larger, cultural tensions Foucault and Habermas make explicit.

Foucault has characterized ours as a confessing society, and he didn't intend it as a compliment.[27] He sees confession as a pervasive structuring principle in the relationship between teacher and child; doctor and patient; psychiatrist and analysand; delinquents and counselors. In all of these relations, the person is called upon—allowed, urged, pressured—to divulge himself, unearthing not only his acts, but also any desires and traits felt to be in any way transgressive. The recitation in *Miranda* of police interrogation techniques designed to undermine the detainee's will is strikingly reminiscent of Foucault, and his account of the way modern institutions pervasively attempt to normalize and regiment their subjects.

Crucial to Foucault's critique of confession is the sense of self that underlies it—a self felt to be deep and mysterious, to harbor secrets that must be hauled up into the light of day, in accordance with some scientific command to seek the truth. The emergence of the individual self—often thought to be the hallmark of Enlightenment thought, and the basis for whatever moral authority the modern liberal state exerts—seems in Foucault to be instead a particularly insidious form of subjugation: the self seeks relief from the burdens of its depth by continuously divulging itself to various "experts." Foucault binds together three different senses of "subject" into a sinister nexus: the autonomous individual characterized by an intricate interior (a "subject" in the sense of one possessing subjectivity) becomes the topic of research (a "subject"—a theme targeted for investigation), and thus becomes subjected, subordinate to various disciplines and their discourses (a "subject"—one constrained by authority).

Foucault calls this process "*assujetissement*": his dark insight is that the appearance of the human "subject" in the Enlightenment and after is a new form of subjugation.[28] The theoretical significance of confession in Foucault is that it captures the distinctive mode in which power by and large operates nowadays. A dispersed power effectively regiments people with discourses of *normality*. It entices and enlists people to subscribe to the authoritative dis-

27. Michel Foucault, *History of Sexuality*, Vol. 1, trans. Robert Hurley (New York: Vintage, 1980), 58–70.
28. On "assujetissement," see Jon Simons, *Foucault and the Political* (London: Routledge, 1995), 19–21.

course. Confession takes place within a power relation that works its effects not so much by issuing commands and demanding compliance as by eliciting self-disclosing speech. The power is not centralized, or indeed easily located; it seems to work its normalizing effects pervasively, invisibly—a thousand points of darkness visible. Confession, in other words, reflects a highly sophisticated and insidious power operation—one that seeks, certainly, to dominate and quell, but does so in ways its subjects do not readily identify as domination. In confessing, the subject seeks to be rid of the onerous burden of specialness, those deeds and traits that set her apart and make her abnormal. Confession is one of the most subtle techniques, then, of Nietzschean *ressentiment*—that massed, furtive pressure that is ever alert to difference and bent on leveling it away.

Foucault essentially denies that anything like the "self" (a profound, separate depth) really exists, and argues that to think in terms of an autonomous center is to blind ourselves to the real nature of our relations to the world. For Foucault, then, it would not make sense to ask whether the state has "overborne" the will of the detainee, because the detainee has already been pervasively shaped by the state. Liberal discourse about the formal equality of rights merely obscures the domination that is brought about by the disciplines.[29]

Foucault's critique of rights and his questioning of the model of the individual self have a powerful resonance in American legal thought, which has been shaped in important ways by legal realism and its "debunking" criticisms of liberal discourse.[30] More specifically, Foucault helps articulate what seems odd in many of the legal decisions addressing the voluntariness of confessions. For the realities of police custody and interrogation seem to point to our suggestibility and weakness, rather than to our rational autonomy. Foucault's analysis makes police custody look disturbingly like a para-

29. See Michel Foucault, *Discipline and Punish*, trans. Alan Sheridan (New York: Vintage, 1979), 221–24. On Foucault's thinking about the law, see Alan Hunt and Gary Wickham, *Foucault and the Law* (London: Pluto, 1994); see also Simons, *Foucault & the Political*, 56–59, 116–18.

30. For a useful account of legal realism and its legacy, see Morton J. Horwitz, *The Transformation of American Law 1870–1960* (New York: Oxford University Press, 1992), 193–212. Of the critical legal studies movement, I will cite as representative examples Mark Kelman, *A Guide to Critical Legal Studies* (Cambridge: Harvard University Press, 1987), esp. 245–46, 257–62; Mark Tushnet, "Following the Rules Laid Down: A Critique of Interpretivism and Neutral Principles," *Harvard Law Review* 96 (1983): 781; and Clare Dalton, "An Essay in the Deconstruction of Contract Doctrine," *Yale Law Journal* 94 (1985): 997. See also Stanley Fish, *There's No Such Thing as Free Speech and It's a Good Thing, Too* (New York: Oxford University Press, 1994), 141–179. See also the discussion in Chapter 3, Section 3, below.

digm, more generally, for the relations between citizen and state: *not* (as rights discourse would have it) autonomous individuals possessing rights the state must respect, but individuals pervasively and deeply formed by their social and political environment. That, indeed, has been the point of much of the "realist" critique in American legal thought: that the state does not neutrally stand outside the private zone of selves, but inevitably molds the actual expectations (and hopes of success) of this or that group of citizens. The insistence on "dignity" and autonomy in an opinion like *Miranda* sounds almost defensive, as though the Court were resisting the implication that the custodial situation was indeed paradigmatic.

Foucault's radical assessment of rationality, the self, therapeutic disciplines, and the state is astringent and deeply unsettling. How plausible is it? Jürgen Habermas has offered a far less sinister picture of confession—one that links it to the central projects of modernity, which he views with far more sympathy than does Foucault. Confession, for Habermas, is a reflex of the waning of traditions, which had once offered compelling and belief-worthy images of the individual and his relation to society, nature, and the universe. Once this traditional amalgam fades, however, the self is thrown back on its own devices. "[I]n place of the exemplary instructions in the virtuous life and recommended models of the good life," Habermas writes, "one finds an increasingly pronounced, abstract demand for a conscious, self-critical appropriation."[31] The individual is now confronted by the demand that "one responsibly take possession of one's own individual, irreplaceable, and contingent life history."[32] The individual is now obliged to reflect on himself or herself. This "intrusion of reflection in the life-historical process generates a new kind of tension." This is the tension between one's new and burdensome consciousness of contingency, and the sense of accountability for one's own existence.[33]

For Habermas, the centrality of confession and self-examination in modern literature—from Rousseau's *Confessions* through Kierkegaard to Sartre—is a sign of the lapse of tradition, and with that, the rise of a posttraditional sense of responsibility for one's self, a new imperative of authenticity. The point of these literary self-examinations is the authors' attempts to work out their orientation or attitude toward their own lives. Habermas concludes that the rise of clinical discourses is hardly a surprise, and is probably inevitable, since the tensions produced by this new

31. Jürgen Habermas, *Between Facts and Norms: Contributions to a Discourse Theory of Law and Democracy*, trans. William Rehg (Cambridge: The MIT Press, 1996), 96.
32. Ibid.
33. Ibid.

self-accountability can manifest themselves in neurotic symptoms if they are not resolved consciously and deliberately.[34]

The decline of tradition has an impact not only on the individual, but more generally on society and the transmission of culture. Once an embracing traditional vision wanes, it is replaced by a pluralism of inconsistent (although not on that account unreasonable) beliefs. Disputes among these different visions mean that the disputing parties must "consciously choose the continuities they want to live out of, which traditions they want to break off or continue."[35] In this way, confession is linked to the discursive practices of law, construed now as the means par excellence of negotiating differences in a post-traditional, pluralist society.[36]

Far from undermining ideas of autonomy, confession is, in Habermas's approach, a closely allied phenomenon.[37] The same responsibility for one's self that calls forth the confessional therapies also requires that a space be cleared out in which individuals can conduct their self-examination and seek out their own autonomous idea of the good life. The need for self-determination ultimately calls into play a moral viewpoint of "equal respect for each person, and equal consideration for the interests of all."[38] Thus, the confessing self joins up with "the expressivist ideal of self-realization, the deontological ideal of freedom, and the utilitarian maxim of expanding one's life opportunities."[39] On this view, it makes perfect sense for courts in custodial confession cases to inquire into voluntariness and to safeguard the rational autonomy of detainees. To be sure, Habermas is not discussing custodial confessions. His line of thinking, however, powerfully supports the relevance and value of judicial scrutiny of voluntariness in such cases.

The differences between Foucault and Habermas suggest that the tensions troubling *Miranda* were in some sense unavoidable: *Miranda* brings to the surface and makes especially clear a painful rift in modern intuitions about the self and its relation to society. Foucault presents the self as something generated by the various disciplines, which create a deep self whose

---

34. Ibid.

35. Ibid., 97.

36. I discuss Habermas's legal theory in more detail below, in Chapter 3, Section 1.

37. I should make clear that Habermas is not talking about custodial confessions, but solely about extralegal forms of confession—e.g., psychoanalysis, autobiographies. On confession in modern literature, and for a rich discussion of its relation to the law of custodial confessions, see Peter Brooks, "Storytelling Without Fear? Confession in Law & Literature," in Peter Brooks and Paul Gewirtz, eds., *Law's Stories: Narrative and Rhetoric in the Law* (New Haven, Conn.: Yale University Press, 1996), 114–34.

38. Habermas, *Between Facts and Norms*, 97.

39. Ibid., 98.

depths ensure that the individual requires the services of an expert, to whom he is encouraged to tell everything. For Habermas, the self emerges rather from the waning of tradition, and the consequent problematization of the individual. One thing seems clear: the autonomous self no longer seems inherent—a necessary, prepolitical fact about us that the state neutrally confronts. It is not a purely natural given. The modern self has a history, or a genealogy. That suggests the pertinence of earlier accounts of the self—earlier chapters in its history—as a way of coming to grips with the tensions and rifts in modern (and specifically legal) conceptions.

I propose now to turn the clock back some 1,600 years, to consider the works of St. Augustine, which constitute one of the most significant milestones in the history of the modern self. Charles Taylor, in his *Sources of the Self,* attributes to Augustine a new sense of the reflexivity and interiority of the self. Augustine is one of the ultimate sources of that conception of the will as central to our personhood. He presents the self as the royal road to God, and therefore an enormously important moral source in our lives.[40] Augustine's *Confessions* is, among a great many other things, a stunning sign of the new centrality of the self, and what Taylor calls its "radical reflexivity."[41] Augustine sought not merely to become aware of the world, but to make his very awareness an object of attention. He tried to experience his own experiencing. The self's capacity for folding over itself—to reflect on itself and to be in some relation to itself—is what Taylor calls its "radical reflexivity." For Augustine, it was what most assimilated the self to God and made it a central route in his quest for God, a potent new source for access to the good.

The rift in modern attitudes toward the self can be traced back to Augustine. His distinctive new sense of "interiority" marks him off decisively and momentously from the classical past, and shows the waning influence of pagan thought: the Augustinian self is, in Habermas's terms, a post-traditional phenomenon. At the same time, the contours of the Augustinian self arise from the overwhelming and incontrovertible authority God has over his creatures: the Augustinian self, in Foucault's terms, is a product of a power or being outside itself. Augustine's early, momentous conception of the self sets in motion for the first time some of the tensions we continue to find in modern accounts.

Augustine's particular relevance for my purposes is that he sketched out an account of the legitimacy of legal systems based on an intricate and

---

40. Charles Taylor, *Sources of the Self* (Cambridge: Harvard University Press, 1989), 127–42.
41. Ibid., 130.

complex model of the self. In *Miranda,* the intricate relations between the person and the state got squelched in favor of a simplifying, but not really plausible, model of the autonomous self. *Miranda* posed a problem central to any jurisprudence: what is the connection between the factual needs of a legal system (e.g., the need for efficient criminal investigations) and its "normative" ones (the need to demonstrate its justice, and therefore its entitlement to citizens' obedience). As I have argued, *Miranda* did not perform too well in this regard; its claim that the legal system fully respects the dignity of its detainees seems on many grounds implausible—not least in its reductive account of willing and voluntariness.

Augustine sketches out a potentially fruitful scheme for the relation between fact and norm in law. He suggests how an account of the legal system might be based on a nuanced, psychologically believable portrait of the self in all its tensions and unresolved conflicts. In addition, he does not stint on the serious human costs any legal system entails. His account of the law's entitlement to citizens' respect is the more remarkable and persuasive, therefore, because it is built upon a highly realistic foundation. Notwithstanding his somber sense of depravity and injustice, Augustine nonetheless has a powerful "eschatological" sense of the futurity of the good. Human life and its institutions do not "possess" justice, but ideally they move toward it, although it will never be attained in this age.

The point here for legal theory is that legal institutions do not *embody* the ideal qualities that make them legitimate. These qualities remain aspirations, and therefore have a certain irreducibly fictive quality. There is a gap between what the law is and what it would have to be to be fully legitimate. This gap does not extinguish law's claim on us; rather, it introduces a dynamic principle thrusting the law always ahead to bridge the ever-changing gap between the "is" and the "ought."

2. Augustine and the Confessing Self

Modern American courts attempting to discern in a custodial confession a "purely voluntary mental action"[42] stand in a tradition beginning with Augustine, who was the first to articulate a conception of the will as a vital and essential part of mental and moral functioning.[43] His conception of the will broke with the past and achieved a psychologically far more com-

---

42. *Bram,* 168 U.S. at 562. See also *Molloy v. Hogan,* 378 U.S. 1, 8 (1964) (voluntariness is the "unfettered exercise of [one's] own will").

43. On Augustine as the "inventor" of the notion of will, see Albrecht Dihle, *The Theory of the Will in Classical Antiquity,* Sather Classical Lectures 48 (Berkeley: University of California Press, 1982), 123–44. See also Charles Kahn, "Discovering the Will: From Aristotle

pelling and plausible account of the person's internal motivations and her troubled orientation toward the good.[44] Augustine considerably complicated the Socratic model, which had presented virtue as a question of knowing the good. For Augustine, as for St. Paul, it was central that one could know the good, but fail to embrace it. Weakness of the will (*akrasia*) was a nagging problem for earlier philosophy; for Augustine, in contrast, as Taylor writes, it was "no problem, but the central crisis of moral experience."[45]

One of the drives behind Augustine's initial conception of the will was his wish to justify the ways of God to man. His early dialogue "The Free Choice of the Will" begins abruptly with the question, "Tell me, please, whether God is not the cause of evil."[46] Augustine's reply, in brief, was to exonerate God and place the blame for evil squarely on humans' perverse abuse of free will. But implicit in this reply was a startlingly new conception of mental functioning, one that began to map out a far more intricate mental interior than any of the models developed up to that time.

Thus, Augustine pursues his exoneration of God by situating evil not in external deeds, but in the internal disposition that motivates them.[47] He does so after demonstrating that no decisive criterion exists for judging external acts on their own terms. One familiar candidate for such a criterion, for example, would be the "golden rule"—that an act is evil when the agent would be unwilling to be acted upon in that way by others.[48] Adultery, on this reasoning, is wrong, because however pleasurable it is, no one would wish to be the victim of adultery. The "golden rule," then,

---

to Augustine," in John M. Dillon and A. A.Long, eds., *The Question of "Eclecticism": Studies in Later Greek Philosophy* (Berkeley: University of California Press, 1988), 234–59; O'Donnell, *Augustine: Confessions*, 3.30–31; Taylor, *Sources of the Self*, 137–38. James Wetzel, *Augustine and the Limits of Virtue* (Cambridge: Cambridge University Press, 1992), offers a detailed exposition of Augustine's "discovery" of the will; see, e.g., 124–25 for a summarizing statement of his argument that Augustine came to deny that virtue reflected purely internal resources of power.

44. Augustine's conception of the self owes something to earlier Stoic thought. See Kahn, "Discovery of the Will: From Aristotle to Augustine." Dihle, however, writes: "The key role attributed to will (*voluntas*) in St. Augustine's corresponding systems of psychology and theology results mainly from self-examination. It is not derived from earlier doctrines in the field of philosophical psychology or anthropology, and seems to mark a turning point in the history of theological reasoning" (Dihle, *Theory of the Will*, 127).

45. Taylor, *Sources of the Self*, 138.

46. Augustine, "The Free Choice of the Will" (*De Libero Arbitrio*), I.1.1. I have used the translation by Robert P. Russell, O.S.A. in Saint Augustine, *The Teacher; The Free Choice of the Will; Grace and Free Will,* Fathers of the Church 59 (Washington, D.C.: Catholic University of America Press, 1968).

47. "Free Choice of the Will," I.3.6–8.

48. Ibid., I.3.6.

might seem to be a criterion applicable to acts themselves, to distinguish objectively just actions from objectively unjust ones.

Still, as Augustine points out, suppose someone were willing to swap his mate in exchange for an adulterous liaison with another's spouse.[49] Plainly, that would be evil, even though it strictly complies with the golden rule. Augustine concludes from this and other arguments that acts are evil only by virtue of an inner disposition, not because of any feature they share as external acts.[50] But Augustine makes the moral life more interior still. For what characterizes an evil disposition is that it feels passion for goods outside its control. A good disposition, in contrast, rests content with what lies within its domain.[51] Augustine is painting a picture of goodness as self-sufficiency—an ancient ideal, but now with a new twist: for what lies within one's control is preeminently the will itself. "For what is more within the power of the will than will itself?" Augustine asks.[52] Implicit in this dialogue is the idea that a good life consists in a *reflexive* self: the will's contentment with the will (as that which can never be lost) is the distinguishing feature par excellence of a good life. "The happy man," Augustine writes, "is the one who values his own good will."[53]

This reflexive interiority made the human a sufficiently complex and autonomous agent that evil could plausibly be said to originate there: that was what Augustine set out to prove in "The Free Choice of the Will." Augustine would not long remain content with this account of the will, but the conception of an interiorized and reflexive self was to remain fruitful throughout his career, and to inform the richest thought of his maturity. The interiorized self became a powerful means of access to God; in particular, Augustine came to link it to the sublime theological mystery of the Trinity. For the mind's functioning evinced that same triune intricacy that lay at the heart of the Divine Mystery.[54] Thus, the mind exists, knows that it exists, and because of this knowledge, loves itself. This mental triad—being, knowing, willing—mirrored the Trinity (the Father, the Son, and the Spirit). Indeed, every mental or emotional activity has a thickness to it—a reference not only to its object, but to its subject. "[T]o understand my true self is to love it, and so with intelligence comes will,

---

49. Ibid.
50. Ibid., I.3.8.
51. Ibid., I.4.9.
52. Ibid., I.12.26. On the significance of self-possession in *De Libero Arbitrio* I, and its backgrounds in Stoicism, see Wetzel, *Augustine and the Limits of Virtue*, 55–68.
53. Augustine, "Free Choice of the Will," I.12.28.
54. See *De Trinitate*, 8.5, 9.1, and, more generally, books 9–15; *City of God*, 11.26; *Confessions*, 13.11.12.

and with self-knowledge, self-love."[55] This persistent self-reference meant, to Augustine, that the mind was itself a community, and, as such, an image of the Trinity, whose eternal singleness harbored, and was most deeply, an intricate and loving rapport.

The cognitive mental apparatus also shows, upon self-reflexive inspection, a coherence—a stepwise ascent—that brings the person to the very brink of true divinity. In book 7 of his *Confessions,* Augustine recounts one of his great breakthrough experiences. His conception of God had always been mired in material ideas, he writes, and it proved very difficult for him to catch a glimpse of truly spiritual, noncorporeal being. A reading of "Platonic books" (presumably the works of the neo-platonist Plotinus) pointed Augustine in the right direction, and enabled him for the first time to achieve a sense of wholly spiritual being.[56]

The "vision" Augustine next presents is heavily indebted to Plotinus, but is nonetheless characteristically Augustinian, in its inexorable movement inward into the interior man. Augustine writes that he was attempting to discern how it was possible for him to appreciate the beauty of nature: his reflections, however, soon turned from the objects perceived to the perceiving subject—he reflected on his own power to reflect on beauty. He proceeded by stages (*gradatim*) from the body to the soul that perceived them. From there, he ascended to the soul's "interior power" (*interior vis*), which receives the sense organs' reports. So far, Augustine has traced a chain to be found even in animals. From that part of the soul that receives and assimilates sense reports, however, Augustine mounts to the "power of reason" (*ratiocinans potentia*) that judges the sense reports. This rational power was not an ultimate, however, since it was itself mutable. Beyond this power of ratiocination there lies intelligence, which is removed from the press of sensory appearances and is the light that illuminates reasoning. Through our intelligence, we have access to those incontrovertible truths we apply when judging the sense reports. These are truths like the superiority of the immutable to the mutable. They are the light that illuminates every mind, and enables each one to reach reliable judgments about the world. The intelligence, then, points inevitably to something outside itself—the Truth, that which is.[57]

To Augustine, it seemed only appropriate to call this immutable and certain truth God. The voyage inward into the perceiving self ended inevitably

55. Taylor, *Sources of the Self,* 136.

56. *Confessions,* 7.9.13, and see O'Donnell's introductory note, *Augustine: Confessions,* 2.413–18.

57. *Confessions,* 7.17.23.

with a leap from the depths of subjectivity into something underlying the self but essentially different from it. Self-reflection arrived at that intimation of the other—to that which is—"in the flash of one tremulous glance" (*in ictu trepidantis aspectus*).[58] In the *Confessions*, this vision represents a milestone in Augustine's spiritual development—his first successful attempt (after years of trying) to conceive of a purely spiritual being, completely purified of body or bodily attributes. The point is that he achieved this by looking inward: the conception that had so long eluded him and troubled his mind was right there all along, implicit in the very mental apparatus he had been exercising without success to find an answer to his puzzle.

But Augustine also describes, with incomparable power and vividness, a counterview of the self that has a special resonance in a postmodern age. This is the self as conflicted and riven, restless, self-consciously aware of its own contingency, and ironic about its commitments and beliefs. It is a view that undermines the optimism of accounts emphasizing rational autonomy and treating the self as fully in possession of itself—able to encompass and direct its desires where it wills. A model of the self very like this emerges almost inevitably from *Miranda*, with its depiction of detainees' susceptibility to clever suggestions, coaxing, and threats, and their being led, little by little, to act against their own genuine best interests.

Augustine, in other words, is an ultimate source for two compelling models of the self that exist in some tension with each other. Far from obscuring or glazing over the conflict, Augustine makes the tension palpable in his *Confessions*. In book 7, as we have seen, Augustine reflects upon himself and finds there an orderly cognitive apparatus that leads him gradually and inevitably to a conception of truly spiritual existence. In book 8, however, when Augustine is again led to consider his reflexive self, he sees a far more conflicted and turbulent interior that leads nowhere, and is painfully at odds with itself. Having achieved an insight into spiritual being, Augustine seeks in book 8 to embrace the life of celibacy (notwithstanding his long history of sexual activity and his evident enjoyment of it). What he finds, however, is that he cannot bring himself to will it, even though he deeply wants it.[59]

Book 8 is central to Augustine's *Confessions*, and reflects a deeply interesting view of the self, but it is in many ways alien to modern sensibilities. In par-

58. St. Augustine, *The Confessions*, trans. Maria Boulding, O.S.B. (New York: Random House, 1997), 139.

59. O'Donnell, *Augustine: Confessions*, 3.30, calls *Confessions* 8 "pre-eminently the book of *voluntas*." On Augustine's attitude toward sexuality, see Peter Brown, *The Body in Society: Men, Women and Sexual Renunciation in Early Christianity* (London: Faber and Faber, 1989), 387–427. On the relation between Augustine's struggles to embrace celibacy and his intellectual acceptance of Christianity, see, e.g, O'Donnell, *Augustine: Confessions*, 3.7–10.

ticular, Augustine's anguished attempts to embrace celibacy may well strike readers nowadays as needless and wrongheaded: no wonder Augustine experienced such resistance to something as perverse as attempting to swear off sex! Still, this was not an idiosyncratic predilection on Augustine's part; celibacy was a widely acknowledged and venerated religious practice. It was an ascetic era, but, as Peter Brown has shown, Augustine's views on sex and marriage were on the whole moderate and balanced.

It is far beyond the scope of this study to address early Christian asceticism and attitudes toward the body. The important point, for my purposes, is the one Augustine emphasizes in *Confessions*, book 8. Celibacy exposed a hitherto unexplored intricacy in the will itself. Augustine thought he was trying to command his will to will something—but the will resisted itself. This was a stunning paradox, for normally the will commanded the body and the body obeyed forthwith.[60] As such, the will seemed the very expression of an integral "I" that was the center of wishes, intentions, and commands: the outcomes one desired flowed readily and immediately from the self's commands. What Augustine discovered in seeking to embrace a celibate life, however, was that the will resisted its own commands: an experience that ultimately called into doubt the coherence of the "I"—the self as an indivisible whole.

Here too, then, Augustine introduces a new reflexivity into accounts of the self: the will is not just a "transitive" faculty that acts upon the external world. It is, to some extent, "in the middle voice": it entails an attitude toward itself and the objects of its own willing. So, for example, one does not merely love external objects; rather, anyone has an attitude or an orientation toward his or her loves. We may wholly approve of what we love, or we may dissent—we may be appalled at one level by the things we yearn for at another. We love or hate our loves.[61]

Augustine finds, then, that his own will resists his control; he is not able to command it to go where he wants it to. This fracture in the will considerably complicates the sense of self, for who is the one who does the willing—the Augustine who desires celibacy, or the Augustine who resists that

60. See *Confessions*, 8.9.21; cf. *City of God*, 14.23.

61. The fruitfulness of this idea, and its continuing suggestiveness, are shown in the contemporary philosopher Harry Frankfurt's theory of "second-order volition"—that is, the desire to have a certain desire. Frankfurt defines the person as one who has these second-order volitions, an attitude or orientation toward one's wants. See Harry G. Frankfurt, "Freedom of Will and the Concept of a Person," *Journal of Philosophy* 68 (1971): 5–20; now reprinted in the same author's *The Importance of What We Care About* (Cambridge: Cambridge University Press, 1988), 11–25. For a discussion of Augustine and Frankfurt on free will, see Wetzel, *Augustine and the Limits of Virtue*, 222–27.

desire? There is no question of this fractured Augustine's "commanding" his will in an autonomous act. Augustine is brought to embrace celibacy at last not by a heroic self-command, but by a congeries of chance meetings, words, events that exert a subtle pressure on his heart and finally bring him to a bursting point, where he is at last able to want what he wants.

Thus, Augustine tells the story of his meeting with Simplician, who in turn told him the story of Victorinus, a prominent orator who publicly converted to Christianity.[62] Augustine yearns to follow his example, but his lust prevents him from doing so. Augustine then meets Pontician, who chances to see a book lying on a gaming table in the house where Augustine is staying. The book happens to be St. Paul's Epistles—not the rhetorical tracts Pontician had expected. Pontician is therefore moved to tell Augustine about the life of St. Anthony of Egypt, and the sudden conversion recently of two courtiers in the emperor's court at Trier.[63] Finally, at the height of his confusion and frustration, Augustine chances to hear a child in the next yard singing "Take and read," a happenstance prompting him to pick up the book at his side—again, Paul's epistles. Augustine lets his eye fall on a passage chosen at random, and at long last finds the strength to embrace what he wants.[64] In all of this, Augustine stresses the role of contingency and luck, and the impact that even apparently random events had on his soul.

The movement from book 7 to book 8 in the *Confessions* reads, on the surface, like a temporal movement leading Augustine ever closer to God. In fact, however, a considerable rupture in Augustine's own thought seems to underlie the striking differences of emphasis in these two books. Augustine's Christianity initially had a deep platonic hue: Christianity, on that view, seemed to complement and complete the work performed by ancient philosophy. Plato and his descendants had adumbrated the full revelation that Christianity brought. When Augustine wrote the first two books of his philosophical dialogue "The Free Choice of Will" in A.D. 387–88, for example, he was still very much under the influence of the neo-platonist Plotinus. Augustine's vision in book 7 reflects his encounter with neo-platonism—and most especially in its optimistic picture of a coherent self leading us, gradually but irresistibly, to God.

But by 397–401, the years when Augustine wrote his *Confessions*, that vision had come to seem at best preliminary. In the 390s, upon rereading St. Paul, Augustine was brought to a very different view of the self, the will, and Christianity—a view that left its trace on the conversion account in book 8. St. Paul's conversion had been visited on him suddenly, gratu-

---

62. *Confessions*, 8.2.3–5.
63. Ibid., 8.6.13–8.7.18.
64. Ibid., 8.8.19–8.12.29.

itously, without any preparation or desire on his part. His conversion experience was plainly the result of grace, a free gift from God that *molded* his will, so that it was now directed toward Christianity. Augustine came to see his own conversion in the light of Paul's.[65]

He wrote of these new insights in seven books *To Simplician, On Various Questions* (396), a treatise written the year before he began his *Confessions*. His treatment of will there differs strikingly from its description in "The Free Choice of Will" (a work that seemed in retrospect tainted by the "school of pride").[66] God's gracious and freely given gift does not merely invite the will to respond; it actually moves the will to do so.

> If we ask whether a good will is a gift of God, I should be surprised if anyone would venture to deny that. But because the good will does not precede calling, but calling precedes the good will, *the fact that we have a good will is rightly attributed to God who calls us, and the fact that we are called cannot be attributed to ourselves . . . . [W]ithout his calling we cannot even will.*[67]

Grace is tailored to the individual personality. People are brought to faith in different ways, Augustine writes, and the same words may deeply move one person while they leave another cold.[68] The will radically depends on having something presented to it that delights and stirs it. But, Augustine asks rhetorically, "Who has it in his power to ensure that something that will delight him will turn up, or that he will take delight in what turns up?"[69] Paul's conversion demonstrates this:

> What did Saul will but to attack, seize, bind and slay Christians? What a fierce, savage, blind will was that! Yet he was thrown prostrate by one word from on high, and a vision came to him where his mind and will were turned from their fierceness and set on the right way towards faith.[70]

In his treatise to Simplician, Augustine has conclusively left behind classical models, and articulated a view of the will that marks an abrupt

---

65. See Paula Fredriksen, "Paul and Augustine: Conversion Narratives, Orthodox Traditions, and the Retrospective Self," *Journal of Theological Studies*, n.s. 37 (April 1986): 3–34.

66. *Confessions*, 9.4.7.

67. Augustine, *To Simplician—On Various Questions*, book 1, question 2, in *Augustine: Earlier Writings*, trans. John H.S. Burleigh, The Library of Christian Classics 6 (Philadelphia: The Westminster Press, 1953), 385–406. The quoted passage is found on 394–95 (Question II, para. 12), emphasis added.

68. Ibid., 396 (Question II, para. 14).

69. Ibid., 405 (Question II, para. 21).

70. Ibid., 406 (Question II, para. 22).

departure from pagan models of self-possession. Augustine remains the great expositor of the will, but the will itself has undergone a profound change: no longer an autonomous, intricately structured internal organ, but something radically dependent on its environment and constantly pressured and pushed by the events presented to it.

Augustine's account of his conversion in book 8 is plainly a narrative illustration of his new account of the will in the treatise addressed to Simplician. The chance encounter with Pontician, the random child's song ("Take and read"), the stories nested within stories (Simplician's story about Victorinus; Pontician's story about the courtiers at Trier)—all of these events embody and convey grace; they show the radical dependency of Augustine's will on his environment and its several impacts on him. They reflect, too, the inability of the will to direct itself: without grace—that is, without a pressure of external events nudging him, pressuring him—Augustine's will is helplessly conflicted.

Augustine's predicament was the occasion for penetrating psychological self-analysis. "Grant me chastity," he prayed, "but not yet."[71] He felt a powerful sense of confusion, unhappiness, and above all shame, since he was not able truly to desire what he knew was the better course. He was "eaten up and confounded" by shame;[72] he "whipped his soul," trying to get it to go where he wanted it to go.[73] Augustine was ashamed to discover in himself not one will, but a tangle of desires, all of varying intensity.[74] It was not that he did not desire celibacy, but rather that he did not wish for it with sufficient fervor; he did not want to want it.

In the inner turmoil leading up to his conversion, Augustine thought he saw evidence of an original, complex unity—a self-reflexive, triune self—now shattered and reduced to countless disordered impulses. Far from expressing the coherence of the self, in other words, will now captured its fatal incoherence. The will's collapse into a tangle of contending wills could only have been a perverse act of will itself—Adam's first disobedience. Augustine read his irresolution as reflecting a foundational act of rebellion, in which the will turned away from its proper object (God) and allowed itself to be dis-tracted (literally, "torn apart") in a continuing stream of narrow gratifications.[75] From that point onward the will was known primarily by the resistance it offered. Far from securing individual autonomy, the will tied the agent to circumstance, and showed his

71. *Confessions*, 8.7.17.
72. *Confessions*, 8.7.18 (*ita rodebar intus et confundebar pudore horribili vehementer*).
73. Ibid. See also *Confessions*, 8.2.4, 8.7.18, 8.8.19, 8.10.22, 8.11.25, 8.11.27.
74. *Confessions*, 8.10.23.
75. See *Confessions*, 8.10.22.

susceptibility to the milieu—not only the objects that commanded his desires, but also the caked habits that prevented him from breaking with the past and achieving true freedom.[76]

Augustine's new appreciation of the internal rifts in the will and the self called forth the specific genre of confession. Confession, for Augustine, entailed an account of one's deeds, but more deeply it was a reflection on the self, and in particular on its contingency—i.e., its incoherence in its own terms, and its radical dependency on a source outside itself. It flowed from the sense of the self as "ec-centric," off center, alienated from its deepest source. To reflect on the internal rifts and incoherence of the self was to reflect on the fallen creature's true relation to Being itself, and was thus a mode of praise.[77]

Augustine's confessing self was one powerful crystallization of what Taylor has called the "dialogic" character of human life. It was a self that is fundamentally relational, and so incoherent except in terms of its relation to another.[78] Confession, as enacted in the *Confessions,* was not an account of one's abnormalities to a worldly authority, but an intimate discourse in which a contingent being dwelled on the depth of its dependency on a foundational other. Augustine may have inaugurated the genre of autobiography, but in doing so he called into question the very concept of an "*autos*"—the unproblematic, well-defined self.[79] Confession is intended almost precisely to shake us loose from something like that sense of ourselves as autonomous centers—self-possessed, self-determining. For Augustine, this sense of the self as a neatly bounded entity is not at all a lofty conception, but an unexamined and misleading one: just what we all tend (wrongly) to think about ourselves.[80]

76. On the power of habit (*consuetudo*) to impede willing the good, see Wetzel, *Augustine and the Limits of Virtue,* 134–38.

77. On confession as praise, see O'Donnell, *Augustine: Confessions,* 2.3–7. O'Donnell's citations show that the connotation of praise was innate in biblical usage of the term, but not in classical usage. Peter Brown, *Augustine of Hippo* (Berkeley: University of California Press, 1967), 175, quotes Augustine's definition of confession as "accusation of oneself; praise of God." In the *Confessions,* he draws the two meanings together into an indissoluble unity.

78. Charles Taylor, "The Politics of Recognition," in Taylor, *Philosophical Arguments* (Cambridge: Harvard University Press, 1995), 227–31.

79. On the *Confessions* and theoretical problems of the autobiographical "self," see, e.g., John Freccero, "Autobiography and Narrative," in Thomas C. Heller, Morton Sosna, and David E. Wellbery, eds., *Reconstructing Individualism* (Stanford, Calif.: Stanford University Press, 1986), 16–29; Elisabeth DeMijolla, *Autobiographical Quests: Augustine, Montaigne, Rousseau and Wordsworth* (Charlottesville: University Press of Virginia, 1994), 13–45; Michel Beaujour, *Poetics of the Literary Self-Portrait,* trans. Yara Milos (New York: New York University Press, 1991), 37–71.

80. See Romand Coles, *Self / Power / Other: Political Theory and Dialogical Ethics* (Ithaca,

Accordingly, Augustinian confession is deeply and pervasively critical. I do not mean by this that the confessant criticizes his past conduct on the basis of some received and unexamined standard. Rather, confession is critical from the ground up: it criticizes first and most fundamentally the very idea of self. It then provides the basis for a searching critique of the social structures that entrench the idea of self and encourage the essentially selfish, power-seeking behavior to be expected of beings construed as well-bounded selves. Confession challenges one's entire affective relation to the world, and calls into question the standards by which one typically discriminates between the better and the worse course of action.

Confession, therefore, represents a turning away from the classical models, the Platonic dialogues, which could not capture the amazing paradoxes of self and speech that Augustine had come to discern. Pagan rhetoric—of which Augustine had been a distinguished exemplar and teacher[81]—had presented language as a tool by which speakers could accomplish their purposes. With its arsenal of persuasive techniques, rhetoric reflected an extreme self-consciousness about the properties of language, and the way these properties could be manipulated to rouse in the audience the emotions most useful to the orator's purposes.[82] Rhetoric, in other words, presupposed that speech had a well-bounded, coherent self as its source, and that the trained speaker could exercise consummate control over the meaning of what he or she said.

This is just the view Augustine rejects in abandoning the dialogue for the confessional format. He strives—how plausibly is another question—to cleanse his speech of his self (conceived as an atomic "center"), so that it becomes the language now of a piece of creation. Such language is "*confessio*"—which for Augustine means not only an account of past sins, but the creature's praise of its creator—language that originates ultimately in the creator.[83] His ideal is speech harboring a wealth of unex-

---

N.Y.: Cornell University Press, 1992), 14–49, on Augustine's confessing self as a critique of autonomy.

81. For an account of Augustine's education in rhetoric, see Henri Irénée Marrou, *Saint Augustin et la fin de la culture antique* (Paris: E. de Boccard, 1938), 47–84.

82. Aristotle's *Rhetoric* represents one of the earliest and still one of the most illuminating rhetorical handbooks. On the nature of rhetoric as a skill at manipulating language, see Thomas Cole, *The Origins of Rhetoric in Ancient Greece* (Baltimore: The Johns Hopkins University Press, 1991), who argues that Plato and Aristotle were the first to distinguish between the "idea" to be conveyed and the verbal medium used to convey it in as persuasive a manner as possible.

83. On the significance of the term *confessio* in Augustine, see O'Donnell, *Augustine: Confessions*, 2.3–4; J. Ratzinger, "Originalität und Überlieferung in Augustins Begriff der

pected, not consciously intended meanings: such profuse meaningfulness reflects a source deeper than the speaker's own narrow intentions.[84]

This aspect of Augustine's thought has perhaps been obscured by Wittgenstein's criticisms of the account of language acquisition at the very beginning of the *Confessions*.[85] There Augustine apparently treats language as a collection of "names" of things, as though a simple one-to-one relation existed between word and object—a view, of course, that Wittgenstein was at pains to refute. But we misunderstand Augustine unless we appreciate that he is making an ethical point about language—viz., that children are induced to learn it as a more efficient way of making their demands known.

The one-to-one approach to word and object is indeed flattening. But that was partly Augustine's point: language loses its richness when it is reduced to a tool of the individual's narrow self-seeking. Morally speaking, children acquiring language are like little orators—bent on getting what they want and using language as a means to do so. The selfishness of the orator and the child results in a greater technical control of language but a marked diminution of meaning. The passage from the *Confessions* Wittgenstein quotes in his *Philosophical Investigations* affords, then, only a very partial view of Augustine's thoughts on language. When language is no longer tied to the speaker's selfish purposes, it takes on that copiousness of meaning, that rich suggestiveness that Augustine hopes his *Confessions* will evince.

The *Confessions* is, among other things, perhaps the earliest account we have of discontent with a law-related career. Augustine's final conversion is marked not only by his embrace of celibacy, but by his resignation from his job as a teacher of rhetoric to future lawyers: no longer would youths buy from him "weapons for their madness."[86] Augustine rejected the "marketplace of eloquence" (*nundinis loquacitatis*, 9.2.2), which was

---

'Confessio,'" *Revue des Etudes Augustiniennes* 3 (1957): 375–92. "*Confessio*" conveys in part a voluntary disclosure of past transgressions, but also has a biblical sense of praise and thanksgiving. In Sermon 67.2, Augustine defines confession as "accusation of oneself; praise of God" (quoted in Brown, *Augustine of Hippo*, 75). In the *Confessions*, Augustine draws the two meanings together into an indissoluble unity.

84. *Confessions*, 12.26.36, 12.18.27. See also 12.14.17: "Wondrous is the depth of your speech, whose surface lies before us, pleasing to your little ones. But wondrous is their depth, my God, wondrous is their depth!"

85. Ludwig Wittgenstein, *Philosophical Investigations*, 3d ed. (New York: Macmillan, 1953), 2, quoting and discussing *Confessions*, 1.8.13. For criticisms of Wittgenstein's analysis of Augustine, see, e.g., O'Donnell, *Augustine: Confessions*, 2.58.

86. *Confessions*, 9.2.2.

premised largely on greed.[87] More deeply, however, Augustine rejected the idea of the speaker as an autonomous master dominating language. The *Confessions*, to be sure, is a consummate piece of writing, and employs the full battery of rhetoric to create a text that is still profoundly moving, even when one cannot accept its premises. The model of eloquence, however, is no longer Cicero, but holy scripture, and the texture of the *Confessions* is skillfully woven in large part from the psalms and Paul's epistles. Thus, Augustine aspires to open up his speech so that the source of his being might speak through him, and his language might express meanings beyond anything he could have intended.

Such a self cannot be understood apart from its environment, and the way it moves and pressures the self into making the decisions it does. Theologically, this is the doctrine of grace—the self's dependence on sources outside itself for the motivation to turn to God. The important point for my discussion, however, is that grace worked through and suffused the host of everyday events that surrounded Augustine and engaged him in a variety of ways. Full, integrated acts of the will were possible, of course—Augustine finally did embrace celibacy—but these did not just flow unproblematically from an internal organ or function ("the will"). They emerged from a host of circumstances, all bearing down on Augustine as he tried to make a decision. The conversion narratives Augustine happened to hear repeatedly during his inner struggles worked on him as unsettling challenges:[88] what prevented him from doing what others had found it in their hearts to do? Their mode was suggestive: instead of arguments, they offered compelling examples,[89] addressed to the will, not the perplexed intellect. Augustine writes of their "insinuating" power—their ability to get under his skin, to rattle and disorient him.[90] All this suggested how circumstances—sundry accidents, the bric-a-brac of life—could suddenly galvanize the will and rouse it to that conviction necessary for resolution. For Augustine, of course, it was not at all accidental. The point, however, is that God was pressuring Augustine's will precisely through the sundry particulars of his milieu.

The whole ideal of "ascent" from this world to an eternal, purely spir-

87.   *Confessions*, 4.2.2 ("Overcome by greed, I sold the art of speaking for victory in the courts"); cf. ibid., 8.6.13 ("I was selling the power of speaking"), 9.5.13.

88.   For a close reading of these narratives and their significance for Augustine's conversion, see Brian Stock, *Augustine the Reader* (Cambridge: Harvard University Press, 1996), 75–111. On the ethical significance of examples, see Charles Larmore, *Patterns of Ethical Complexity* (Cambridge: Cambridge University Press, 1987), 1–21.

89.   *Confessions*, 8.2.3 (*insinuari*), 8.2.4. (*quibus modis te insinuasti illi pectori*), 8.6.14 (*insinuans*).

90.   *Confessions*, 8.12.29.

itual world—which Augustine achieved in book 7—now came to look seriously incomplete and misleading. "Ascent" failed to capture the radical dependency of the soul on its environment. Grace, perhaps paradoxically, gave a new importance to the actual, physical details and concrete episodes of the individual's life. This pointed to a new importance for society and the love of one's neighbor: the fallen world now emerged as the means through which creatures were moved by grace and in which they were constrained to seek out the creator. The political implications Augustine saw in this new model of the self will be described in the next section. Before turning to that, however, I need to show the multiple pervasive effects Augustine's new model of the self brought in its train.

For example, because grace worked through a thickly detailed environment to move the conflicted will to action, *narrative* took on a new centrality. It conveyed a sense of the self immersed in the world, a part among other parts. The philosophical dialogue, in which two people deliberately reasoned their way toward a conclusion, by its very nature subtly distorted how the soul attained the truth. Augustine, we might say, went from conceiving will philosophically (as something internal to the self and knowable) to conceiving it *narratively* (as something borne upon—both for good and ill—by one's circumstances).

So, the narrative in *Confessions*, book 8 captures implicitly that mix of free will and grace that proved so difficult to formulate theoretically.[91] It would be impossible to parse out to what extent Augustine exerted his free will to choose a life of celibacy, and to what extent he was prompted by grace. The narrative modality shows the considerable pressure events exerted on him, and thus points irresistibly to the pervasive presence of grace. At the same time—and, again, thanks to the narrative modality—it is clear that Augustine's own personality has not been sidelined: he truly wills the decision he makes. The superficial polarities between an autonomous self and external pressure made no sense in Augustine's bracing vision of a radically contingent self. Narrative became expressive of that vision; it enabled Augustine to show how an individual's life-changing decisions are deeply embedded in circumstances over which he or she has no control.

Underlying and impelling these insights into the contingency of the self and its immersion in a material world was Augustine's attempt to ex-

91. How to reconcile grace and free will was a vexed problem for Augustine. For an account of the controversy and Augustine's attempts to formulate the relation between grace and will, see Wetzel, *Augustine and the Limits of Virtue*, 161–218; Brown, *Augustine of Hippo*, 365–75.

plain evil.[92] As we have seen, Augustine's ground-breaking theory of the will took its inception from the need to show the cause of evil. Augustine moved beyond the conceptions set forth in "The Free Choice of the Will," but when he did so, the result was a yet more compelling account of evil. This was partly a matter of the new model's greater psychological realism: the fragmented self Augustine unforgettably captured in the *Confessions*—particularly in book 8—reflected (in Augustine's view) the pervasive effects of evil, the creature's perverse turn away from the source of his being. Just as important, the self's immersion in the material, created world gave the evils of this world a greater urgency, an ineluctable reality that could not be so easily transcended.

Augustine thought that ancient eudaemonist philosophies failed especially in their refusal to take seriously the pressing reality of evil. It was his willingness to give evil, suffering, injustice their full weight that, in his view, distinguished his Christian beliefs from those of the pagan past. In Augustine's view, ancient philosophers not only ignored large stretches of reality—slavery, war, disease, death, and anyone's constant exposure to these and other serious harms—but also offered a bland and unpersuasive account of the individual's internal life.

Augustine's radical criticism of the philosophical tradition finds its most forceful expression in book 19 of the *City of God*. There, Augustine reproduces an argument that there exist 288 possible schools of ethical thought. He begins by indicating four different schools of thought, distinguished by their view of the natural good for man—pleasure, repose, a combination of the two, or what Augustine calls the "primary natural blessings." But in each of these four possible schools is posed the question whether the goods are desired for the sake of virtue, or virtue for the sake of them, or both are to be desired for their own sake. These three distinct possibilities increase the number of possible philosophical schools from four to twelve. But the good may be sought either for one's own sake, or for the sake of one's fellow-man: thus, the twelve sects double to a possible 24.[93]

It would be tedious to follow this ingenious reasoning all the way. It is sufficient to indicate its general tendency and purpose in Augustine's argument: this *omnium gatherum* afforded a point of view from which to assess ancient philosophy as a whole, the better to expose the unexamined, and no longer plausible, assumptions that underlay all of them. For all these schools of thought presupposed that felicity was attainable in this life. They made that presupposition because they also assumed a certain

92. On the centrality of evil in Augustine's thought, see G. R. Evans, *Augustine on Evil* (Cambridge: Cambridge University Press, 1982).

93. *City of God*, 19.1.

model of the self as capable of deciding where the highest good in life lies, and then securing that good in the individual's life. But Augustine's model of the riven, conflicted self denied both these assumptions: the internal stresses and contradictions dividing the self ruled out happiness—stable, ordered, secure—as a possibility in this life.[94]

As Augustine points out, each of the candidates for a supreme good can be snatched away from us. This is obviously true of physical goods. ("For is there any pain. . . any disturbance . . . that cannot befall a wise man's body?" Augustine asks.) But it is true even of such noble ideals as virtue. Virtue makes no sense except as a constant struggle with its opposite: it is not the secure possession ancient philosophy made it seem. "Although it claims the topmost place among human goods, what is its activity in this world but unceasing warfare with vices, and those not external vices but internal. . .for it is never true, in this life, that vice does not exist."

Augustine criticizes the Stoics for their failure to treat ills as genuinely evil—capable of seriously diminishing or even ruining a life. The reality and power of evils to dash human lives rouses Augustine to the heights of his considerable eloquence:

> There is a mighty force in the evils which compel a man. . .to rob himself of his existence as a man . . . There is a mighty force in those evils which overpower this natural feeling which makes us employ all our strength in our endeavour to avoid death—which defeat this feeling so utterly that what was shunned is now wished and longed for . . . There is a mighty force in those evils which make fortitude a murderer.[95]

If ancient philosophers had taken suffering and evil really seriously, Augustine writes, they could not have supposed that philosophy (or anything at all in this life) could successfully achieve happiness. That Augustine insisted on the grievousness of these flaws—as on the authentic evils posed by death, disease, and madness[96]—may seem surprising, given his rooted belief that we were made for happiness in another world: surely, we might have thought, for Augustine the evils of this life are not really worth grieving, given that a greater and more reliable reality awaits us.

94. On this passage, see R. A. Markus, *Saeculum: History and Society in the Theology of St. Augustine,* paperback edition (Cambridge: Cambridge University Press, 1988), 82–84.

95. The quotes are all from Augustine, *City of God,* book 19, chapter 4. Trans. Henry Bettenson.

96. See *City of God,* 19.4–8.

But not at all: Augustine is convinced not only that happiness is deeply impossible in this world, but that this world is for now an inescapable reality for us, not to be transcended by flights of faith. To be sure, we look forward to another world; but we do so as parts deeply embedded in a material world. Augustine has a "disenchanted" sense of the inescapability of this world—the impossibility of fully escaping its gravitational pull on us by meditation or mystic ascent.[97]

The ineluctability of the world and its evils gives Augustine's thought a distinctly *tragic* sense. In other words, in marking himself off from what he took to be the pagan philosophical tradition, Augustine in effect links up with a different strand in classical antiquity—Greek tragedy. Tragedy was the genre of human suffering par excellence: it presented spectacles of unmerited suffering in human life, and presented this suffering as capable of inflicting real damage—just the point of Augustine's contention with the Stoics and other ancient philosophers. Moreover, a tragedy like Aeschylus' *Oresteia* evinced many of the paradoxes of decision and responsibility Augustine was later to elaborate in distinctly Christian terms. Agamemnon's decision to sacrifice his daughter Iphigeneia was voluntary on his part, an official act in his role as commander-in-chief of the Achaean troops—in other words, truly a decision. At the same time, however, his act makes no sense except as part of a supernatural plan that fulfills an ancient curse on the house of Atreus. Nor does it make any sense apart from the exigent circumstances in which Agamemnon was compelled to make it. His decision manifested both character and destiny, inextricably tied—a distinctly human agency and a divine power that gets worked out in individual human acts. The tragic agent was not the sufficient cause of his own acts; rather, as Jean-Pierre Vernant writes, "it is his action, recoiling upon him as the gods have . . . ordered, that reveals him to himself, showing him the true nature of what he is and what he does."[98]

As Vernant points out, Greek tragedy was the literary genre that, for perhaps the first time in Western history, sought to portray man in his condition as a deliberate agent: the dramatic action unfolded on the basis of acts to which the hero was fully committed, and for whose consequences he was responsible.[99] Yet what emerged from these explorations of the human as committed agent was how incomplete this description was, how incoherent action was when considered purely in terms of human agency. The tragic hero was "tugged in two opposite directions."

---

97. See R. A. Markus, *Conversion and Disenchantment* (Villanova, Pa.: Villanova University Press, 1989).

98. Vernant, "Intimations of the Will in Greek Tragedy," 80.

99. Ibid., 79.

Sometimes he was to blame for his actions, to the extent that they expressed his character; sometimes—or, really, at the same time—he was a "plaything in the hands of the gods."[100]

Augustine's conceptions of the will and the self evince a similar complexity and instability. On the one hand, the will secures autonomy and hence full responsibility for one's own acts—that is the conception Augustine describes in "On the Free Choice of the Will." In book 8 of the *Confessions,* however, Augustine presents a far more complex view of the will as fragmented and radically dependent on grace. Although Augustine is regarded as the first to articulate a recognizable concept of will (*voluntas*), the will turns out to be but another, internalized site for the ambiguities surrounding human agency that had earlier been explored in Greek tragedy—the tensions between the active and the passive, between human intent and environmental constraints on intention, between the spontaneity of human desire and an overarching pattern of divine destiny.

The will—originally conceived as an emphatic expression of human autonomy and responsibility—inevitably attracted to itself ideas of the agent's radical dependence on his or her environment. Augustine himself was embarrassed by these tensions in his own thinking. In his last years, the Pelagians (who denied Augustine's teaching on grace, and taught that happiness was indeed attainable in this life) were able to quote, against Augustine, several passages from his own treatise "On the Free Choice of the Will." (That was the early Augustine who could insist that "man. . .can live an upright life whenever he so wishes.")[101] But it was precisely the inability to will oneself to lead an upright life that formed the basis for Augustine's later conception of the self.

These tensions that mark the agency of tragic heroes and the "confessing self" have not abated; in fact, they have found some of their most striking expressions in case law—above all in the custodial confession cases prior to *Miranda.* Justice Frankfurter's opinion in *Culombe v. Connecticut,* for example, eloquently shows how courts attempted to do justice at once to the idea of an autonomous will and to the obvious susceptibility of the individual to his environment. Frankfurter wrote that because "the concept of 'voluntariness' is one which concerns a mental state," a court must engage in "the imaginative recreation, largely inferential, of internal, 'psychological' fact."[102] The

100. Ibid., 81.
101. "On the Free Choice of the Will," II.1.1. Augustine cites the passages from "The Free Choice of the Will" that Pelagius quoted to support his own rival theories of free will and grace. See Augustine, *Retractations,* 1.9.3. On the Pelagian controversy, see Brown, *Augustine of Hippo,* 340–75.
102. *Culombe v. Connecticut,* 367 U.S. 568, 603 (1961).

court was faced with the task of inferring this "internal, psychological fact" from the (unavoidably, and often deliberately, disorienting) circumstances attending the confession. "For the mental state of involuntariness upon which the due process question turns can never be affirmatively established other than circumstantially—that is by inference."[103] The court was only too aware that it was inescapably chasing its own tail. The very concepts a court can use to express a mental reality, Frankfurter wrote, are "generalizations importing preconceptions about the reality to be expressed."[104] *Culombe* shows how custodial confession cases had obliged courts to wrestle with problems of agency and responsibility that had long before engaged the theologians, and before them the tragedians.

In *Miranda,* the Supreme Court wisely decided to get off the seesaw: the rule announced there made voluntariness a relatively simple determination for courts to make, since it now depended in large part on the question of whether the detainee had been properly advised of his rights. On the other hand, as we have seen, *Miranda* seemed to squelch the implications of the individual's suggestibility, and to adhere—almost defensively—to a far simpler model of the self as rational and autonomous. *Miranda* can scarcely be said to have resolved the tensions and ambiguities surrounding the idea of will and autonomy. What kind of legal theory might be constructed on the basis of the more complex psychological model that seemed implicit in the case? I believe Augustine is suggestive here too.

3. The Limited State and the Intricate Self

The *Confessions* could be understood as the account of Augustine's search for a model of the self that could capture his own complex and conflicted experience. The model he suggests is still powerful, and certainly more plausible, psychologically speaking, than the paradigm of a responsible and fully rational self the *Miranda* court pressed into service. But perhaps this psychological richness is beside the point in a legal framework. After all, there exist excellent reasons for *not* using a psychologically "profound" model of ourselves in a legal setting: to think of ourselves as responsible citizens is a natural complement to the attractive and compelling idea of a liberal state that respects the dignity of persons and of individual rights. It is not obvious how such a state could rest on the model of the fragmented self Augustine presents. Augustine considerably deepened the interior self, and found mysterious depths in the individual soul. That

103. Ibid., 605.
104. Ibid., 604.

deepening of the self into a self-reflexive subject, however, introduced the need to confess, as a way of excavating these depths in the hopes of finally squaring oneself with authoritative Being. This is a disturbing vision, for it looks deeply incompatible with our own political arrangements.

Augustine has, in consequence, been attacked for the deplorable political consequences that seem to flow from his ideas of the self. Elaine Pagels, for example, has criticized Augustine for turning away from a rich tradition of thinking that celebrated the "freedom" of Christians, and the new infusion of power over one's life and capacity for good that baptism brought with it.[105] Even more trenchantly, William Connolly has attacked Augustine for the sinister, Foucauldian implications of the confessing self.[106] Connolly treats Augustine as an especially clear example of the way a political order based on morality needs to condemn and exclude those who fail to support its ontology and its way of structuring the world. Augustine was indeed a defender of orthodoxy: he wrote diatribes against "heretical" sects (the Manicheans, the Donatists, the Pelagians) and defended the use of state power to force individuals into the church.[107] This was not just an unfortunate but dispensable aspect of Augustine's teaching. Animating his *Confessions* is the underlying sense that it really matters what one believes: so long as Augustine was gripped by the Manichean teachings, he could not attain a sufficiently complex and responsive sense of himself. After struggling through to his fascinating and hard-won ideas on the fractured will, Augustine was not likely then to engage in dialogue with the Manicheans, or to respect the difference of the "other." Notwithstanding what I will argue was the prescient secularity of his views of the

---

105. Elaine Pagels, *Adam, Eve and the Serpent* (New York: Vintage, 1989), 98–126.

106. William B. Connolly, *The Augustinian Imperative: A Reflection on the Politics of Morality*, Vol. 1 in Morton Schoolman, ed., *Modernity and Political Thought* (Newbury Park, Calif.: Sage Publications, 1993), 85. See also Coles, *Self / Power / Other*, 14–53. While Coles is more sympathetic than Connolly to Augustine—and in particular to the richness of Augustine's confessing self—he nonetheless criticizes Augustinian confession as the beginning of a "new form of power intent on extirpating all that does not accord with the voice of the 'one true God.'" Coles, *Self / Power / Other*, 10.

107. On Augustine and the suppression of the Donatists, see Peter Brown, *Augustine of Hippo*, 240–42, 334–36. On Augustine and coercion in general, see John M. Rist, *Augustine: Ancient Thought Baptized* (Cambridge: Cambridge University Press, 1994), 239–45; Markus, *Saeculum*, 133–53; John Milbank, *Theology & Social Practice* (Oxford: Blackwell, 1990), 417–22. For a withering critique of Augustine, see, e.g., John M. Rist, "Augustine on Free Will and Predestination," in R. A. Markus, ed., *Augustine: A Collection of Critical Essays* (New York: Doubleday, 1972), 218–52, and esp. 243–48. Others argue that Augustine's willingness to use state force to coerce his religious adversaries is inconsistent with the thrust of his mature thought on the state and law. See Markus, *Saeculum*, and Milbank, *Theology & Social Practice*.

state, Augustine nonetheless managed to square them with using political force to coerce others into the church.

For Connolly, Augustine is the very prototype of the Nietzschean ascetic, whose will to power takes the indirect road of self-negation—he invented a supreme authority to whom he could then bend his knee. Augustine sought to articulate an encompassing order, whose inevitable tendency was to become an official reality that then distinguished between the true and the heretical. Augustine purported to glean this containing order by looking deep within himself. His own internal experiences became a kind of map to reach and explore a wholly nonmaterial existence. But once we step outside Augustine's own perspective, Connolly writes, the "humble confessor emerges as the wily creator of the one fiction he is willing to bow before."[108] Augustine projected himself into a fictive divinity and then represented the fiction as an "order" he counseled himself and others to read.

I don't believe Connolly's attack tells the whole story, but there's no doubt he is on to something. As James O'Donnell writes, "few proponents of Christian humility have obtruded themselves on the attention of their public with the insistence (to say nothing of the effectiveness) that marks [the *Confessions*]."[109] It is a curious feature of Augustine, at least to a modern sensibility, that having gotten such a powerful grasp on psychological complexity, he should think of it as an evil to be eschewed or wished away. The renowned acuity of Augustine's psychological self-analysis was at bottom an exploration of what he took to be the pervasive effects of evil. In Augustine's view, however, that evil irresistibly pointed to a supervening good, whose goodness consisted, to a degree we tend to find troubling, in its simplicity. Augustine was too astute an observer of humanity to believe that evil would ever be cured or disappear in this age; nonetheless, he looked forward to a different era when the good city of God and the wicked city of man would be finally distinguished. This attitude led him to the most repellent features of his teaching—his willingness to countenance the eternal torment of the "unjust" as the price willingly paid to secure an eternal and unambiguous good. Augustine has been called the first theoretician of the Inquisition.[110] From a Foucauldian perspective, his evident intolerance and authoritarianism seem at one with his confessional "therapy."[111]

108. Connolly, *Augustinian Imperative*, 45–46.

109. J. O'Donnell, *Augustine: Confessions*, 1.xlii.

110. Brown, *Augustine of Hippo*, 240; Rist, *Augustine: Ancient Thought Baptized*, 241 n. 65. Brown goes on to make the point that Augustine was in no position to be a Grand Inquisitor, nor was he bent on maintaining the status quo in a totally Christian society. The Donatists, for example, were not a small sect Augustine sought to rub out, but a body of Christians as large as his own congregation, and in many ways similar to it.

111. On confession as therapy, see Brown, *Augustine of Hippo*, 165, 176–81.

Augustine is in some ways inconceivably remote from modern readers. In other ways, however, he seems stunningly contemporary. When first embarking on Augustine's *Confessions,* Oliver Wendell Holmes (then a justice in the Supreme Court) commented that it was a "rum thing to see a man making a mountain out of robbing a peartree in his teens." After completing it, however, he wrote of being deeply moved by the *Confessions,* even though he heartily disagreed with the religious views animating it.[112] The ambivalence felt by Holmes—that great progenitor of modern legal theory—points to the complex relations between Augustine and modernity. The *Confessions* continues to stir and challenge its readers. Its portrait of the conflicted self, its deconstruction of time and memory, its self-consciousness about language—all these give it a special resonance for a late-twentieth-century audience.

On the other hand, Augustine's most piercing insights into the contingency of the self, time, language all flow from a rooted, and insistent, view of a purely spiritual and unquestionably authoritative being. The fragmented self turns out to be an oblique way to reconstitute an orthodox conception of God and creation. Augustine captures the anxieties and rifts of this life, but only because he is supremely confident about his theism.

In particular, Augustine's theory of the moral obligation to obey the law rests on views about humans' intrinsic nature—their inevitable orientation toward peace. It is difficult in a modern democratic society to conceive of an acceptable jurisprudence based on an account of a universal, core human nature. Nonetheless, I propose in this section to articulate what I take to be an attractive model of the state that is sketched in Augustine's work. I attempt not to present an objective account of the entirety of Augustine's political thought, but to sketch in detail a significant feature of it, one that is, admittedly, at odds with his actual practice (and, indeed, with other aspects of his political thought). As a thinker, Augustine was rich and complex, but not systematic. He lived in a transitional and unstable era, and his thought evolved considerably over the course of his writings. He was the sort of person, as he wrote to one of his correspondents, who "wrote as he progressed, and progressed as he wrote."

The point of isolating and exploring an important strand in Augustine's political and legal thinking is that he succeeded in doing something that, in my view, has escaped modern theory. Justice, for Augustine, was an ideal that no legal system could ever "possess," but that nonetheless gave it a moral claim on citizens' respect. The real achievement in Au-

112. See *Holmes-Laski Letters: The Correspondence of Mr. Justice Holmes and Harold Laski, 1916–1935,* vol. 1, ed. Mark deWolfe Howe (Cambridge: Harvard University Press, 1953), 300, 307–8.

gustine's legal theory is not so much the debunking realism of his account (although that, too, is a fascinating part of it), but his movement beyond the negative critique to show the basis of its affirmative claim to the saint's active concern. To be sure, Augustine's solution can no longer enjoy broad acceptance: he projected the ideal into an eschatological future that was certain to come and that would work a final, authoritative separation of good from evil. Nonetheless, the challenge to any modern jurisprudence is (as it was for Augustine) to show the legitimacy of the state, even granting its serious imperfections. It is worthwhile, then, to consider book 19 of Augustine's *City of God*, where he sketches an account of adjudication (and, more generally, of the secular state) that presupposes his fascinating model of the complex self.

Augustine's rereading of St. Paul—a watershed in his thinking about the self and the will—was also a turning point for his thinking about law and the state.[113] The more complex psychological model of the self depicted especially in book 8 of the *Confessions* had unavoidable political connotations. First, Augustine had come to see the self as inevitably grounded in and dependent on its actual milieu. This meant that the self was deeply social, and that society was not something that one could or should transcend. Augustine had initially contemplated a monastic life, as an escape from the follies of society. He continued to praise that life, but now as a model for what society ought to be.[114] In his earlier thought, when the ladder of ascent and the possibility of transcendence formed the core of his spirituality, love of neighbor played a distinctly secondary, ancillary role to love of God. His new model of the self, however, meant that love of neighbor was now the preeminent means of loving God—

113. Interest in Augustine's theory of law and the state continues to flourish. Among recent works, see, e.g., Dorothy F. Donnelly, ed., *The City of God: A Collection of Critical Essays* (New York: Peter Lang, 1995), section I ("Political Thought"); Jean Bethke Elshtain, *Augustine and the Politics of Limits* (Notre Dame, Ind.: University of Notre Dame Press, 1995); Rist, *Augustine: Ancient Thought Baptized,* 203–55; Eugene TeSelle, "Towards an Augustinian Politics," in William S. Babcock, ed., *The Ethics of St. Augustine* (Atlanta: Scholars Press, 1992), 147–68; Milbank, *Theology & Social Practice,* 380–438; Graham Walker, *Moral Foundations of Constitutional Thought* (Princeton, N.J.: Princeton University Press, 1990), esp. 65–112; Markus, *Saeculum,* esp. 72–104.

For an overview of Augustine's political thought, see Herbert A. Deane, *Political and Social Ideas of St. Augustine* (New York: Columbia University Press, 1963), esp. 116–53, although his treatment tends to obscure how Augustine's ideas evolved over time. The evolution in Augustine's views of law and the state is well brought out in Markus, *Saeculum.* See also F. E. Cranz, "The Development of Augustine's Ideas on Society before the Donatist Controversy," in *Augustine: A Collection of Critical Essays,* ed. R. A. Markus (New York: Doubleday, 1972), 336–403.

114. See Rist, *Augustine,* 205–6.

saints were constrained to conduct their quest for God from within a fallen and deeply flawed world.[115]

This meant that one could no longer think in terms of the Christian simply cultivating his private spirituality, apart from secular society and without regard for it. Augustine's thinking became more incarnational over time: saints were now inevitably "in" society, even if not entirely of it. Community was the proper form of life for human beings. "There is nothing so social by nature and so anti-social (*discordiosum*) by corruption as the human race," he wrote.[116]

At the same time, the model of the self as riven and conflicted—psychologically rather more persuasive than the models Augustine inherited—called for a more realistic model of the state. The assembly of conflicted beings, only precariously in charge of their own lives, could hardly be thought to be in stable possession of justice. Augustine, accordingly, insists on the grave defects from which any government, and any system of administering law, must suffer. The state is made necessary by humans' perverse turn away from God, and their collapse in upon their own wills and narrow interests. The earthly city, Augustine writes in the ringing introduction to *City of God*, "aims at dominion, which holds nations in enslavement, but is itself dominated by that very lust of domination (*libido dominandi*)."[117]

The relation between ruler and ruled, he suggests, is essentially a master–slave relation: both are forms of dominion brought about by sin.[118] A state bears a disturbing resemblance to a band of thieves,[119] and law may well serve merely to further the selfish interests of the propertied classes.[120] The ruler, moreover, does not govern because of some natural superiority.[121] Augustine stresses the inner turbulence and the instability of the rulers themselves.[122] Far from achieving the rule of reason over passion, law reflects the very unruliness of the passions, and the need to apply extremely strong and direct methods to ensure their control.[123]

There is no question, therefore (at least in Augustine's mature

115. Ibid., 159–68.
116. *City of God*, 12.28.1.
117. Ibid., 1.1.
118. Ibid. See Markus, *Saeculum*, 93, 199–200.
119. *City of God*, 4.4.
120. Ibid., 2.20.
121. Ibid., 19.15. "[God] did not wish that a rational creature made in his own image have dominion over others except for irrational things; he did not want man to rule over man, but man to rule over beasts."
122. Ibid., 19.4.
123. Cf. ibid., 19.4 (the virtues reflect the disorderliness of the passions).

thought), of the state's mirroring an overarching, cosmic order, or of its embodying some natural hierarchy. To the contrary, war is the inevitable tendency of the earthly city—the "coercive power inseparable from the social existence of fallen human beings," as Robert Markus writes.[124] "Tension, strife and disorder are endemic" in society, Markus notes. "Human society is irremediably rooted in this tension-ridden and disordered saeculum." "It was this radically 'tragic' character of existence for which ancient philosophy, in Augustine's view, could find no room."[125]

It is striking how frequently, in treatments of Augustine's views on law and politics, writers have recourse to the word "tragic." At the risk of being overly schematic, Augustine's historical position looks rather like a mirror image of the historical shift reflected in Greek tragedy, which looked back upon a heroic past from the perspective of a civil society, a *polis*. Just as the fading heroic myths afforded an external perspective and critique of the civil ideals, so did Augustine's Christianity furnish him with an exterior point of view from which to assess the Roman ideal of law and government. Aeschylus and Augustine stand, respectively, at the beginning and the end of the ancient *polis*. In both cases, the view emerges of a world structured by war or *eris* ("strife"). Law is an institution that cannot quite "do justice to" us, and that demarcates a region in which it settles for a second best—to keep the peace.

Thus, Augustine's mature thought on the state stands in marked contrast to earlier, classical conceptions of the *polis*. In the *City of God* he rejects the definition of the state given in Cicero's philosophical dialogue *De Republica*. Cicero defines the republic as "a people united in association by a common sense of right and a community of interest."[126] If we bear in mind Augustine's psychological model of the conflicted will, we can appreciate how untenable Cicero's classical definition of the state must have seemed. Augustine criticizes it as necessarily implying that the state is just ("a common sense of right")—something he denies states in fact are or could ever be. Augustine revises the requirements downward. A state is "the assembly of a rational multitude joined in fellowship by their agreement on the things they love."[127]

The change in direction Augustine takes is characteristic of him. He substitutes a realist criterion (things actually loved) for an ideal one (justice). This new, psychological criterion presents the state as expressive of actual human purposes and preferences. The state and its laws are one

---

124. Markus, *Saeculum*, xii.
125. Ibid., 83.
126. See *City of God*, 2.21; Cicero, *De Republica*, 1.25.42.
127. See *City of God*, 19.21, 19.24.

highly visible crystallization of a people's character—a magnifying glass for the drives actually motivating most people within a society. The state is the fallen and conflicted human will writ large.

By focusing on people's loves as determining the character of the state, Augustine also suggests the possibility of a dynamic character to the state. Augustine distinguishes between more and less evil purposes among essentially fallen loves: the old Romans' dedication to individual glory, for example, inspired them to some genuinely admirable feats of self-denial.[128] Thus, while Augustine believed the state was bound to suffer grave defects, he seems to allow for a difference between better and worse states, and for the possibility of a change in character of the state over time.

The point is that Augustine's dark and skeptical view of the state did not lead him simply to dismiss it: it had its distinct character and its own potential for improvement or deterioration. In all of this, Augustine moves away from the "classical" definition of the state as founded on a static, essentially timeless justice. He presents a far more realistic and "immanent" account, and one that rests upon a psychologically complex model of the person. Augustine was not concerned with the best constitution, or with the state's educational function—the themes of much political philosophy before him—but, as John Rist states, with "the basic flaws that must be discerned in each and every form of political society."[129] For all his debunking emphasis on the state's grievous defects, however, Augustine nonetheless held that the law genuinely obligates citizens. In particular, Christians owed it not simply their passive obedience, but their affirmative concern and respect: Christian jurists, for example, had a duty to serve it in the capacity of judges, when asked. More generally, the heavenly city not only defends, but guards and actively seeks out (*tuetur atque appetit*) the compromise of human wills that constitutes the earthly peace.[130] Augustine's "legal realism" did not land him in nihilism, or an inability to explain why the state imposed genuine obligations.

This is the aspect of Augustine's teaching that seems potentially richest and most suggestive for modern jurisprudence. Although Augustine did not believe that any state could plausibly claim to *possess* justice, he did hold that justice was nonetheless relevant to a state's claims on its citizens. The state reflected an aspiration toward peace, even though this aspiration reflected the sadly warped conditions of fallen mankind. Christians were to serve the state because of the true peace darkly reflected in it. Augustine thus points to what we might call the *ironic* character of the Chris-

128. See ibid., 5.18.
129. Rist, *Augustine*, 217.
130. *City of God*, 19.17.

tian's duty toward the state: saints owed a duty to the state even though they knew that it could never lay claim to achieving a final and stable justice. Their duty to it was based partly on ideals that the state darkly reflected, but could never possess.

We can bring out what is most distinctive in Augustine's mature thinking about law and the state by comparing it with his earlier thought. Again, the early treatise "The Free Choice of Will" will be our point of departure. There, Augustine presents a view of temporal law as an image of the eternal law: he writes that whatever is just in temporal law derives from the unchanging dictates of eternal law.[131] Indeed, in another treatise written about the same time ("On True Religion"), he goes so far as to state that a law that failed to cohere with eternal law would not be a law.[132] The early Augustine's rather conventional view of temporal law "deriving" from eternal law is obviously indebted to neo-platonism. It presupposes an encompassing order linking immutable, purely spiritual realities to transient, bodily ones.

Apparent evils in the state, on this view, make sense once they are situated within the larger, fully coherent order of things. So, for example, Augustine writes, "What is more horrible than the public executioner? Yet he has a necessary place in the legal system, and he is part of the order of a well-governed society."[133] Order, he continues, is that which leads us to God; a wise prince is the best means of achieving order.[134] The state, then, is part of a "ladder of ascent" that leads easily to a more sublime order. Augustine's early view of the state and law parallels his early view of the interior life as a well-ordered apparatus that leads irresistibly to ever more sublime modes, and ultimately to God.

Nonetheless, even in these earlier writings Augustine displays a marked realism about the law, which would continue and deepen in his more mature thinking. Thus, in "The Free Choice of the Will," he presents law essentially as a form of damage control: it is above all addressed to those inordinately attached to earthly goods. "As long as they fear to lose these goods," he writes, "they practice a kind of moderation in their use capa-

131. "On the Free Choice of the Will," 1.6.15.

132. "On True Religion" (*De Vera Religione*), 21.38. *De Vera Religione* was written in A.D. 390, a little after Augustine had written the first two books of "On the Free Choice of the Will." Herbert Deane writes, "As far as I have been able to discover, in none of the works written [after the early *De Vera Religione* 21.38] does Augustine ever state that positive law must conform to God's eternal law or to the law of nature to be valid." Deane, *Ideas of St. Augustine*, 90.

133. "On Order" ("*De Ordine*"), 2.4.12. Augustine wrote "*De Ordine*" in A.D. 386, the year before he wrote "The Free Choice of the Will."

134. Ibid., 1.9.27, 2.8.5.

ble of holding together a society that can be formed from men of this stamp."[135]

This formulation is deepened in his later work. In book 19 of the *City of God*, for example, Augustine writes that "the earthly city seeks out an earthly peace and there draws a limit to the citizens' agreement about the giving and obeying of orders, so that they have a kind of compromise among human wills (*compositio voluntatum*) concerning the things relevant to mortal life."[136] Augustine's account here sounds at first distinctly modern: it envisions a limited state that addresses a zone of overlapping concerns—the matters everyone is concerned about, whatever else they want or value. The state is a kind of clearinghouse in which a host of individual wills get assimilated, assessed, and coherently directed. The state is a "composition" (*compositio*) of wills.

Underlying these ideas, however, is the notion that the state places boundaries on the mass of essentially selfish individual wills. For without these limits, coercively enforced, no life together among the fallen would be possible. Law is a kind of exoskeleton: it supplies the stable structure and cohesiveness society needs, and thus prevents the worst consequences of people's disordered loves and lives. Its purpose is confined to canceling out at least some of the effects of sin; it aims solely to resolve at least some of the tensions inevitable in human society.[137] It exists, as Augustine elsewhere wrote, so that there might be a "secure innocence among the wicked."[138]

Augustine's view of law bears some resemblance to Holmes's debunking account of law from the bad man's point of view: as Holmes was at pains to show, the law is there for no sublime purpose, but rather to set limits to what the bad man can do.[139] Holmes's theory, like Augustine's, implies that the bad man will prudently pursue his self-seeking activities up to but not past the limits allowed by law. Holmes sought to lance some of law's inflated claims to being a system of moral reasoning; his "bad man's" view of law pointed to law as a matter of public policy and wise so-

135. "On the Free Choice of the Will," 1.15.32.

136. *City of God*, 19.17 ("*ita etiam terrena civitas, quae non vivit ex fide, terrenam pacem appetit in eoque defigit imperandi oboediendique concordiam civium ut sit eis de rebus ad mortalem vitam pertinentibus humanarum quaedam compositio voluntatum*").

137. Markus, *Saeculum*, 93–94.

138. Augustine, *Epistles*, 153.

139. Oliver Wendell Holmes, "The Path of Law," *Harvard Law Review* 10 (1897): 457, 459: "If you want to know the law and nothing else, you must look at it as a bad man, who cares only for the material consequences which such knowledge enables him to predict, not as a good one, who finds his reasons for conduct, whether inside the law or outside of it, in the vaguer sanctions of conscience."

cial engineering.[140] Augustine's view, too, implicitly rejects views of the Roman state as a vehicle for God's purpose, and takes a far more realistic view of law. Part of Augustine's appeal as a legal theorist is this protorealist quality: as did the legal realists of this century, Augustine's procedure was to debunk the idealist claims of received theory.

The discontinuities between Augustine's earlier and later thought served to bring out and emphasize the darker elements that were there from the beginning. Augustine abandoned the idea of an easy, natural "ascent" from the temporal state and its laws to the eternal order, and made the relations between the state and the heavenly city considerably more complex. The evils of the state came to seem truly evil—not softened or mitigated, as they had been in earlier writings, by their containment within an encompassing and knowable order. Yet even as he emphasized the enormous costs imposed by the state, and the grave flaws infecting it, Augustine also insisted on the Christian's immanent situation within it. It was a feature of his earlier thought that the good man was not really governed by temporal law, but solely by eternal law.[141] In his later thinking, Augustine moved away from this: even the Christian remained subject to the temporal laws, and obligated to serve them above and beyond mere obedience. That was because even saints could not hope to "transcend" the world in the rather facile way the young Augustine had imagined. The depth of the physical creature's immersion in physical creation—so to speak, a part among other parts—made the world, and more particularly society, not only inescapable, but the difficult, steep, and oblique road by which the Christian approached God.

Augustine's later thoughts on law and the state are most succinctly crystallized in his account of the judge in book 19 of the *City of God*. Augustine cites the judge in the course of his attack on pagan philosophy, and his insistence on human wretchedness and the sheer reality of evils in this life:

> What about those judgments passed by men on their fellow-men, which cannot be dispensed with in cities, however much peace they enjoy? What is our feeling about them? How pitiable, how lamentable do we find them! For indeed those who pronounce judgement cannot see into the consciences of those on whom they pronounce it. And so they are often

140. Ibid., 460–61, 467–69.
141. "The Free Choice of Will," 1.15.31: "I think that men whose happiness derives from their love of things eternal come under the eternal law, whereas the temporal law is laid upon the unhappy."

compelled to seek the truth by torturing innocent witnesses in a case which is no concern of theirs. . . .This means that the ignorance of the judge is often a calamity for the innocent.[142]

The judge's misery flows partly from the highly imperfect information on which he must base his decisions. This flaw is especially clear in the case of confessions. For in deciding whether a defendant is guilty and so deserving of punishment, the judge must use torture to ensure that witnesses and the accused will speak the truth. The judge can never know whether the accused spoke the truth or was simply trying to escape the torturer.

> Even more difficult to bear, more to be grieved over and if possible bewailed with fountains of tears: when the judge has the accused tortured (to avoid killing an innocent person through ignorance), it happens through his wretched ignorance that he kills an innocent man after torturing him . . . . When this man has been condemned and killed, the judge still does not know whether he has killed someone innocent or guilty. [143]

Nor can the judge ever know whether the sentence he has imposed will serve any purpose.[144] Nonetheless, it is imperative that a society have institutions to make these judgments, even though decisions are reached in an unavoidable ignorance of all pertinent facts.

Judith Shklar has shown the pertinence of Augustine's insistence on the pervasiveness of injustice and social ills, and the inability of any state finally to eradicate them. As she argues, injustice is much more than the simple inverse of justice. It has an urgent, imperative reality in the outrage felt by the victims of injustice, and indeed is felt more passionately than the rather theoretical claims of justice could ever be. The normal model of justice, Shklar writes, "does not ignore injustice, but it tends to reduce it to a prelude to or a rejection and breakdown of justice, as if in-

---

142. St. Augustine, *City of God,* 19.6 (Bettenson translation).

143. *City of God,* 19.6.

144. See Augustine, *Epistle* 95, 3:

> What shall I say about punishment or non-punishment, since this is something we intend for the good of those who are to be punished or not punished according to our judgment? And, in setting the limit of the punishment, are we to proportion it to the kind and degree of the offenses, as well as to the endurance of the individual soul?. . .And here is a dilemma which often occurs: if you punish a man, you may ruin him; if you leave him unpunished, you may ruin another.

Trans. by Sister Wilfrid Parsons, S.N.D., in *Saint Augustine: Letters,* Vol. 2, Fathers of the Church 18 (Washington, D.C.: Catholic University of America Press, 1953), 117–18.

justice were a surprising abnormality."[145] Augustine's skepticism about
the normal model of justice has the signal merit of making these evils
stand out more starkly than they often do in conventional political or
legal philosophy.[146]

For Augustine, it is the mark of maturity to acknowledge the reality of
the evils inevitably entailed in administering the laws, and not to insist
that the evils do not really matter or that the judge is really happy. To be
sure, Augustine grants, the judge is not morally culpable for carrying
out his duties. That does not mean, however, that the judge is therefore
happy:

> Yet if it is through unavoidable ignorance and the unavoidable duty of
> judging that he tortures the innocent, are we to be told that it is not
> enough to acquit him? Must we grant him happiness as a bonus? How
> much more mature reflection it shows, how much more worthy of a
> human being it is when a man acknowledges this necessity as a mark of
> human wretchedness, when he hates that necessity in his own actions and
> when, if he has the wisdom of devotion, he cries out to God, "Deliver me
> from my necessities!"[147]

Although he grants that the judge is not blameworthy for the harms
he causes, he refuses either to ignore those harms or to call the judge
happy. For Augustine, optimism about the law's legitimacy is callow
when it insists that the judge is blessed in doing his duty, because the
duties are genuinely fulfilling. In his view, it requires maturity, and is far
worthier of the human being, to dispense with the illusion that law must
reflect and express its subjects before it can exert a moral claim on
them. The Augustinian jurist cries, "Deliver me from my necessities!"
For Augustine, law has a legitimate claim both to the judge's allegiance
and to his grief.

Augustine's portrait of the judge certainly has the ring of truth: he anticipates that anxiety often expressed by modern American courts faced
with custodial confession cases.[148] His anguished judge is a far cry from
Dworkin's "Hercules," who has all the serene, classical virtues Augustine

145. Judith N. Shklar, *The Faces of Injustice* (New Haven, Conn.: Yale University Press), 17.
146. Ibid., 20–21, 24–26.
147. *City of God*, 19.6 (Bettenson translation).
148. See, e.g., *Haley v. Ohio*, 332 U.S. at 606 (Frankfurter, J., concurring): "Unhappily
we have neither physical nor intellectual weights and measures by which judicial judgment
can determine when pressures in securing a confession reach the coercive intensity that
calls for the exclusion of a statement so secured."

denies. Hercules is Olympian, saturnine, jovial—supremely competent and assuredly happy. For Dworkin, the legal system can obligate us morally only if it meets certain criteria. Only essentially just institutions—those evincing a certain integrity—can exert a moral authority on us. Hercules' wholeness and serenity reflect what Dworkin asserts is the coherence and sufficiency of the legal system.

But from an Augustinian point of view, Hercules' confidence is self-deluding. He shows his true colors only in those rare "hard cases" that require the court in essence to characterize the kind of legal system we have. Hercules (like Dworkin's jurisprudence more generally) is designed to deal with the loftiest of judicial tasks. It is the lowlier problems facing the Augustinian judge, however, that seem the more intractable and unsettling. Long before we even get to the courts' power or right to decide the underlying philosophical issues posed by our political institutions, we must reckon with the courts' ability (or inability) simply to gather the facts and to pronounce sentence. Augustine's darkly hued portrait of the anxious judge has the virtue of giving full *theoretical* scope to the gnawing uncertainties Dworkin treats as dispensable—as if they were the sort of thing that can be ignored at the theoretical level.

The judge's wretchedness is a reflex of Augustine's skepticism about the possibility of justice in this world, and his deep conviction about the genuine lamentability of law's serious imperfections. Even while he insists on the gravity of these ills, however, Augustine is at pains to show that the legal system exerts a real obligation on Christians. This seems to me the heart of what Robert Markus has elegantly called the "complexity and poise" of Augustine's mature political and legal theory.[149] Even one who appreciates the "darkness that attends the life of human society" will agree to serve as a judge, because of the claims society has on him. Indeed, it is unthinkable that he should neglect his duty.[150]

But why and how can such an imperfect and coercive institution as the law properly lay claim to the saint's respect? Augustine's answer, briefly, was that although the saints are like captives in this "earthly city," they obey the temporal laws to preserve a harmony (*concordia*) with the citizens of the earthly city as to things relevant to the temporal order.[151] Law supports an earthly peace, which reflects that perfect or "heavenly" peace that will come after the end of history, when the city of God is perfected.[152]

149. Markus, *Saeculum*, 102.
150. *City of God*, 19.6.
151. *City of God*, 19.17.
152. *City of God*, 15.2.

To appreciate the significance of this position, we need first to ask what Augustine means when he says the earthly city "reflects" or "signifies" the heavenly one. In his earlier writings too Augustine indicated that the temporal order "reflected" the eternal one; what he meant there was that the temporal state derives its authority from its containment within an overarching order. But his emphasis on the deep and grievous flaws of the state throughout *City of God* shows that there is no longer any question that the temporal order proceeds from the eternal order. In the *City of God*, the state is emphatically *not* part of a natural order.[153] Rather, Augustine has come to think of two "orders"—a natural order and "an order of wills."[154] The first reflects the perfection of divine providence as it arranges a beautiful and coherent creation that perfectly embodies divine justice: everything is in its place and has its due. The second order also reflects divine providence, but does so by showing how God's justice is asserted even in the face of perverse human choices, and humans' turn away from the source of their being. Augustine's point is that this fateful turn away from the Creator does not destroy divine justice, but moves it into a new register: justice now finds harsh expression as the just punishment visited on mankind for its sins.

The important point for my purpose here is that for Augustine, this second order—the order of wills—was the preeminent mode in which fallen creatures were to discover God and their own oblique relation to Being. To seek transcendence by contemplating some coherent natural order could only be a partial ideal; it risked ignoring the reality of our situation, the depth of the creature's immersion in a fallen world. The saint did not escape society; rather, he saw more deeply into it, and appreciated (as the worldly-minded could not) how this fallen and grievously imperfect order pointed to something beyond itself.

To see how the saint does this, we should remember Augustine's experience of his own conflicted will in book 8 of the *Confessions*. It showed, indeed, his own perversity and his fallen state, but it also showed the internal complexity of the will: the fragments that now warred against themselves were once part of an integrated and coherent order. Augustine's later doctrine of the self-reflexive, "trinitarian" aspect of the mind owes much to his first humiliated sense of his will's resistance to its own commands. The very experience of disorder became a way of construing—indirectly, obliquely—what the original order was like. Flaws and imperfections, which might seem to be merely obstacles to the soul's search

153. See, e.g., *City of God*, 19.21.
154. See Markus, *Saeculum*, 88–92. As Markus states, Augustine developed this distinction between two orders in book 8 of his *Literal Interpretation of Genesis*.

for God, became (at least for the Christian) the distinctive, postlapsarian way of catching a glimpse of the mortal's relation to God.

Thus, in the *Confessions*, even Augustine's youthful errors and wayward paths are ultimately illuminating. The mature Augustine tells us that as a young man in Carthage he was "not yet in love, but in love with love (*amare amabam*)."[155] The phrase captures his immersion in sensation for its own sake: it conjures up the frivolity and selfishness of the young Augustine sowing his wild oats. As it turns out, however, it also captures the self-referentiality of genuine love—the fact that love is itself an object of love—an insight intended to show the likeness between the creature and the triune creator. Augustine's confessional theology is drenched in the paradox that the richness and profundity of God's Being presses itself upon his creatures, even when they are most distant from it and distracted by their own narrow, self-regarding pursuits. The expression "love of love" crystallizes this paradox linguistically. The mature Augustine sees, even in the distorted and frivolous sensuality of his youth, a refracted version of the mind's original triune wholeness.

So, too, with the earthly city: the saint sees through the disorder to what the original order must have been like. The earthly city, as Augustine stresses throughout *City of God*, was founded on fratricide, and this outrage to the natural ties of kinship pervades every aspect of the city. Cain, the first fratricide, was also the first founder of a city; and the founding of Rome, notoriously, was tainted by Romulus's murder of his brother Remus.[156] This fratricidal strain runs through Roman history, for Rome's expansion included the conquest and domination of its mother cities, Alba Longa and Troy.[157] Later, after Rome had conquered the world and so lacked any external foes, the fratricidal strain exploded again in civil war, as individual citizens sought to arrogate power to themselves.[158]

Even Rome's most sublime ideals bore the taint of the originary fratricide. In the *City of God*, Augustine recurs to the old Roman hero Brutus, who fulfilled a supremely difficult duty by pronouncing judgment against his own son for treason against Rome.[159] Brutus certainly displayed the kind of lofty impersonality that duty requires, but it is plain that he is to be pitied, for he was obliged to condemn his own son to death. Augustine does not question Brutus's courage, but duty plainly evinces some dread-

---

155. *Confessions*, 3.1.1.
156. See *City of God*, 3.6, 15.5.
157. See ibid., 3.7, 3.14.
158. See ibid., 5.13; and see the overview of Rome's bloody history in book 3.
159. See ibid., 3.16, 5.18. On duty (*officium*) and its backgrounds in Stoic thought, see Milbank, *Theology & Social Practice*, 412–15.

ful miscarriage in the violence it can do to one's most natural sentiments. Augustine admires the self-discipline, but deplores the whole framework in which such duties are posed.

What the saint can appreciate is how such terrible disorders in the state "refract" an aboriginal community of love and mutual concern, before each one turned aside to his or her own purposes. What was this original community like, whose degenerate reflection constitutes the state? One model for this idyllic fellowship, in Augustine's writings, is his own climactic conversation with his mother Monica at Ostia, shortly before her death, as recounted in book 9 of the *Confessions*. In other words, the city's fratricidal disorder—a family tearing itself apart—points to an aboriginal order whose shape and texture are strongly familial in nature. As recounted in *Confessions* book 9, Augustine and Monica spoke not so much as son and mother, but as two pilgrims in a quest for eternal life. Their blood relationship fed into the mutual concern and delight they felt, but their sense of themselves as joint searchers transformed anything that was limiting in the mother–son relationship. They became a community of equals, in which Augustine's maleness, his intellectual prowess, and his earthly prestige ceased to distinguish him in any important respect from a woman lacking his education and worldly success.

The "community" of mother and son points to an ideal fellowship of which the city, tainted from its very inception by fratricide, is the sick mirror. Augustine and Monica's joint vision at Ostia embodied that communal peace that Augustine describes at the close of book 19 of the *City of God*.[160] The city and its laws represent the badly warped, coercive, and fallen kind of "peace" for which a fallen society must by and large settle. The earthly city too loves peace, though in a severely distorted version:[161] this love of peace is the vestigial trace of man's original, unfallen nature. Serving it is the saint's acknowledgment of his or her containment within that fallen world. As Augustine stresses, in this age the two cities are inextricably intermingled.[162] Good and bad alike share this earthly peace, but only the good catch glimpses of the heavenly peace of which the earthly is a degenerate form.

Citizens of the heavenly city remain deeply engaged in this world, and work out their dedication to a perfect heavenly peace within the severely flawed conditions of this world. Promoting the earthly peace is one important way in which one shows allegiance to the heavenly peace. To be sure, Augustine places a good deal of stress on the necessity of passive obedience to the state: his insistence that even despots are entitled to the Chris-

160. *City of God*, 19.27.
161. Ibid., 19.12.
162. Ibid.

tian's obedience is one of the repellent features of his legal thought.[163] On the other hand, it seems implicit in Augustine's thought that one ought to try correcting the worst excesses of a legal system. Augustine's catalogue of human miseries does not sound like someone who was indifferent to suffering. Indeed, the judge's gnawing anxiety demonstrates that he cannot be indifferent to the suffering he brings about. Deepening earthly peace, making it less imperfect, is the painful, laborious way in which citizens of the heavenly city work during this age toward heavenly peace. They live out an ethic of duty in the hopes of a final flourishing once this *saeculum* has finished. Most important, then, is that no present order can be final. Any legal system, any state, is seriously imperfect, and these imperfections are a motor that drives them forward, in an effort to become less unfairly coercive. As Markus writes, the *City of God* resists

> the divinisation of any form of social arrangement, whether existing or proposed. It points to a radicalism which will not permit any endorsement of what is, and will reject no less uncompromisingly any plan for what is to be. We can, and in Augustine's view, we must, dedicate ourselves to the pursuit of a justice we know to be unattainable here: to a quest which is doomed, and yet, is an inescapable duty.[164]

In sum, law does not "possess" legitimacy. It exerts a moral authority because it is oriented toward, or reflective of, a genuinely valuable peace, which it is nonetheless incapable of wholly embodying. The source of law's legitimacy is partly destabilizing, for those who honor what is truly worthy of respect in the law are moved to make it less transgressive of its sources. Its moral authority requires that its practitioners correct its injustices, without expecting that law could ever attain anything like justice. Political activity to improve the laws is marked by a sense that it can never reach an end in this age. The law's power to obligate flows from sources it can never hope to possess fully or stably.

This view of law is relevant to the custodial confession cases, and in particular to *Miranda*. Suppose the court had in fact looked upon the detainee as in some measure paradigmatic, and as indicating something like Augustine's model of the conflicted self—a will fragmented, uncertain, and sug-

---

163. Augustine emphasized the importance of passive obedience to the powers that be. See, e.g., P.L.R. Brown, "Saint Augustine and Political Society," in Donnelly, ed., *The City of God*, 18–35, esp. 20–22. Nonetheless, Augustine seems to allow for political action leading to changes within the state. See Peter Burnell, "The Problem of Service to Unjust Regimes in Augustine's *City of God*," in Donnelly, ed., *The City of God*, 37–50.

164. Markus, *Saeculum*, xx.

gestible. The court would not have tried to show that the state respects the detainee's "autonomy," nor would it have pinned autonomy on the possibility of a free (that is, uninfluenced) act of will. Instead, the court would have been far more conscious of the state's inability ever to fathom or fully reflect the individual's complex psychological interior. The court might still have arrived at the same holding and required that henceforth detainees be advised of their legal rights before police begin the interrogation. But it would have placed this holding on the firmer basis that such warnings secure a rough-and-ready fairness to the investigation. That, in the final analysis, is the best to which an instrument as blunt as law is can aspire.

4. LAW AS PRACTICE

Denying the justice of legal systems—emphasizing their serious flaws and blind spots, the disparity between their rhetoric and their reality—is a fruitful and illuminating step. As Judith Shklar has argued, injustice is not just an absence of justice, but a powerful reality in its own right—in the toll it takes on the life of its victims, in the fury it rouses and the violence it invites. The consciousness of injustice is passionate, vivid, and subversive. Justice, in contrast, seems pallid and theoretical—something we think about mainly when it is absent.[165]

To focus on injustice is a fruitful step because it undermines the pretensions of theory—its bright way of directing our attention to the positive. The focus that insists on the grave flaws of any legal system deepens sensitivity to the pervasive human responsibility for making the world we inhabit, and to the imperative of correcting the world's manmade injustices. More to my point here, emphasizing the serious imperfection of law is a royal road to the central problems of jurisprudence. This focus makes arguments emphasizing the justice (or the fairness, or the integrity) of legal systems seem bland and partial (in both senses of that word—both incomplete and tendentious).

But then, what is the next step? It might seem best, for example, to abandon efforts to treat law in moral terms altogether, and to situate it on another basis. For example, one might articulate a view of law as a rational tool for effecting scientifically informed policy—the view associated, say, with Oliver Wendell Holmes, and more recently with Richard Posner. Yet another approach would be to treat law's pretensions to goodness as hypocritical lip service, which the politically engaged should try to manipulate in order to advance their own political vision.

165. Shklar, *Faces of Injustice*, 15–50.

This is a view associated variously with the legal realists and the Critical Legal Theorists.

Neither of these stances, however, seems to me maintainable in the long run, mainly because law will never be cleansed of its moral aspirations and these will always remain pertinent to it. Since law uses coercion, fairness in the way its force is deployed must remain a relevant issue. Beyond that, law, far from being just a body of commands, inevitably reflects ideas of the person. Law has a certain stubborn "inwardness"—a self-reflexive reference to the political and moral conceptions underlying its enactment and application. Law is too much with us; we are inside it. To dismiss its moral dimensions, then, is to treat a pervasive aspect of ourselves as somehow dispensable.

Here, then, is a central problem of jurisprudence: how to acknowledge the pertinence of moral conceptions to the law (which Holmes and the legal realists failed to do), without claiming implausibly (as do Dworkin and Rawls) that a legal system successfully achieves these ideals. To put it another way: how to incorporate a genuinely persuasive conception of ourselves into a model of a legal system that (a) acknowledges that law fails in important ways to respect these complexly modeled persons and (b) nonetheless has a genuine claim to their respect?

Augustine's legal thought is still worth considering, if only because he posed this central problem in jurisprudence. What is intriguing in Augustine is that he shows how moral conceptions like justice or peace are indispensable aspects of a legal system without, however, claiming that any legal arrangements could possibly secure them. If his account is not wholly successful—and, in any event, no longer workable—that is partly a measure of the difficulty of the problem.

The picture of law I sketch in this study—law as a practice—attempts to address the problem of how to offer a plausible, "realist" view of the law that nonetheless shows its claim to our allegiance. As we have seen in Chapter 1, law as practice has a certain *breadth:* adjudication, for example, is not simply a question of judges interpreting the principles underlying our political system. A theoretical model needs to accommodate as well the advocates who articulate the broadest public dimensions of the client's position, and elaborate persuasive narratives that marshal the facts into a compelling vision of where justice lies.

We might add now that law as practice also has a *depth in time.* To put this as pointedly as possible: to think of law, even for theoretical purposes, as a "body" or a "system" or anything to which time is not absolutely essential is to distort it. Law is a practice, and, as such, is immersed in time—or, to use an Augustinian term, "distended" in it. Only by appreciating this "distention" in time can we hope to give an account of the legitimacy of law. For the morality of law requires a sense of both its past and its future. The familiarity of law—its age-old quality—is one of its most important stabilizing features (certainly more significant as a practical stabilizing property than any theoretical demonstrations of its essential justice). To say that law is a traditional practice and rooted in the past is not at all to say that it is an unchanging one. As a practice, law inevitably responds to the contemporary milieu, even as it is guided by the past.

Moreover, law-as-practice is distinguished by its futurity. The present of the law is always unstable because of the disparity between its rhetoric and reality. This disparity—the injustice existing in any legal system—prevents it from having a claim on citizens' respect to the extent that the law prevents or forecloses change. The mutability of the legal system, then, its openness to revision, is essential to its having any such claim. Law is not a rational system that possesses some specified excellences; instead, the values animating a legal system are a destabilizing feature, a principle of movement ensuring that law never stops in a single place. The futurity of law, then, is crucial to the way we think about its legitimacy.

We must be careful, however, in the way we conceive of this "futurity." Augustine is a powerful cautionary example here. He too thought law was tethered to the future; indeed, the importance of the future in Augustine's account is one of its most suggestive and still relevant features. However, he also thought of this future as harboring a final, unambiguous, and unchanging good: thanks to his confidence in this future, he was able to countenance the use of state coercion in matters of belief. How, then, to model the legal system in a way that keeps the future always in the future, that ensures that law will always be imperfect, always a practice? This will be the subject of Chapter 3, which explores the links between law and poetry—both of them "interminable" practices that do not look forward to any conclusion. Not only does law-as-practice never come to an end; more deeply, there is no end for it to achieve. Its ideals are self-conscious inventions, immersed in the flux of time.

Rationality and Imagination in the Law: Jürgen Habermas and Wallace Stevens

It has become a fundamental part of much thinking about law that it is a fiction. The essential idea is that law has its roots in human making, not in the structure of the world. It is not something that humans "read off" from the cosmos, or descry in the essential nature of "man." Rather, it is the massive and pervasive product of human decisions and efforts, reaching back deep into the past, extending into most (if not all) aspects of human life and open to continuous revision and reworking. No one individual could possibly encompass it—design it, plan it, or even understand it entirely. Nonetheless, it is the house in which we live. ("We" here has an embracing sense that extends far into both past and future.) To model law as a practice immersed in time reflects this conception of law as a fiction.

But, of course, "fiction" can mean different things. It can mean, for example, that something is a lie—the sort of thing that has a grip on us, but which we ought to dispense with. Fiction, in this sense, is the opposite of truth. But "fiction" can also be used as though it were almost synonymous with truth: our fictions are, or can be, especially expressive of our values and the conflicts and tensions between them. Fiction, in other words, offers us a true mirror of ourselves.

Just so, the idea that law is a fiction can be used to different effects—as a way either to debunk law's claims to justice (it is "merely fiction"), or to celebrate its expressive powers. As I noted at the end of Chapter 2, neither of these arguments seems to me persuasive, because neither is a conception we can really maintain in the course of our actual practice of law. A practice requires that we take it seriously—not trifle with it as though it were essentially meaningless. By the same token, a practice requires that we view it realistically without an artificial overlay of idealization.

The idea that law is a fiction may come too easily to us. To claim that our legal arrangements are rooted solely in human decisions is, or at least should be, genuinely disturbing. Just how unsettling the "fictionalization" of law is may be best appreciated by considering the case of individual rights. The easiest way to conceive of a right is to understand it as abiding innately in the individual. On this view, because the individual is inherently endowed with reason and the capacity to endorse some conception of the good, he or she has rights over against the state, whose legitimacy depends on its respecting those rights. Rights, then, are not a fiction, but a reality, a deep truth about our innate nature.

Idealizing ourselves this way, however, no longer carries much conviction: we do not think of ourselves in terms of essences much anymore, and to speak of our "innate nature" sounds retrograde and oppressive. But removing the imaginative prop of the intrinsically rational, autonomous self turns out to be troubling indeed, and makes it difficult to account for rights. What is a right, after all, if not something possessed by an individual who has certain prerogatives the state must leave undisturbed? Because we absolutely need rights to carry on our practice of law, we still talk about them, of course, invoke them and deal with them as living realities. But there is the nagging sense that we are talking gibberish—words drained of meaning, words that have lingered on mainly by force of habit.

In this chapter I explore the idea of law as a fiction, in a way that tries to respect its power to unsettle some fundamental ideas about law, without falling into nihilism. I want to be realistic about, but not dismissive of, law's need for idealizations. I will focus on the jurisprudence of Jürgen Habermas, because he seems to offer the best and richest account of the fictive elements in law. These elements are above all the idealizations the practice of law requires to get off the ground. It is Habermas's intriguing point that pervasive human practices—e.g., conversation, law—necessarily bring about idealizing (fictive) conceptions of the practice and the persons who carry it on. Habermas's great virtue is that he can show how ideas like the rationality of law or the rights-bearing individual are necessary extensions of our ongoing democratic practice of deciding what laws will govern us. The ideals do not presuppose any metaphysical commitments, and do not stake out any claim about the structure of the cosmos. They are grounded in our ongoing practices and are essential to their functioning.

Rich as Habermas's account is, it is not without its problems. The difficulty is partly that, as he presents it, the practice of law seems insufficiently historical. The idea of individual rights is just given with the practice, and therefore seems to be essentially static. He fails to capture—at a theoretical level—the dismaying sense that this central feature of our legal systems is not a bedrock reality, but fluid and mutable, just because it is the product of human invention. Habermas takes the fictional quality of law seriously, but it seems to me that his account sidelines some of its most unsettling features. He makes rationality appear less conflicted, more "rational" than it really is.

In the first section below, I explore Habermas's ideas on the rationality of law, as a way of showing both their richness and what I take to be their shortcomings. I suggest that the legal concept of the autonomous, rights-bearing individual is an imaginative projection, part of whose value, at least, rests in its *not* being reducible to some objectively existing and demonstrable state of facts. This is an idea that Habermas has worked out with considerable rigor. At the same time, Habermas's account seems to me excessively optimistic and too static. I therefore draw an elaborate parallel between poetry, as presented by Wallace Stevens, and law, in order to show first how Stevens's poetic intuitively captures some of Habermas's best insights, and next how it corrects for the excessive optimism that marks Habermas's account.

In the second section I focus on the idea of evil in Stevens to show how this feature of his poetry illuminates one of the blind spots in modern jurisprudence. Habermas (like Dworkin and Rawls) presents legitimacy too much as something securely established and surely possessed by legal systems; they leave no doubt that law is entitled to the respect of its subjects. Poetry corrects the excessive rationalism of jurisprudence. It does so not only because it speaks about the evils that persist in human life, but more deeply because, as Stevens presents it, evil is an implicit, constitutive element in poetry. Thus, Augustine's insistence on the reality of evils troubling the administration of law is still pertinent, and still necessary—it seems to me—for a credible jurisprudence.

In Section 3 I try to show how the relation between poetry and law illuminates some of the practical problems posed by interpreting the Constitution. I will explore some of the most important currents in twentieth-century constitutional law and show how they have been deeply "poetic." Finally, in Section 4, I address one of Stevens's most striking formulations of poetry (as an "imagining of the normal"), and show the relevance of this formulation for an understanding of law, which in its own way, too, is an imagining of the normal.

A word, finally, about the relation between this chapter and the preceding one. Augustine's super-realities—God, a sure and univocal

good, an ultimate winnowing of the good from the evil—are theological versions of the kind of immutable "verities" that get debunked in
realist accounts of law. In a way, then, a theist like Augustine throws the
essential arc of realist twentieth-century jurisprudence into high relief.
Writers like Habermas and Stevens show that debunking a concept like
"God" as a human invention does not extinguish it, but should lead to
a more complex sense of ourselves and, in particular, the role our need
for idealizing fictions plays in the sense we have of ourselves and our
institutions. Habermas and Stevens both see modernity as partly filter-
ing the past, siphoning away what is no longer useful or persuasive in
it, and deciding what parts of the past shall continue to be valid. I believe Augustine is a supremely eloquent proponent of a past that gets
filtered by modernity. Partly, what Habermas and Stevens do is to give
Augustine's already considerable self-reflexiveness an extra turn, so
that now God, paradise, the angels—the unquestioned super-realities
of Augustine's universe—are seen as themselves figments of human desire, whose apparent reality is ultimately a tribute to the extraordinary
fertility of the imagination. What links Habermas and Stevens is the
sense that debunking these super-realities does not dispense with
them, for they are indispensable; they live on precisely as fictions,
which nonetheless exert a powerful grip on us.

To say that rights are "fictive" is unsettling. It might seem that, once the
metaphysical superstructure is dispensed with, we are left merely with a
sprawling tangle of words—tedious, implosive, ineffectual. To be sure,
there is no goal to be attained—no final reality, no *Ding-an-sich*—to which
language delivers us and then falls silent. One never breaks out of language into an unmediated, real world. This was just Augustine's anxiety,
in fact—that because language can never be silenced (at least in this life),
we have always to do with mere signs, a talkative world that, at best, can
only refer us to an Other, whom we can never attain in this age. Poetry,
however—the blithe celebration of words—intrinsically refutes this: to be
left with language is not to be utterly bereft. Stevens, I think, shows how
the concept of the poetic affords the bare, but sufficient, minimum
needed to explicate a workable legal system.

1. The Rationality of Law

Law has traditionally put a premium on reason and rationality.
Natural law theory, for example, construed law as right reason in accordance with nature. Aquinas viewed reason as the criterion in general for
human conduct, and assumed that reason had standards of correctness

that led, or should lead, everywhere to the same conclusions.[1] Positivism—the modern view that law is simply the rules that get laid down—seems initially to deny the rationality of law and to present it simply as will (the will of the sovereign, or, in a democracy, the will of the sovereign people).[2] The point of much work in recent jurisprudence, however, is to show exactly how rationality is a feature of law even within the considerations of positivism.

Modern jurisprudence presents rationality in ways that are subtly, but deeply different from natural law theory. Rationality is no longer understood transcendentally, as inhering in the cosmos. Instead, it is conceived *pragmatically,* and this in several senses. First, law is intended to settle and coordinate expectations in situations where traditional beliefs are no longer available or no longer suffice to secure a stable communitywide consensus. In a disenchanted and pluralistic world, law performs some of the functions once served by religion. Whereas religion seemed to be a stable, incontrovertible amalgam—a super-reality in which fact and value were indissolubly fused—law in modern society is a steering mechanism, designed to maintain order under conditions of pluralism.

Rather than appealing to a settled and uncontroversial belief, law now appeals to reason: it offers arguments that those affected by the laws could be expected to understand and accept. This rationality is wholly immanent: it makes no appeal to transcendent standards, nor does it assume that others share one's fundamental beliefs.

Public debate across the broad spectrum of society, and, more formally, within the popularly elected legislatures may be expected to issue in decisions that avoid any provincialism of interest or perspective. It converges

1. For a statement of the Stoic conception of natural law, see, e.g., Cicero, *De Republica,* III.33. Julia Annas, *The Morality of Happiness* (Oxford: Oxford University Press, 1993), 302–11, offers a useful overview of the Stoic position on natural law, together with references to the primary sources. Aquinas's position is set forth in relevant part in *Summa Theologica,* Quaestiones 90–91, available in translation in T. McDermott, ed. and trans., *Thomas Aquinas: Selected Philosophical Writings,* The World's Classics (Oxford: Oxford University Press, 1993), 409–21. The Stoic and Thomistic conception of natural law is found in Grotius and Pufendorf, as well as Hobbes and Locke. On the natural law tradition, see Lloyd L. Weinreb, *Natural Law and Justice* (Cambridge: Harvard University Press, 1987). For an excellent statement and defense of natural law theory, see John Finnis, *Natural Law and Natural Rights* (Oxford: Oxford University Press, 1980).

2. See John Austin, *The Province of Jurisprudence Determined* (New York: Noonday Press, 1954), Lecture I, 13. See also Thomas Hobbes, *Leviathan,* Part II, chapter 26 ("Of Civil Laws"): "Civil Law is to every subject those rules which the commonwealth has commanded him by word, writing, or other sufficient sign of the will, to make use of for the distinction of right and wrong—that is to say, of what is contrary and what is not contrary to the rule."

on what an informed, objective observer might conclude is the best, or most reasonable course. Law's rationality aspires to be pragmatic in this utilitarian sense, in that it selects the best means to achieve its stated ends. It would be misleading, therefore, to treat positive law solely as an expression of the will: the democratic procedures used to generate law tend to make it a rational tool—that is, a sensible and efficient one.

Positive law is rational in a deeper sense than this, however. Law is not simply a transitive instrument, a means of affecting the world by carrying out certain programs. It is also self-reflexive: any law reflects its own legality. As Hart, for example, showed, a law is not just any kind of command regarding conduct; it must possess certain formal properties if it is to qualify as a law.[3] These formal features include, above all, generality, but also clarity and prospectivity, as well as consistency with other commands.[4] Thanks to these formal features law is intrinsically rationalizing: its commands, if they are to be recognized as *legal* commands, must apply equally to all, and generally across all situations. Law bears a distinct affinity to Kant's concept of universalizability: it supplies general rules that guide conduct whatever the circumstances.

In a democracy, these formal features are self-reflexive in the additional sense that they bear the traces of the law's democratic origins. The equality of the obligations the laws impose and the protections they afford mirror the formal equality of the citizens, who have enacted the laws. In the absence of any transcendent, "metasocial" guarantees, the only conceivable basis for law's legitimacy is its source in the very people who are subject to it. Only in this way can law, in a disenchanted era, be more than force, or the will of the most powerful classes.[5]

Law's self-reflexivity, then, makes it rational because it embodies the democratic conditions of its own genesis—that is, it shows that citizens (as the authors of the law) have good reason to obey it. Partly in consequence, law is a predominant form of public reason, the means to which a political community turns when it is compelled to reflect on itself and the principles animating it. This is another way of saying that law now bears the burdens of embodying and fostering solidarity in the rational community (a community of rational beings) that generates it. The law

3. H. L. A. Hart, *The Concept of Law* (Oxford: Oxford University Press, 1961), chapter 2 ("Laws, Commands and Orders").

4. Lon Fuller, *The Morality of Law,* rev. ed. (New Haven, Conn.: Yale University Press, 1969), chapter 2 ("The Morality that Makes Law Possible").

5. See Jürgen Habermas, *Between Facts and Norms: Contributions to a Discourse Theory of Law and Democracy,* trans. William Rehg (Cambridge: MIT Press, 1996), 30–33, 102–4, 118–20, 135, 408–9.

and the political community mutually inform and promote each other. The rationality of the community is not a given, independent reality that lies outside the political or legal process. Rather, this community arises in and through practice: it constructs itself through the continuing activity of rational argument and debate.

For these reasons, positive law is not a more or less naked expression of will. Although law must express the popular will if it is to be legitimate, rationality nonetheless inheres in the democratic procedures for marshaling and identifying the popular will. The rationality characterizing law, in other words, is largely internal to it. It has to do with the formal and procedural qualities of the law, and arises from law's self-reflexive quality.

We notice two things about the rationality of law, as so conceived. First, this pragmatic rationality is a *minimalist* conception: rationality comes to mean something like reasonableness. Rationality characterizes the laws because principled reasons could be given in support of them—reasons those affected by the law could reasonably accept. The reasonableness of any given law does not mark it out as uniquely correct: other possible enactments, incompatible with the law in question, might nonetheless be just as reasonable. Reason, on this view, does not issue in determinate conclusions, since it is not a standard imposed from without. Indeed, disagreement is only to be expected as the outcome of reasoned debate. On the other hand, reason should suffice to identify a course of action that is at least acceptable to all those affected.

A legal system that is rational in this pragmatic sense is necessarily dynamic, because the reasons supporting an enactment are always liable to being overcome by other, more persuasive reasons.[6] Reasonableness means that a legal system never attains a final order of optimum rationality; it is inherently ongoing and interminable. One of the important features of reasonableness, then, is that it serves to structure and facilitate change. The stability of a legal system, in other words, consists not in some final order, but in the system's ability to incorporate dissent and to change.

The second feature of rationality as reasonableness is its *ideal* quality. To appreciate this, we must recall the two aspects of rationality distinguished above—the objective rationality (or efficiency) of a statute, and the intrinsic, self-reflective rationality. The former is not an ideal quality, since it can be assessed objectively by experts or other disinterested observers: rationality in this utilitarian sense is at least theoretically demonstrable. But this aspect of rationality is not necessarily what makes it the source of legitimacy in a legal system.

6. Habermas, *Between Facts and Norms*, 35–36.

Rather, legitimacy arises primarily from the self-reflexive properties of law: because it reflects and embodies its own genesis in the democratic procedures of debate and discussion, the law is entitled to the citizens' respect. But this is an *ideal* feature: to think of ourselves as a political community dedicated to rational debate is to abstract from reality and to simplify ourselves. To be sure, this ideal quality must have a footing in actuality—as, for example, in universal adult suffrage and equality of access to office. The point, however, is that it cannot be *reduced to* fact. It is a projection, one way of construing ourselves. There is no objective way, finally, of demonstrating that a society amounts to a political "community." It is an internal model for viewing ourselves, valid only to the extent that it seems "true to" us—that is, to the extent that it captures some vital aspiration that is deeply characteristic and widely recognized as such.[7]

This points to one of the central dilemmas in modern jurisprudence. Disenchantment calls for law to be legitimate purely as a human practice. Accomplishing this, however, requires considerable idealization—which strains plausibility, particularly in a disenchanted world. When belief in an otherworldly authority is widespread and well settled, law need not be idealized, because it lives off an already idealized world. This was the case, for example, with Augustine's theory of law, which he presented as inevitably falling short of the ideal. When, however, law cannot claim to reflect (however imperfectly) a transcendent, ideal realm, it nonetheless requires some notion of an ideal to which it can attach itself. The notion of a political community, for instance, is clearly central to efforts to show the legitimacy of law, yet this community is highly stylized and deeply troubling to our realist sense. The idealization must occur in a material, political context where its counterfactual character is immediately apparent.

Between the minimal and the ideal features of pragmatic rationality, then, an ineradicable tension exists. The minimalism of rationality reflects a realist thrust in modern jurisprudence that dispenses with any notion of a transcendent realm, an objective fusion of fact and value. The idealism of rationality, on the other hand, shows that even with a reduced ontology, law does not avoid recourse to idealizing conceptions.

This tension between the real and the ideal runs throughout law. So, for example, law is at once a social fact and a normative system. It uses coercion to ensure compliance, yet claims a moral authority, entitling it to citizens' obedience. Legal rights are partly zones of amorality in which

---

7. This necessarily ideal quality of law is one of the central problems explored by Habermas in *Between Facts and Norms*. See ibid., 9–21, 28–41, 42, 129–30, 197–98, 322–23, 461–62.

one is free to live however one pleases; yet they are also the basis of a legal system's claim to moral authority.

The point I wish to make now is that the combination of minimalism and idealism yields a rationality that is strikingly *fictive* in conception—not false or deluded, but an admittedly non-demonstrable, idealizing self-description. The realist, or minimalist, thrust in modern legal thought does not rid law of its idealizations. Instead, it reveals them to be human projections (that is, fictions), not mirror images of an objective super-reality. We can put this differently. The idealized political community required by modern jurisprudence is the precipitate of an earlier conception of an objective, rational cosmos: it is what remains once that cosmos has been filtered through a modernist screen.[8] Minimalism shows how indispensable the ideal is to an institution like law: even when the ideal rational order supposedly mirrored by law has been jettisoned, legal theory must still find some way to incorporate it.

Naturally, this fictive quality is a disturbing feature in jurisprudence, and has prompted many efforts to avoid or evade it. One way is to confine rationality in law to efficiency. This was the line taken by Holmes in his famous lecture on "The Path of the Law," where he described the man of the future as the social engineer, not the legal expert versed in the letter of the law. Law, for Holmes, was best understood from the perspective of the "bad man," who treated law purely as a fact, something to be taken into account in the rational effort to maximize his own opportunities.[9]

Richard Posner develops the line adumbrated by Holmes, and argues that law should be a relatively unselfconscious, "transitive" tool for bringing about rational outcomes. In *Sex and Reason,* for example, Posner offers statistics about abortion and the social effects of forbidding it or permitting it, and concludes, on the whole, that abortion before viability should be permitted. The normative question of women's reproductive rights—or the connection between women's autonomy and legislation outlawing abortion—does not play a major role in his argument.[10] Indeed, in *Overcoming Law,* Posner provocatively argues that we should dispense with theories of constitutional law—that is, reflexive theories that seek to define and justify a certain zone in which judicial review is legiti-

8. Cf. ibid., 99, on human rights and the principle of popular sovereignty as the post-metaphysical "precipitate" left behind by a religious and metaphysical tradition.

9. Oliver Wendell Holmes, "The Path of Law," *Harvard Law Review* 10 (1897): 457, 462.

10. Richard A. Posner, *Sex and Reason* (Cambridge: Harvard University Press, 1992), 271–90, although he concludes (ibid., 337) that *Roe* was badly reasoned in terms of due process law.

mate and appropriate.[11] For Posner, the legal system should be more robustly outer-directed: courts do better to amass the facts and then decide which policy makes the most sense. "Overcoming law" means quitting the bad habit of worrying about the conditions necessary if law (any law) is to be legitimate.

A diametrically opposed response to the fictiveness of legal rationality is to insist on it, and in this way to deny that law is rational. This was the approach of the legal realists,[12] and more recently of the Critical Legal Theory school. In a well-known article, for example, Duncan Kennedy argued that law was conflicted at its core—torn between self-regarding and altruistic impulses. Attempts to rationalize law, accordingly, were bound to fail because of its core irrationality.[13] The tendency of this approach is to reduce law to an exercise of will, and in particular the will of the most powerful classes: law appears to be inevitably political. Law's claim to be reasonable and coherent is, on this reading, *merely* fictive—that is, false and obscuring.

Realism leveled a powerful critique at law's claim to rationality. It debunked as pretensions—falsehoods, fictions—the claims of law to be somehow above the fray, neutrally adjudicating disputes according to uncontroversial, objective criteria. Law, for the realist, was right *in* the fray: immanent and inescapably political. Law's vaunted rationality—for example, its formal neutrality—served the political interests of some at the cost of others. To appreciate that law is something we actually *do*—to find in it the traces of contingency, partiality, and self-seeking that are the mark of human works—was to reject law's transcendental claims as self-deluding.

Realism is more than simply a "school" within jurisprudence. It is an unavoidable feature of the modern sense of what law is, most especially in its critique and rejection of a transcendent conceptual apparatus that purports to yield objectively correct legal answers. Realism is what I called above the "minimalist" thrust in modern jurisprudence. Ronald Dworkin and, more recently, Jürgen Habermas attempt to retrieve a sense of the rationality (and therefore the legitimacy) of law within this now unavoidable realist perspective.

11. Richard A. Posner, *Overcoming Law* (Cambridge: Harvard University Press, 1995), 207–14.

12. On the history of the Legal Realist movement, see Morton J. Horwitz, *The Transformation of American Law 1870–1960* (New York: Oxford University Press, 1992), chapters 6–8; Robert Samuel Summers, *Instrumentalism and American Legal Theory* (Ithaca, N.Y.: Cornell University Press, 1982). See also Cass Sunstein, *The Partial Constitution* (Cambridge: Harvard University Press, 1993), 51–57; Habermas, *Between Facts and Norms*, 200–01.

13. Duncan Kennedy, "Form and Substance in Private Law Adjudication," *Harvard Law Review* 89 (1976): 1685, 1774–78.

Habermas in particular stresses the ideal or "counterfactual" aspect of rationality. It is Habermas's point that this ideal element cannot be eliminated: it arises together with the practice of law and is essential to its functioning. Rather than an imitation of an external order, law is evidently a human construct for channeling and coordinating uses of power, and as such it is inevitably political. It is not *merely* political, however; if it were, it could scarcely count as law. In order to be perceived as law—that is, to function at all as a normative system with claims to citizens' respect—law must at least be reasonable, in the sense described above. That is, law must flow from and reflect the free discourse and debate of autonomous and equal citizens. But this reasonableness rests on idealizing models: it simplifies concrete and complex persons into beings who are autonomous and equal to others; it abstracts from the intricate political, economic, religious and historical bonds of society, and treats it instead as (at least partly) a community in which autonomous citizens undertake to govern common affairs in accordance with rules worked out in common.[14] Habermas's point is that the practice of law requires us to assume something like this: these abstract and simplified ideal models of the self and society are what we must suppose if law is to function as law at all.

Habermas traces out a middle path between the two critiques of rationality in law distinguished above—the utilitarian and the realist. As against the utilitarians, he argues for a less arm's-length relation between the individual and the law. It is an assumption of Posner's approach, for example, that law is a tool we consciously choose to utilize—an efficient means of social engineering. The thrust of Habermas's approach, in contrast, is that we are always already within the practice. Law is an environment that has deeply formed us. In effect, there is no such thing as a "pre-legal" person who then decides to establish law, just as there is no such thing (for example) as a "pre-linguistic" person who consciously decides to speak. Rather, there are persons within the law who, by virtue of being within it, are committed to a certain ideal sense of themselves.

On the other hand, by arguing that ideal concepts are a part of the actual practice of law—that such concepts are necessary if the practice is to continue—Habermas answers realist critics who jettison rationality altogether and assert that law is essentially a mask for individual or class self-aggrandizement. Although the ideal cannot be reduced or dissolved into the factual, it is nonetheless immanent within our practices, which require us to credit them once we engage in the practice.

14. Habermas, *Between Facts and Norms*, 84–104, 118–29, 454–55.

Habermas's notion of an ideal presupposed by practice is suggestive, but elusive. It emerges in sharper focus, however, if we consider language—an even more fundamental practice, and one that is, in Habermas's view, foundational for law. In *Between Facts and Norms,* Habermas situates jurisprudence within the larger contours of his celebrated "communication theory." Habermas's idea is that inhering in language itself are ideal, counterfactual presuppositions to which one is committed simply by speaking with another. Participants in a conversation, for example, necessarily presuppose that they can understand each other—an assumption that entails the idealized view that words have identical meanings for the speakers. The conversation will go nowhere unless the participants nurse the assumption, even though it may be plain to an outside observer that words do not have an identical meaning for all speakers.[15]

Furthermore, statements made during conversation (at least in conversations intended to reach mutual understanding) do not primarily purport to reflect a truth existing independent of language. Their aim is to persuade, and so, statements implicitly claim that they could be supported by yet other statements showing their reasonableness. The "truth" of a statement boils down to an ideal claim that addressees of any time or place would find it persuasive. A participant accepts a statement as true essentially because he or she finds that anyone, anywhere would accept it.[16]

In other words, Habermas treats the "truth" of a statement as essentially a question of validity, and presents validity, in turn, as rational acceptability. The validity claim, Habermas writes, "overshoots" the immediate situation and implicitly claims not merely to be persuasive for the specific addressee, but to be equally persuasive for all possible addressees.[17] We notice how Habermas has dispensed with an ideal, extralinguistic realm of "truth" (to which language neutrally refers), and then shows how idealizations are intrinsic to the very practice of conversing (the acceptability of a statement to any and all addressees).

Conversation serves, in turn, as a model for law, in its self-reflective quality as creating and promoting solidarity.[18] The decision to govern the collective aspects of life together according to rules jointly worked out is a larger, public version of a conversation in which participants try to reach agreement. As with a private conversation, deciding to work out rules in common already commits participants to certain positions. Most notably,

15. Ibid., 11–12, 19–20.
16. Ibid., 12–13, 15–17, 20–21, 34–35.
17. Ibid., 14–15, 21.
18. Habermas stresses, however, that law is not confined to this function of promoting and expressing solidarity. See ibid., 25–27, 31, 40–41.

perhaps, the decision to work out rules in common with others presupposes a general and mutual recognition of one another as free and equal: only on this supposition does one enter into a conversation with others. This conception of the individual as free and equal to others is an idealizing one. Habermas's point is that it is unavoidable if one wants to carry on a practice of hammering out the governing rules in common.[19]

Habermas's theory evinces that minimalism we discussed above: in order to establish rights to individual autonomy he assumes nothing more than a mutual effort to work out rules in common (public autonomy). There is no need to suppose, in particular, that rights are somehow inherent in the individual, prior to any intercourse with others. Rather, rights of private and public autonomy "co-originate": they come about together with the decision to enter into a communitywide conversation about the rules governing life in common.[20] In other words, the idea of individual rights is an idealization that arises with the practice of law, and is necessary to its continued functioning. Only if we suppose that individuals bear certain rights can we understand law as a means by which a group decides to work out together the rules that will govern their life in common. Thus, Habermas presents a view of the individual as emerging from and through society. He tries in this way to dispense with a theory of the subject—a mischief-maker in jurisprudence, since it tends to make society secondary to the individual, and, as a result, to make social rules look suspect from the start, as curbs on the individual's natural freedom.[21]

Habermas, in sum, treats law's rationality as an ideal model—in other words, a fiction, but a fiction intrinsic to the practice of law. His approach is at once stimulating and unsettling. For Habermas is in effect saying that rationality contains within itself a component of the irrational: ultimately, the rationality of law cannot itself be rationally demonstrated. We do not rationally choose to make law. Rather, we understand that for law to maintain its legitimacy—and so to be effective as law—it must be rational. The rationality of law is, so to speak, imposed on us as a necessary condition of its being law at all.

Although Habermas builds his jurisprudence on the "ideal" quality of law, he nonetheless tends in various ways to silence or marginalize this "irrational" element in law's rationality. He makes law appear more rational than, on his theory, it really is. To see how this is so, consider his account of informal opinion- and will-formation, which is one of the distinct ad-

---

19. Habermas, *Between Facts and Norms*, 82–104, 118–31.
20. See ibid., 84, 88–89, 103–4.
21. See ibid., 1, 13–14, 84, 103–4, 298–99, 301.

vances on previous thought Habermas makes in his jurisprudence.[22] Rather than focusing (like Dworkin) on the single "herculean" figure of the judge, Habermas situates the formal procedures of law within a far more embracing context of informal opinion- and will-formation that takes place (or should) *throughout* a free society, in discussions, reports, debates by and among citizens.[23] The formal institutions of law then "live off" the informal, but ingrained and pervasive habits of informal conversation and comment about public affairs. Legal institutions, in effect, formalize these democratic habits: they institutionalize the popular opinion and will-formation that exists informally in the society at large.

Habermas's point is that legal commands are entitled to respect (i.e., will be laws, rather than naked commands) only to the extent that citizens can look upon themselves as the authors.[24] The formal procedures for enacting and administering law, however, are not a sufficient condition for attaining this. Rather, the legitimacy of law ultimately requires that legal theory take into account the informal modes of discussion among citizens.

Habermas's distinction between informal and formal modes of forming opinion and will represents a considerable advance on Rawls's discussion of public reasoning. Rawls presented public discourse unrealistically, as something confined to reasonable arguments. He seemed to presuppose a division between the public realm (where only reasonable arguments could count) and a private one (where one might have recourse to beliefs others could not reasonably be expected to accept).[25] Habermas's concept of "informal opinion- and will-formation" allows for a robust, embracing popular debate, without a priori strictures on what counts as public discourse. The formal processes of lawmaking then serve to channel and focus the relevant considerations that have been generated informally.

Habermas presents a kind of flow chart in which the informal "sluices" into the formal, and the two are complementary components in a smoothly functioning system.[26] The rationality of law, which rests on the representativeness of these processes, looks coherent, organic: the formal legal apparatus translates informally generated opinions into legal concepts. But here Habermas may give too untroubled a picture: it seems unlikely that popularly generated ideas, fears, and preferences are unproblematically transformed into legal concepts without any loss. In

22. See ibid., 298–302, 304–8, 313–14, 359–66.
23. For Habermas's critique of Dworkin, see ibid., 211–25.
24. See ibid., 32–33, 135, 408–9.
25. On Rawls, see above, Chapter 1, Section 1.
26. See, e.g., Habermas, *Between Facts and Norms*, 298–302.

fact, the formal procedures of law seem designed partly to repress the sheer proliferation of ideas that informal discussion excites.

Law, in other words, partly cuts itself off from the informal public discourse from which it grows. It is at the same time grounded in and uprooted from its social milieu. Law's rationality consists partly in its self-reflexive sources in the political community of citizens—including debate and political agitation that can be raucous and subrational. These subrational features, however, are supposed either to be squelched by the formal procedures of law or refined into legitimate reasons. Law's rationality consists partly in just this squelching and refining. This suggests that Habermas simplifies rather too much in his implicit claim that a coherent system of informal and formal will-formation imbues the law with reasonableness and legitimacy. It seems fairer to say that rationality is something wrested from the tumult of public debate and serves to a considerable extent to suppress it.

Habermas's treatment of language also makes law appear more uncomplicatedly rational than it is. Law for Habermas is not only modeled on language; it seems almost like a ripple effect, something that necessarily eventuates as a consequence of language use.[27] Habermas treats language above all as a means of conducting a conversation intended to reach consensus from an initial position of disagreement. As we have seen, this model of language-as-practice brings with it certain ineluctable idealizations—for example, meanings identically understood by all participants, or "truth" as universal acceptability. But this is to present language as inchoately serving the purpose law serves: law too is a means by which societies as a whole work out common understandings across rooted differences of outlook and belief.

Here too, however, Habermas makes language (and therefore law) appear more rational than it is. To begin with, the features he treats as inherent in language seem rather to be limited to one particular use of it. Language is not especially predisposed to the conversational mode between equals. It can be used to issue commands, express pain, or reflect on its own power to convey meaning through sound. Speakers may at-

27. See, e.g., ibid., 17–18, 25, 35. Thus, Habermas writes, for example, "as soon as the illocutionary forces of speech acts take on an action-coordinating role, language itself supplies the primary source of social integration." Ibid., 18. In order to serve this function, speakers must want to reach an understanding with each other about something in the world. This seems to be a fairly minimal condition, however: Habermas nowhere indicates that this is an exceptional or extraordinary use of language. As shown above, moreover, Habermas seeks to dispense with a theory of the subject—that is, to do without a specific decision to put language to a particular use.

tempt to dominate their listeners, or they may throw themselves at their mercy. Language does not yield democratic institutions because of some genius inherent in it.

To be sure, in a "post-metaphysical" era, when traditional beliefs are subjected to increased scrutiny and skepticism, there arises a more acute sense of language in its own right, and its power to affect belief. This rhetorical use of language is highly self-conscious about the linguistic properties calculated to stir others and rouse conviction in listeners. Therefore, it seems to be persuasive rhetoric, rather than language as such, that has a special affinity with democracy, where a premium is placed on persuasion.[28] Habermas treats as inherent in language features that seem characteristic of a late, rather sophisticated development of it.

Habermas, then, may beg the question by planting within language the conclusions he will then draw from it. It is not surprising that he can show such affinities between law and language, since the model of language he offers is tailor-made to support them. Habermas draws a politically tinged view of law from something supposedly inherent in language itself. This is not so different from drawing political conclusions from such concepts as "human nature" or "individual autonomy": the conclusions lurk as assumptions within the concepts.

Rather than being inherent in language, the properties Habermas describes seem to arise from a more or less deliberate decision to use language in a particular way—a decision, that is, to converse with a mutual view toward persuasion. Habermas, then, does not quite avoid having recourse to the individual "subject," who is able to use language in different ways (even though he or she does so from a position inevitably within language). Projected out into law, Habermas's model exaggerates the inherent rationality of the law, and affords too little scope to the will.

Once the breadth of language's uses is borne in mind, the supposed inherent link between law and language seems rather too simple. At least in *Between Facts and Norms*, Habermas ignores the poetic uses of language, which stress the opacity or density of speech—language so overloaded with meaning that communication is impeded or stopped. In the preceding chapters we have contrasted the semantically rich properties of language with a "thinned out," more easily managed style better suited to

28. See Thomas Cole, *The Origins of Rhetoric in Ancient Greece* (Baltimore: The Johns Hopkins University Press, 1991). See also Aristotle's *Rhetoric*, and Jürgen Sprute, "Aristotle and the Legitimacy of Rhetoric," in David J. Furley and Alexander Nehamas, eds., *Aristotle's Rhetoric: Philosophical Essays* (Princeton, N.J.: Princeton University Press, 1994), 117–128.

rational argument and debate. In the first chapter, for example, we saw that the *Oresteia* could be read as moving away from a thick and menacing ambiguity toward the linguistic stability necessary for rational argument to work. In the *Confessions,* too, Augustine presented language as inherently inexhaustible in its significance. Law, then, requires a pared-down style, with transparent meanings that are readily understood and shared. Far from being an inherent property of language, however, this style is more like a precarious achievement—an ideal never fully realized because of the semantic richness of language.[29]

Habermas thus tries to avoid some of the consequences of his claim that law has an irreducibly ideal element. He makes the rationality of law look more coherent and straightforward than it really is. That he does so testifies to just how unsettling it is to treat legal concepts as "idealizations" or fictions. Rights, we feel, should have a bedrock foundation; to approach them as idealizations evidently threatens to make them look flimsy and vulnerable.

I have dwelt on Habermas because his jurisprudence—so richly suggestive, despite its imperfections—points to the fruitfulness of using literature as a means of approaching law. Habermas's work points to the "poetic" quality of law, and, although he himself has not followed this line, he makes it possible to formulate the links between poetry and law with a new rigor. In tracing out this affinity here, I hope to show that poetry can genuinely illuminate the troubling idea that law entails the use of fictions.

29. Habermas has discussed poetic language elsewhere. See Jürgen Habermas, *The Philosophical Discourse of Modernity,* trans. Frederick G. Lawrence (Cambridge: MIT Press, 1987), 185–210 ("Excursus on Leveling the Genre Distinction between Philosophy and Literature"). There Habermas affirms the distinction between poetic and philosophical language, as against Derrida and his collapsing of philosophy into poetic discourse. Citing Roman Jakobson, Habermas treats "poetic" language as language self-conscious about the linguistic medium as such. Although such reflexivity may crop up in all kinds of utterances, it becomes "predominant" and "structurally determinative" in works generally recognized as "poetic." See ibid., 199–200. Although no "bright-line" distinction exists, then, separating poetic from other kinds of discourse, a distinction nonetheless remains relevant and useful: it is a question of this reflexive element predominating over other features.

Habermas seeks to refute the argument that *no* distinction between poetry and philosophy exists. As Habermas concedes, however, there is no question of absolutely marking off the dense, "world-creating" usage of language from a transparent, "problem-solving" one. In elaborating his legal theory, he seems to proceed from the background assumption that "normal," "everyday" language (language used to solve problems) is primary, and that poetic language is a later elaboration, and as such is separable enough from everyday uses to be ignored for theoretical purposes. Part of my argument in this study challenges that background assumption, and asserts rather that law, at one level, is engaged in the process of separating itself out from opaque and self-referential speech, and achieving a transparent, outer-directed language.

The intuition underlying the idea that law and poetry are linked is that law is in substantial part an institution *expressive* of a society's conceptions of order and justice, and that its authority rests partly on this expressive quality.[30] Law is not so much a body of rules as it is one of the ways people actively make sense of the world, and as such it is comparable to other institutions—art, poetry and religion. Debate about laws and legal cases amounts to what Clifford Geertz has called a "public square version" of our values. Law is "an *Anschauung* in the marketplace."[31]

Literature, as the work of the imagination, has a new centrality, once the pervasively fictive character of human institutions is laid bare. The imagination is not confined to the novel or poem, but is a force at work throughout our lives, and lies at the basis of the great super-realities—the religious doctrines of heaven and earth—that have traditionally served to orient people and help them live their lives. The poem, then, is but one especially clear instance of the imagination's work, and as such is potentially illuminating about the "fictive" element of law that is so deeply unsettling.

The kinship between law and poetry was noted as long ago as ancient Greece, when the poet Hesiod described the "sweet dew" the Muses pour on the tongue of the king, who "speaking surely, soon brings an end to even a serious quarrel."[32] But the affinity between the law and poetry has a distinctly modern thrust. For poetry, I want to argue, is characterized by just that "minimalism" and "ideality" that law evinces in the modern era, as well. It is striking that both modern jurisprudence and modern poetics present themselves as differentiations from an earlier religious consensus. "In an age of disbelief," the poet Wallace Stevens writes, "it is for the poet to supply the satisfactions of belief."[33]

The "minimalist" character of poetry emerges once traditional beliefs

---

30. Oliver Wendell Holmes, for example, wrote, "The law embodies the story of a nation's development through many centuries; and it cannot be dealt with as if it contained only the axioms and corollaries of a book of mathematics." Oliver Wendell Holmes, *The Common Law,* ed. Mark DeWolfe Howe (Cambridge: Harvard University Press, 1963), 5. To that extent, law is a "mirror"—the image Theodore Ziolkowski has adopted as the title of his law-and-literature study, *The Mirror of Justice* (Princeton, N.J.: Princeton University Press, 1997). Ziolkowski offers an array of quotes from distinguished legal thinkers on the expressive qualities of law (3–4).

31. Clifford Geertz, *Local Knowledge* (New York: Basic Books, 1983), 175.

32. Hesiod, *Theogony,* 86–87.

33. Wallace Stevens, "Two or Three Ideas," in *Opus Posthumous,* rev. ed. (New York: Knopf, 1989), 259. On Stevens and the pertinence of his poetry to legal theory, see Thomas C. Grey, *The Wallace Stevens Case* (Cambridge: Harvard University Press, 1991). Grey argues, in essence, that Stevens's poetry embodies pragmatism of a kind that should inform the work of lawyers as well. I have learned much from Grey, although my own discussion traces the connection between Stevens and law at a more abstract level.

ebb and fade. The decline of such beliefs exposes them as contingent and transient works of the human imagination, rather than cosmic and indisputable "super-realities." Once religious conviction splits into a variety of incompatible beliefs, religion begins inevitably to look more like poetry—an imagining of reality, rather than reality itself. From a poetic point of view, religion is the imagination hidden from itself. Poetry, as Stevens presents it, is the imagination now made self-aware and conscious of its pervasive role throughout human affairs. Individual poems crystallize the activity of the imagination; more broadly, however, they reflect our own role in creating the "lifeworld"—the world of orienting values, of fundamental realities. Poetry traces even the most exalted concepts to the restless, fertile human mind. Properly understood, it embodies and confronts us with a sense of our own finitude and contingency—not just because it often speaks of death and the transience of life, but because inherent in it as a medium is the intimation that no transcendent or metasocial guarantees exist.

Poetry, then, comes to epitomize modernity, for it reflects the modern consciousness of human responsibility for making the world. It is one symptom of the disenchantment of the world. If poetry is "destructive," as Stevens once wrote,[34] that is because it dispenses with a populous metaphysical realm, and supposes the existence only of actual human beings. Poetry harbors a markedly realist thrust. By celebrating the imaginative power that creates such vivid intimations of order, it implicitly debunks claims that an objectively existing order is discoverable and demonstrable.

At the same time, poetry also has an obvious "idealizing" quality. What is left over when the gods have departed is not a knowable world, wholly accessible to rational control. Rather, the decline of religion faces society with the singular power of the imagination to create the world it inhabits. The disenchantment of the world does not, in other words, leave it less enchanting, or wholly susceptible to rational control. Rather, we realize something of the structure of enchantment, how seeing is always and unavoidably what the philosopher Richard Wollheim has called a "seeing-in"—not just dispassionately registering the world, in other words, but seeing memories, hopes, metaphorical extensions implicit in it.[35] Poetry is an especially intense example of seeing-in. Because it is *we* who enchant the world, its enchantment cannot dictate how to live, or what to do. Belief in some incontrovertible order yields, then, to a self-conscious, ironic

34. Wallace Stevens, *Collected Poems* [hereafter *CP*] (New York: Knopf, 1954), 192.
35. Richard Wollheim, *Painting as Art* (Princeton, N.J.: Princeton University Press, 1987), 46–75.

sense of the deep desire for some orienting reality, and the role this desire plays in spurring the imagination to create what Stevens calls "supreme fictions."

Poetry does not signal the death of belief, but rather the rise of a new, ironic, and self-conscious version of it: one believes in a "supreme fiction," despite being aware that it is fictive, not literally or demonstrably true.[36] It is not true in some absolute sense, but rather "true to us" because it captures us in an aspect of ourselves. One believes in it because it satisfies a need, and because one has become aware that belief is in large part need-satisfaction.

Poetry, then, evinces a distinctively modern kind of credibility—one that dispenses with belief in the literal truth of what is believed in. This suggests on the one hand the continuing importance of belief, but also the troubling claim that belief is no longer in the literal or objective existence of that which is believed. The plight of Stevens's "poetic man" (*homo poeticus*) is that he deeply wants satisfactions (a containing order, the whole of harmony) that he knows are, at one level, merely desires. Poetry suggests our irrationality, and our disparate, *dis-tracted* quality: our deeply wanting satisfactions we then invent; the reality-producing quality that desire possesses, thanks to the imagination.

Desire, however, is not a distraction from reality, something we can dispense with. It is extremely potent: its fruitfulness and its central role in human life are shown in the historical reality of religious belief. Religion becomes one of the most impressive demonstrations of the world-shaping power of desire and the imagination. As the long history of religious belief shows, desire has populated reality with a host of divinities, powers, and dominions. At the very least, then, desire is itself a part of reality, not

36. One of Stevens's recurring ideas was that belief could only be in something conceded to be fictive. See, e.g., Holly Stevens, ed., *The Letters of Wallace Stevens* (New York: Knopf, 1966), 430, 443, 820. See also "Asides on the Oboe," *CP*, 250 ; "Adagia," in *Opus Posthumous*, 189. Stevens's name for this belief was the "supreme fiction," the subject of one of his greatest poems, "Notes toward a Supreme Fiction," in *CP*, 380–403. The idea of belief in a fiction may owe something to William James, "The Will to Believe," in *The Will to Believe and Other Essays in Popular Philosophy* (New York: Longmans, 1905). See the discussion in Milton J. Bates, *Wallace Stevens: A Mythology of Self* (Berkeley: University of California Press, 1985), 205–10.

With Stevens's idea of belief in a fiction, compare Joseph Schumpeter's observation, "To realise the relative validity of one's convictions and yet stand for them unflinchingly, is what distinguishes a civilized man from a barbarian." Quoted in Isaiah Berlin, *Four Essays on Liberty* (Oxford: Oxford University Press, 1969), 172; and Richard Rorty, *Contingency, Irony, Solidarity* (Cambridge: Cambridge University Press, 1989), 46. Rorty's chapter on "The Contingency of a Liberal Community" (44–69) is an elaboration and defense of Schumpeter's remark.

an external intrusion that clouds or confuses an otherwise transparent and flat reality. The poet—more generally, *homo poeticus*—searches out what will suffice now that our desires have been disenchanted. More precisely, poetry simply *is* what suffices: it is the belief-worthy fiction that does not insist, implausibly, on the literal truth of its propositions.

Poetry exists at the conjunction of these two thrusts—the minimalist and the idealizing. By acknowledging its own fictiveness, its sources in human desire, it aspires to offer the just-sufficient satisfaction of the human longing for the transcendent. Poetry is a taking responsibility, now, for those compelling, belief-worthy visions that sustain life and give it its vitality and interest.[37] Poetry mobilizes or activates that normative background that orients and gives direction to individual lives. This background is now self-consciously created by the powerful imagination of individual poets, whose words become the imagination of their fellows.

Poetry offers ideas of order, but patently does not aspire to offer "the" idea of order; it celebrates "parts of *a* world," rather than attempting to define "the" world.[38] It does not point to a conclusion—an objectively correct order we achieve, after which we can rest. Kant's definition of art as "*Zweckmässigkeit ohne Zweck*" (purposefulness without purpose) is suggestive here. Poetry embodies the sense that a final destination (a *Zweck*) does not exist: what we have, instead, are self-reflective parts of reality—minds—continually grappling with other parts. It is deeply characteristic of poetry that it continues to be written—that it goes on and on, without stopping or reaching some destination. Poetry is interminable in principle: implicit in it is the sense that there is no *Zweck* out there to be achieved.

Poetry and law are in some sense twin and complementary crystallizations of modernity. Each embodies in its distinctive way the decline of shared, fundamental beliefs that orient action within a society. Positive law presupposes dissensus and provides a means of coordinating expectations in the absence of agreement about fundamental reality. Poetry, for its part, embodies the sense that the fundamental realities that seemed unshakeable and absolute were of human making (that is, poetic), and therefore contingent and partial. Law and poetry alike are characterized by their interminability: neither looks forward to achieving a culminating *telos*, and in fact both are partly defined by the very absence of a *telos*. It is part of their very nature that they are spurred forward by an ideal vision that on principle can never be achieved.

37. See Wallace Stevens, "The Noble Rider and the Sound of Words," in *The Necessary Angel* (New York: Vintage, 1951), 30.
38. I allude here to the titles of two of Stevens's collections of poetry: *Ideas of Order* (1936) and *Parts of a World* (1942).

To a degree, then, law and poetry are twin offshoots of an earlier religious amalgam, a shared and encompassing belief. That amalgam constituted a super-reality that provided a firm basis for social solidarity and satisfied individuals' need for a sense of identity and purpose. Law and poetry now serve these two needs. Roughly speaking, law is a means of securing social solidarity without consensus. Poetry, in turn, satisfies the desire for order without commanding belief in it. Law and poetry alike, then, reflect dissensus, contingency, and interminability. Within these minimalist conditions, however, they satisfy (respectively) society's need for settled expectations and the individual's need for a compelling sense of self.

Seeing this connection between poetry and law may serve to make the ideal, or "counterfactual," character of rights a little less unsettling. To be sure, rights do not "really" exist in some objective, clinically demonstrable sense of the word "real." That makes them dispensable, however, only so long as you suppose that reality can be reduced to the rationally demonstrable. Poetry implicitly rejects that model, and suggests that the ideal is inherent in our practices—that we are pervasively, inevitably poetic. The "order" articulated in poetry remains always an idea—one that exists chiefly in its own articulation. It is a figment of language, but not, for that reason, trivial or merely false. To conclude that poetry is negligible because fictive is to assume that non-poetic language has no "fictive" element—that it plainly mirrors an objective reality lying beyond it. Poetry is our most characteristic activity, however, because it embodies the modern, ironic sense that language itself powerfully creates our reality. This was Habermas's point as well. Law, at least to the extent that it embodies and promotes solidarity, is like an ongoing conversation. It consists in the back-and-forth of language—less in what is exchanged than in the conversational exchange itself.[39] Rights, then, reflect the power to imagine ourselves—to produce paradigms or models of the self.

So far, I have been exploring the connections between poetry and law. I have tried to situate a troubling paradox of legal theory (viz., that the legitimacy of law partly rests on fictive idealizations) within a more encompassing sense of the poetic nature of any human activity. But what about politics, that other activity deeply characteristic of modernity? Once "metasocial" guarantees have been discarded, politics—the competition among co-beings for power—begins to look paradigmatic; it seems to be what most public activity (certainly law) boils down to. A debunking, realist thrust, linking law to politics, has distinguished much of the shrewdest legal thinking in this century. Legal realism is hardheaded, clear-eyed,

39. See Habermas, *Between Facts and Norms*, 414–15, 437, 445–56.

free of illusions. To insist on the pertinence of poetry and the fictive to law, in contrast, may seem soggy and soft. What can we say in defense of linking poetry and law?

To answer this question, I plan to follow the lead of Wallace Stevens, and in particular to elaborate some of his thoughts on the relation between poetics and politics. Stevens, who has been a recurring reference point in the chapter thus far, may seem like a peculiar choice: he is sometimes thought of as an elitist poet—remote and apolitical.[40] No one would mistake Stevens for a poet for the masses. Nonetheless, historical events of the first half of the twentieth century forced him to ask of what use or worth his extraordinary lyric talents were, in a world torn by global wars, economic depression, and mass uprisings. Although he never agreed that a poet had a social obligation, Stevens came to see poetry and politics as closely related and overlapping—to the extent even that poetry was in danger of being altogether effaced by politics.

Poetry, for Stevens, was a "destructive force": it emerged as a central practice partly because of those turbulent realities that had destabilized traditional beliefs. Industrialization, immigration, and war had all had their hand in changing the spiritual landscape of Stevens's youth, and in exposing the verities of his religious upbringing as no longer credible figments. The emergence of a new, more violent "reality," in other words, disenchanted the old world and pointed to the centrality of the poetic—the contingent, historically situated human imagination—as creating the super-worlds it deeply desired. Poetry, then, emerged as central together with the new violent reality: in a sense, poetry lived off a newly secular-

---

40. See, e.g., Frank Lentricchia, *A Modernist Quartet* (Cambridge: Cambridge University Press, 1994), 124–79, a revised (and even less sympathetic) version of an essay that originally appeared in the same author's *Ariel and the Police* (Madison: University of Wisconsin Press, 1988), 135–244. See also Marjorie Perloff, "Revolving in Crystal: The Supreme Fiction and the Impasse of Modernist Lyric," in Albert Gelpi, ed., *Wallace Stevens: The Poetics of Modernism* (Cambridge: Cambridge University Press, 1985), 41–64.

Perloff's piece seems to me intemperate and unfair, but it has stimulated much work addressing the political implications of Stevens's work. See, e.g., Melita Schaum, "Views of the Political in the Poetics of Wallace Stevens and H.D.," in Melita Schaum, ed., *Wallace Stevens & the Feminine* (Tuscaloosa: University of Alabama Press, 1993), 171–89; the articles in *The Wallace Stevens Journal* 13 (1989), a special issue dedicated to "Stevens and Politics"; Alan Filreis, *Modernism from Left to Right: Wallace Stevens, the Thirties and Literary Radicalism* (New York: Cambridge University Press, 1994); and the same author's *Wallace Stevens and the Actual World* (Princeton, N.J.: Princeton University Press, 1991).

Stevens's (often inconsistent) political statements are usefully collected in Harvey Teres, "Notes toward the Supreme Soviet: Stevens and Doctrinaire Marxism," *The Wallace Stevens Journal* 13 (1989): 152. Bates, *Wallace Stevens: A Mythology of Self,* 170–94, trenchantly discusses the inconsistencies and ambiguities in Stevens's politics.

ized, pluralist, industrialized society. Poetry, Stevens wrote in the midst of World War II, was a "violence" from within pitted against the violence offered from without.[41]

These same violent upheavals threatened to overwhelm poetry, and to trivialize it as a merely *individual* act of imagination in a time when the concept of the self and the individual seemed increasingly to be only one more metaphysical—and therefore dispensable—entity. Poetry, it might have seemed, was only a transient phase in an ever greater realism whose ultimate trend was to dispel all fictions as illusory and false. Poetry itself might stand to be disenchanted, as resting on that spurious fiction known as the "individual." Such, indeed, was precisely the Marxist critique of poetry.

Marxism proved a powerful catalyst for Stevens's poetic.[42] It represented a powerful new conception of history, and a compelling vision of the future. As a conception, it may have been the work of sheer reasoning, but its existence as a worldwide movement grew from its power to fire the imagination of the masses. Marxism resembled poetry: it was a destructive force; it rejected the accumulated conceptions that obscured reality. Plainly, its vision of the future spoke deeply to many—many more, it had to be admitted, than poetry did.[43]

Marxism could be understood as continuing the work of scouring the world of its accumulated fictions—including ultimately poetry, which (on this view) represents a halfway point or a phase, in which the world had been only partly disenchanted and the mythology of the "self" still had currency. Marxism called into question the very significance of the individual, and with that the vitality of art as the product of the individual imagination. In an essay titled "The End of the Novel," the Russian poet Osip Mandelstam trenchantly wrote:

It is clear that we have entered a stretch of powerful social movements, of massed organized actions, when the class struggle becomes the real, commonly recognized event, [and] when the individual's stock is declining in the minds of contemporaries, and at the same time the novel's strength and influence are declining. . . . The further fate of the novel will be noth-

41. See Stevens, "The Noble Rider," in *Necessary Angel,* 36.
42. For useful discussions of Marxism and Stevens, see Bates, *Wallace Stevens: A Mythology of Self,* 170–94; Teres, "Notes toward the Supreme Soviet," 156–63. Both treatments center on the group of poems titled *Owl's Clover* (1936). My discussion focuses, rather, on Stevens's later, and I think more penetrating, lecture "Imagination as Value" (1948), reprinted in *Necessary Angel,* 131–56.
43. See "Imagination as Value," *Necessary Angel,* 143.

ing but the history of the pulverization of biography as a form of private existence; it will be even more than dispersal—it will be the catastrophic perishing of biography.[44]

Stevens's poetic was forged in this difficult moment, when poetry itself seemed on the verge of melting into history. Rather than presenting this as a struggle between "art" and "science," or between the "rational" and the "irrational," Stevens came to see a contest between two forms of the imagination—the poetic and the political. "One wants to consider the imagination on its most momentous scale," he wrote. "Today this scale is not the scale of poetry, nor of any form of literature or art. It is the scale of international politics and in particular of communism. . . . Surely the diffusion of communism exhibits imagination on its most momentous scale."[45]

Stevens was far indeed from seeing the imagination as a simple "value," indisputably good,[46] for it was in some sense pitted against itself. Its worldwide, world-creating powers were at last apparent for all to see after the violent upheavals of the early part of the twentieth century had undermined the stability of beliefs in an overarching world structure. But the very forces that showed the centrality of the imagination also tended to make the lyric poem seem outmoded and irrelevant, for it rested on a concept of the individual (the individual poetic sensibility) that might seem one more delusion.

Poetry and politics were contending over what was to be the new "poem of the earth." The political imagination (Marxism) offered an earthly paradise of bodily needs satisfied. The poetic imagination, in contrast, sought to satisfy the needs that had originally called forth the ideas of paradise and hell.[47]

This tension between poetry and politics is an enduring one in the history of literature. It goes back at least as far as the classic Roman poets, who were supported by powerful politicians but insisted on the integrity of their own calling, and wrote *recusationes* (or "refusals"), declining to use

44. I am indebted to Anna Brodsky for bringing the passage to my attention and for the translation used in the text. The complete essay can be found in Osip Mandelstam, "The End of the Novel," in Jane Gary Harris, ed., *Mandelstam: The Complete Critical Prose and Letters*, trans. Jane Gary Harris and Constance Link (Ann Arbor, Mich.: Ardis), 198–201. Mandelstam's essay appeared in 1928.

45. Stevens, "Imagination as Value," in *Necessary Angel*, 142–43.

46. Ibid., 133. On Communist Russia as an example of the imagination at work, see Stevens, *Letters*, 620, 685.

47. See *Necessary Angel*, 145.

their poetic talents to celebrate state-imposed themes.[48] The poetic that insists on the independence and integrity of the poem has implicit in it a certain political vision. Indeed, some strands of liberalism—as, for example, the work of Richard Rorty—seem in essence to be drawing out the political consequences of poetry and its need for a certain independence. Rorty projects a poetics into a politics.[49]

The tension between poetry and state, therefore, bears implications far beyond those of literary history and poetics narrowly conceived. For the poet is, at one level, the individual par excellence, and poetry is in some sense the best case that can be made on the individual's behalf. This point is implicit in the Mandelstam passage cited above. Poetry is based on the individual experience, and transmutes it into statements of general significance. To undermine the individual, therefore, is to threaten the very existence of art.

Stevens's defense of poetry amounted to a defense of the individual—but the individual now modeled in a way that reflected the pervasiveness of politics. His underlying premise was that there exists a deep-seated and ineradicable need for a self-image, an orienting model for oneself. His argument, then, was that poetry alone—not politics—was sufficient to satisfy that need. Religion had once afforded men and women a sense of their own "nobility"—that is, a sense of their own significance or dignity—by situating them within a large cosmic drama of good and evil. Once the shared, communal imagination of this drama had faded, however, only extraordinarily vital imaginations could offer the satisfactions traditional beliefs had once provided. Such an extraordinary imagination is the province, however, of the individual, who thus becomes newly relevant in a time of violent reality. The individual alone is the source of something vitally necessary to society at large and to the individual members of it.[50]

The need for ennobling self-images was poorly served by mass political movements like communism. This latter Stevens dismissed as a "grubby faith," which in effect offered only minor wish-fulfillments to persons construed as wholly absorbed by their circumstances. What it provided was in-

48. See, e.g., David O. Ross Jr., *Backgrounds to Augustan Poetry* (Cambridge: Cambridge University Press, 1975), 123–29.

49. See Rorty, *Irony, Contingency, Solidarity*, 53–69. Rorty urges that liberal society become aware of its contingency and drop the attempt to ground itself metaphysically. This would represent, in his view, a "poeticization" of the political culture. I address Rorty in more detail at the conclusion of Section 2 and in Section 4, below.

50. See, e.g., Stevens, "Imagination as Value," in *Necessary Angel*, 149–50, 153–55; "The Noble Rider and the Sound of Words," ibid. , 27–36.

sufficiently "abstract"; it failed to offer a sense of self apart from and independent of one's immediate circumstances. Marxism, then, represented an inferior kind of imagination—trained too much on bodily needs, and crudely reductive of the range of human aspirations.[51]

The inability of religious beliefs to satisfy the need for an ennobling image does not extinguish the need. Instead, the noble now inheres in the mind's very act of creating ennobling fictions. Nobility, in other words, consists in the ability to construe oneself as noble. This self-referring imagination—an imagination aware of its own activity—is more adequate to us than an imagination that conjures up this or that satisfaction, but ignores or denies the self-creative, self-reflective intricacies of the self.[52] Stevens then did not see poetry and politics (especially Marxist politics) as locked in a life-or-death struggle. Rather, because he found politics ultimately less satisfactory as a piece of imagination, he felt sure that poetry of his sort must survive.

Only to an extent, then, is poetry "pitted against" politics. To the extent that it is, it stands for the significance of the ideal and the nonpragmatic, as against the leveling reality of politics, and its tendency to dissolve the individual into the mass. Just as important, however, is the considerable overlap of the poetic and the political. For politics too incorporates this sense that mankind *creates* reality. Stevens's conception of the poet, then, was strikingly, if not quite conventionally, political. The "politician" is a recurrent figure in Stevens's poetry and is closely related to the poet, for both are extraordinarily sensitive to the undercurrents that pervade people's lives but that remain unspoken. The politician hears the words "[t]hat have rankled for many lives and made no sound."[53] (Of the two, it seems important to emphasize, poetry is the more basic and encompassing practice: it is more self-consciously aware of the creativity that informs it and links it to other human pursuits.)

The affinity between the poet and the politician reflected Stevens's distinctive view of the poet's calling. Stevens stoutly resisted the idea that there was something odd about a lawyer writing poetry, as though he presented a strange combination of vatic poet and worldly lawyer.[54] Rather, he insisted that the poet was just a man among men. Despite the apparent oddness, Stevens's law work was essential to his conception of the poet, as

51. See Stevens, "Imagination as Value," in *Necessary Angel,* 139, 143; see also Teres, "Notes toward the Supreme Soviet," 154–63, esp. 156–57.

52. Stevens, "Noble Rider," in *Necessary Angel,* 33–36.

53. Wallace Stevens, "Sketch of the Ultimate Politician," *CP,* 336. See also "Sad Strains of a Gay Waltz," *CP,* 122.

54. See, e.g., Stevens, *Letters,* 412–416.

one whose gift consisted mainly in his ability to project out into articulate utterance what was implicit in any human life. Stevens's life as a lawyer, in other words, showed his conviction that poetry was inextricably woven into life's fabric.

To require the poet to opine on this or that political issue would be to miss the genuine political significance of poetry, as an affirmation of the individual and the imaginative, the ineluctability of the fictive. The true political significance of poetry is the demonstration it affords of life lived inevitably *within* the imagination, even at our most rational. This significance is botched badly if the poet undertakes to be topical—as though he or she had some obligation to be so.[55] The political significance of poetry is finally that it shows high instances of imagination in its purest form: the poem is a distillate of the embrace of the imagination and the world.

To link law to poetry, then, is not to sever it from politics. It is rather to suggest that even in its political dimensions law entails the imagination, because we are irreducibly imaginative beings. The imagination is a part of reality, or, to put it paradoxically, the "unreal" inheres in the "real." The rational is not cleanly distinct from the imaginative, as though these were two mental departments. Reason is the "methodizer" of the imagination: it works out what the imagination has already conceived.[56] Because the imagination is an organic part of our makeup, it is important that political and legal institutions have an adequate conception of it.

The relevance of poetry to law is that it points to what an adequate conception would be. On this view, the fictiveness of law is not at all a deficit, but something downright essential if it is to be adequate for beings like us. It is possible to conceive of law in a way that tries to dispense completely with idealizations—such is the effort, from different points of the political spectrum, by Richard Posner and the critical legal theorists. To link law to poetry, however, is to claim that any theory of law that dispenses with fiction is to that extent flawed. To treat the self solely as rational would simplify us unduly by excluding altogether the imagination, and its self-reflective possibilities for imagining a self. On the other hand, to deny the rationality of the law and the self altogether would also be an undue simplification, reducing the imagination to the merely false or delusive and ignoring the potent reality of its projections.

While legal theory expounds on the rational as legitimating law, poetry merges or blurs reason into its backgrounds in the imagination. Law portrays its subjects as rational and autonomous, and as such possessing an

---

55. See Stevens, "Noble Rider," in *Necessary Angel,* 27–31.
56. See ibid., 154.

innate dignity. Poetry, it seems to me, deepens the analysis, and locates the source of dignity in something more fundamental than the reason. It is the power to conjure up a vision of ourselves and others as rational beings that is fundamental; our dignity is really just this power to imagine dignity and so confer it.

2. STEVENS ON EVIL

Charles Larmore has recently suggested that the explorations of evil and violence in modern art do not point to an amoral aesthetic—an autonomous "art-for-art's-sake" that deliberately flaunts its disregard of morality. Rather, the aim of this aesthetic is to "point to the permanence of evil, the inevitability of violence, to which optimistic views of history refuse to face up."[57] One optimistic view Larmore has in mind is that of Habermas, in particular his overly harmonious definition of science, morality, and art as three complementary forms of reason.

According to Habermas, to be rational is to have reasons for asserting the truth of factual claims (it is the task of science to set forth these reasons); or, again, to have reasons for the rules of conduct one invokes (morality states those reasons); or, finally, to have reasons for being in a particular state of mind (art explores the reasons for feeling the way one does).[58] The individual domains of science, morality, and art in this way complement each other and are fundamentally at one: all grow from the different facets of an essentially unitary reason. Against this, Larmore points to the artistic concern with evil as reflecting a split or disharmony within modernity, in which the optimism of reason and rationality is questioned or undermined.

In this section I explore the concern with evil in the poetry of Wallace Stevens, as a way of elaborating Larmore's suggestive comments: in Stevens's poetic, poetry incorporates the idea of evil, and so poses an implicit challenge to legal theories that rest upon premises of rationality and self-availability (Habermas's theory is a distinguished example). "*Death is the mother of beauty*," Stevens wrote,[59] and in his poetry he frequently explored the intimacy between poetry and evil—the latter under-

57. Charles Larmore, *The Morals of Modernity* (Cambridge: Cambridge University Press, 1996), 201.

58. Habermas, *Between Facts and Norms*, 365; *The Philosophical Discourse of Modernity*, 336–41; *Vorstudien und Ergänzungen zur Theorie des kommunikativen Handelns* (Frankfurt: Suhrkamp, 1984), 441–72 ("Aspekte der Handlungsrationalität"); Larmore, *Morals of Modernity*, 191.

59. "Sunday Morning," VI, *CP*, 69.

stood broadly as finitude, contingency, partialness: in a word, mortality. For Stevens, however, mortality was not simply a biological fact we inevitably recognize as such. Our physicality, our transience were exceedingly difficult to grasp, and could be realized only by exerting the imagination.[60] Mortality, then—in this "thick" sense of a fully achieved orientation toward ourselves as contingent, historical, transient—is a part of one's ethical history, a deeply assimilated insight into the transient self. This "achievement" of mortality represents an overcoming of metaphysical schemes that present us to ourselves as something different from and more permanent than physical beings in a physical world.

Political, economic, and social turbulence—Stevens's word is "violence"—prepares the way for this achievement by making transcendent metaphysical structures seem implausible. Evil, in other words, is partly a restatement of Habermas's concept of the "postmetaphysical" condition, but it captures an aspect of pluralism, demythologization, and secularity that Habermas's picture omits—namely, that these phenomena deny the satisfaction of an evidently deep and enduring desire for an objective, uncontestable truth. To miss the "evil," wish-denying aspect of these pervasive social realities is to be overly optimistic about them, and unduly simplifies them. "How cold the vacancy," Stevens writes,

> When the phantoms are gone and the shaken realist
> First sees reality.[61]

This sense of cold vacancy—of being shaken and perplexed—is pivotal to Stevens's conception of modernity and its pervasive realism. Like Habermas, Stevens is a defender of the modern; but unlike Habermas, his sense of the good is rooted in his distinctive sense of the bad. His poetry suggests that rationality itself is built on and embodies a certain disappointment. It is not the simple good that Habermas presents, partly because its centrality arises only after we have been compelled to recognize the fictiveness of the lifeworld. Stevens's poetic, I think, better captures the heady emotions of terror and freedom excited by the decline of transcendent concepts.[62]

Evil, then, stands for the continuing pertinence, even in a "postmetaphysical" age, of the transcendent as an object of desire. The exposure of metaphysical verities as fictions is not merely the end of a painful and turbulent ethical history. It is also the ground from which a new, distinctively

---

60. See "Esthétique du Mal," XV, *CP*, 325.
61. Ibid., VIII, *CP*, 320.
62. See ibid., XI, *CP*, 322.

poetic conception of the good arises. Stevens puts it paradoxically: "The good is evil's last invention."[63] This good, now expressly premised on contingency and partialness, manages to grant our desires (minimally, but sufficiently), without denying the lessons evil has taught. It is poetry's distinctive excellence that its affirmations incorporate the Mephistophelean "no."[64] Only "in this bad" do "we reach / The last purity of the knowledge of the good."[65] Stevens reconceives the lyric and its situation within a world of violence. More pertinently, for our purposes, he restates the ideas of autonomy, individuality, and freedom as tragic themes, and so throws a distinctively "poetic" light on these central legal concepts. I want to draw out the implications for legal theory of Stevens's claim that reason itself is an imaginative construct produced in part by turbulent historical conditions.[66]

To get a grip on the centrality of evil in Stevens's poetry (*mal* is his ironically distanced name for it), I first want to look briefly, and by way of contrast, at Shelley's great defense of poetry. Shelley and Stevens were in the same boat: both faced doctrines, hostile to poetry, that were materialistic, efficient, and unillusioned. In Shelley's case the doctrine was Benthamite utilitarianism, in Stevens's a kind of practical and pervasive materialism that seemed to be the "spirit of the age" and that received one (but by no means its only) formulation in doctrinaire Marxism. Shelley's reply to the Benthamites was that poetry conferred a benefit on society by feeding the moral faculties.

To begin, the imagination was the organ of man's moral nature because the "great secret of morals is Love." Poetry did not so much offer edifying examples of moral conduct, then, as nourish the power to imagine the world and others. "A man, to be greatly good, must imagine intensely and comprehensively; he must put himself in the place of another and of many others; the pains and pleasures of the species must become his own." Poetry "enlarges the circumference of the imagination,"[67] which is "enlarged by sympathy with others' pains and passions; the good affections are strengthened by pity, indignation, terror, and sorrow." Shelley makes the bold claim that the best poetry regularly accompanies good

---

63. "Extracts from Addresses to the Academy of Fine Ideas," II, *CP*, 253.

64. See "The Well Dressed Man with a Beard," *CP*, 247. Cf. "Esthétique du Mal," VIII, *CP*, 320.

65. "No Possum, No Sop, No Taters," *CP*, 294. Cf. "Asides on the Oboe," III, *CP*, 251.

66. See, in this regard, "Man and Bottle," *CP*, 239.

67. Shelley, "A Defence of Poetry," in Donald H. Reiman and Sharon B. Powers, eds., *Shelley's Poetry and Prose* (New York: Norton, 1977), 487–88.

conduct and habit, and that the highest perfection in human society correlates with the highest dramatic excellence.[68]

Stevens's defense is strikingly different. Like Shelley, he presents the imagination as a central and pervasive phenomenon in human affairs, but he does not claim that it helps anyone to become "greatly good," nor that it has an improving moral effect on its readers. For Stevens, poetry does not primarily arouse pity and terror; indeed, he considers pity just what poetry should *not* seek to arouse.[69] Stevens has little or none of Shelley's moral fervor: Shelley contrasted poetry and "Mammon"; for Stevens, notoriously, money itself has a poetic quality.[70]

Nonetheless, I think Stevens speaks more directly to us. His claim is not that poetry makes us good, but the far more modest one that it helps us to live with evil.[71] Stevens offers a minimalist idea of poetry, one that dispenses with optimistic and implausible claims about poetry's beneficial practical effects. Unlike Shelley, he does not suppose that the goodness of individuals and of eras can be so readily assessed and differentiated. His idea that poetry helps people live their lives has the disabused air of, say, Freud's famously modest claim for psychoanalysis—that it helped patients achieve a life of ordinary unhappiness.

The thrust of Stevens's poetic is more political than moral. The focus is not on individual perfection, but rather on people's general ability to get on with life. The stimulus for his elaborating a poetic was in large part the continuing global upheaval on all fronts—political, social, economic—throughout the first half of the twentieth century. For Stevens, these extraordinary conditions revealed or underscored a persistent feature of reality: World War II, for example, reflected the persistent, warlike structure of existence.[72] The poet's role, then, is conceived within this essentially warlike context: poetry enables us to live our lives within a world whose deepest structure is one of strife ("violence" or "chaos" are two other Stevensian formulations).

Even this considerably pared-down claim may seem implausible: I will show in this section that it is in fact an interesting and challenging view, and a fruitful one for legal theory. Preliminarily, however, we need to realize how distinctive Stevens's poetic is, and how it rejects deep and pervasive assumptions about poetry and literature. For example, Habermas's

68. Ibid., 490, 492.
69. In "Esthétique du Mal," III, *CP*, 315, Stevens wrote that the Christian God, in pitying humankind, was akin to self-pity.
70. See Shelley, "A Defence," 502–03; contrast Stevens, "Adagia," in *Opus Posthumous*, 191.
71. Stevens, "Imagination as Value," in *Necessary Angel*, 150.
72. Stevens, "Noble Rider," in *Necessary Angel*, 21.

point that art states reasons for being in particular mental or emotional states links up to Shelley's defense of poetry: for Shelley, too, poetry nourished the imagination's power to conjure up the reality of others—that is, to appreciate the way they felt and the reasons they felt that way. This view of literature, moreover, has informed many, if not most, studies of the links between law and literature, which present literature as making its readers more empathetic, better able to understand another person's experience.[73] What law should learn from literature, on this view, is how to state the reasons for being in a particular state of mind. The resultant increase in empathy is thought to improve the quality of practitioners' legal work: judges will be better judges if they appreciate the parties' reasons for feeling the way they do.

I have indicated why I think such a view of law is misleading, and why it unduly simplifies law to think of it as unambiguously improved by an increase in sympathy. Stevens's poetic therefore is of interest because it points to a view of poetry (and therefore of the relation between poetry and law) quite different from the predominant account. Stevens rejects the idea that poetry's office is to offer consolation—to rouse pity for suffering, or to excite its readers into action meant to relieve others' distress. Poetry, rather, reflects on the unavoidability of evil as a constitutive feature of life.[74] Stevens's point was not the ethical one that we should accept evil in the world, but the significantly different one that evil should be incorporated into our self-image, as a part of who and what we are.

This conception of poetry, however, is deeply problematic in a liberal democracy, in which "evil" tends to strike us as injustice—something to be

73. See Chapter 1, Section 3.
74. It should go without saying that Stevens was not advocating that nothing be done to alleviate others' suffering. We know, for example, that Stevens was personally quite generous in helping others. He assisted his older brother Garrett financially, and did so graciously and ungrudgingly. See Joan Richardson, *Wallace Stevens: A Biography, The Later Years, 1923–1955* (New York: Beach Tree, 1988), 141–42. He consistently helped out at least one young man at his office with money, and helped him obtain loans to finance his way through law school. See Peter Brazeau, *Parts of a World: Wallace Stevens Remembered* (San Francisco: North Point Press, 1985), 34–37.

Stevens was not preaching the idea of happiness through acceptance of evil, and was far indeed from presenting "the idea of a richly self-sufficient self. . .upon whom other lives can have no disturbing impact." Mark Halliday, *Stevens and the Interpersonal* (Princeton, N.J.: Princeton University Press, 1991), 33. It was just one of Stevens's points that the modern world made it impossible to ignore suffering. See "Noble Rider," in *Necessary Angel*, 18–19 (commenting on the shrinking of the world and our new intimacy with people living far away).

set right, and therefore fundamentally within rational control.[75] The views of poetry in Shelley and Habermas supplement this sense: by rousing pity (or showing reasons for mental and emotional states), poetry helps ensure that injustices will be remedied.

To insist on the intractability of evil, therefore, as Stevens does, runs counter to some of our deepest assumptions and most important commitments. Evil, we feel sure, should ideally call forth a deeply personal, engaged response of pity—one result of which might well be a resolution to correct the injustice.[76] As against this, Stevens sought to write an impersonal poetry, one that distanced or depersonalized the response to evil.[77] In her significantly titled *Words Chosen Out of Desire,* Helen Vendler has insisted on the roots of Stevens's poems in his own lived experience.[78] We must supplement this, however, by recognizing Stevens's effort in and through his poetry to depersonalize his own experience. He attempted to get past the individual occasions—this or that misfortune that befalls anyone—to a sense of an inherent and inevitable evil.

Because he goes against the grain of deep moral beliefs, it is hardly a surprise that Stevens has been accused of being effete and irrelevant, and that his poems about evil have often been condemned. Yet poetry, for Stevens, implicitly corrects the pervasive belief that evil is an essentially political phenomenon that can be eradicated by human effort. "Esthétique du Mal," for example, is one of Stevens's most important treatments of the affinities between poetry and evil, and a central text for my discussion in this section. The "Esthétique" treats poetry as an account of pain and death, but one that does not essentially look forward to their eradication. More particularly, poetry does not address transient mental states, nor does it seek to articulate this or that evil or misfortune that befalls one from outside. That seemed to Stevens to be the core of sentimentality.

75. See Judith N. Shklar, *The Faces of Injustice* (New Haven, Conn.: Yale University Press, 1990), 1–14; Bernard Williams, *Shame and Necessity,* Sather Classical Lectures vol. 57 (Berkeley: University of California Press, 1993), 127–29. See also Guido Calabresi and Philip Bobbitt, *Tragic Choices* (New York: Norton, 1978), discussing some problems of allocating scarce resources in life-and-death contexts.

76. See Halliday, *Stevens and the Interpersonal,* chapter 1 ("Stevens and the Suffering of Others"), criticizing Stevens for his failure to address the suffering of individual others.

77. Stevens expressly denied that poetry was personal. See Stevens, "Adagia," in *Opus Posthumous,* 186.

78. Helen Vendler, *Words Chosen Out of Desire* (Knoxville: University of Tennessee Press, 1984).

The centrality of "Esthétique du Mal" in Stevens's oeuvre has been rightly stressed by Harold Bloom.[79] As Bloom writes, "Esthétique du Mal" is uneven, but no section of it is "without its own greatness."[80] The poem was Stevens's attempt to address the relation between poetry and pain[81]— not willed or chosen evil, but, as Bloom writes, "necessary evil, the pain and suffering inseparable from a consciousness of self in a post-Christian or Nietzschean world."[82]

In his "Esthétique," Stevens is at pains to scour poetry of any taint of mere sentiment. He jokingly refers to a book title—*Livre de Toutes Sortes de Fleurs d'après Nature* ("all sorts of flowers")—as epitomizing sentimentality,[83] which tries to address "all sorts of misfortune." This sentimentality never plumbs beneath the individual occasions of evil to an understanding of the perennial shape of evil, its enduring place in human life. The true poet, Stevens continues, resembles a pianist: it would be misleading to say that the virtuoso plays "all sorts of notes." Better to say that he plays "only one in the ecstasy of its associates."[84] Neither does the poet drum up emotions for this misfortune or that (all sorts of misfortune); instead he captures the evil that underlies them all.

Nor does Stevens assume that poetry helps us better understand others' states. He expressly rejects pity as a falsifying response to evil. Pity has often been treated as the moral sentiment par excellence, the source of all fellow feeling, and hence the fount of the moral life.[85] Yet in offering his "esthétique du mal," Stevens presents pity as seriously flawed, too close to self-pity, and so an evasion of evil.[86] Pity simply does not suffice as

79.   Harold Bloom, *Wallace Stevens: The Poems of Our Climate* (Ithaca, N.Y.: Cornell University Press, 1977), 225–26; see also Henry Weinfield, "Wallace Stevens' 'Esthétique du Mal' and the Evils of Aestheticism," *The Wallace Stevens Journal* 13 (1989): 27–37. I have also found instructive Joseph N. Riddel, "Metaphoric Staging: Stevens's Beginning Again of the 'End of the Book,'" in Frank Doggett and Robert Buttel, eds., *Wallace Stevens: A Celebration* (Princeton, N.J.: Princeton University Press, 1980), 308–14. Helen Vendler treats the poem rather coolly in *On Extended Wings: Wallace Stevens' Longer Poems* (Cambridge: Harvard University Press, 1969), 206–17.

80.   Bloom, *Wallace Stevens*, 226.

81.   See Stevens, *Letters*, 468.

82.   Bloom, *Wallace Stevens*, 226.

83.   "Esthétique du Mal," IV, *CP*, 316.

84.   Ibid.

85.   See, e.g., Edmund Burke, *A Philosophical Enquiry into the Origin of Our Ideas of the Sublime and Beautiful* (Oxford: Oxford University Press, 1990), 41; Adam Smith, *The Theory of Moral Sentiments* (New York: Augustus M. Kelley, 1966), 3; Jean-Jacques Rousseau, *"The Social Contract" and "Discourse on the Origin of Inequality"* (New York: Washington Square Press, 1967), 203.

86.   Here Stevens is in the company of not only Nietzsche, but Plato. For a discussion of pity and its proponents and enemies, see Brian Vickers, *Towards Greek Tragedy*

a minimalist aesthetic, for it obscures the ability "plainly to propound" evil. Rather than informing its readers about others' states of mind (for example, the poet's), poetry primarily articulates for them their own deepest sense of themselves:

> . . . the genius of misfortune
> Is not a sentimentalist. He is
> That evil, that evil in the self, . . .[87]

This "evil" is internal and constitutive; in one of its avatars it is time, which ultimately destroys the mind.[88]

Poetry is the acknowledgment of evil as constitutive of us. It rejects the myths presenting evil, for example, as the province of a diabolic agent bent on our destruction.[89] Once we have rid ourselves of no longer plausible explanations like this, Stevens suggests, we can get by with the astringent, barely sufficient pleasures of poetry:

> It seems as if the honey of common summer
> Might be enough,. . .
> As if pain, no longer satanic mimicry,
> Could be borne, as if we were sure to find our way.[90]

Poetry is the expression of "the race that sings and weeps and knows not why."[91] The lyric moment comes about through our disenchantment, a deepened sense of our finitude, of the newly vivid transience of time. The fleetingness of time is one of the oldest stock lyric motifs, going back for example to Horace's *carpe diem* ("seize the day"). Stevens situates this lyric moment within a highly sophisticated, disenchanted sense of finitude, contingency, partialness—a vivid sense that emerges from the lapse of Christian verities under the pressure of violent, cataclysmic events. The intensity of the lyric moment contains within it a sense of grief, and of the fragility of being.[92]

The significance of the claim that evil is inherent and constitutive comes into yet sharper focus once we appreciate how at odds it is with

(London: Longman, 1979), chapter 2, esp. 64–70; and my *Poetics of Supplication* (Ithaca, N.Y.: Cornell University Press, 1994), 11–12, with references.

87. "Esthétique du Mal," IV, *CP*, 316.
88. "The Pure Good of Theory," *CP*, 329.
89. "Esthétique du Mal," III, *CP*, 316.
90. Ibid.
91. "A Thought Revolved" (Romanesque Affabulation), *CP*, 186.
92. "On the Adequacy of Landscape," *CP*, 244.

some deeply rooted political commitments. Indeed, many of Stevens's formulations about poetry make it sound like a kind of antipolitics, in which several cherished political conceptions are almost systematically reversed. For example, political freedom presupposes a containing order; the poet, in contrast, may articulate ideas of order, but he always remains a "connoisseur of chaos."[93] When Stevens hears (in the poem "Idiom of the Hero") "two workers say, 'This chaos / Will soon be ended,'" he stoutly insists, "This chaos will not be ended . . . Not ended, never and never ended." This short poem is given over entirely to denying a "cure" for various ills: weakness and poverty will not be conquered. Indeed, the poet's native condition is one of poverty:

> I am the poorest of all.
> I know that I cannot be mended.[94]

Again, political freedom in a liberal democracy seems to presuppose the power to articulate one's views confidently and clearly. But for Stevens, poetry is "flawed words and stubborn sounds."[95] The poet's freedom consists in lacking words, of "be[ing] in the difficulty of what it is to be," a kind of paradoxical aphasia.[96] Here again we need to appreciate how deeply Stevens's poetic implicitly challenges some cherished political commitments. We can certainly imagine a poetic that would complement a political conception of freedom: poetry as the teacher of eloquence, of speaking compellingly what is on one's mind.

But this is not Stevens's poetic.[97] For him, freedom is to be emancipated from outmoded conceptions of the world, and no longer to have a "doctrine" that substitutes for a fresh imagining of reality. It is "to be without a description of to be."[98] If liberal theories of law and government place a premium on articulateness, Stevens celebrates poetry as the "organic boomings" of an ox,[99] and situates poetic freedom precisely in this inability completely to encompass and articulate one's thought.

93. "Connoisseur of Chaos," *CP*, 215.
94. Stevens, "Idiom of the Hero," *CP*, 200–201.
95. "The Poems of Our Climate," III, *CP*, 194.
96. "Notes toward a Supreme Fiction" (It Must Be Abstract I), *CP*, 381.
97. Stevens endorsed Bertrand Russell's remark that to "acquire immunity to eloquence is of the utmost importance to the citizens of a democracy." Stevens, "Noble Rider," in *Necessary Angel*, 10.
98. "The Latest Freed Man," *CP*, 205.
99. Ibid. The reference seems to be to an old, pious tale about St. Thomas Aquinas, who was taunted by his fellow students as a "dumb ox." Aquinas's teacher, Albert the Great, corrected the students: "The bellowing of that ox will one day fill the world." For the story, see, e.g., Anthony Kenny, *Aquinas* (New York: Hill and Wang, 1980), 3. Aquinas

Poetry aims at this eloquent sub-speech: it trades in presence (the confident, doctrinal knowledge of the world) for a kind of pregnant presense that "resist[s] the intelligence almost successfully."[100] Stevens is far indeed from presenting poetry as an emblem of perfection, a kind of unblemished "rounded whole." Rather than embodying or even pointing toward some Utopia, poetry is a medium for the deeply flawed. "The imperfect is our paradise," he writes, and it is this refusal of perfection even as an ideal that distinguishes Stevens's poetic: "Since the imperfect is so hot in us, [delight] / Lies in flawed words and stubborn sounds."[101]

Poetic freedom, then, is a matter of chaos, aphasia, poverty, ignorance— the antithesis of the political conception of freedom, which stresses order, articulateness, knowledge, and a certain power over one's life and projects. These brisk inversions of crucial political and legal conceptions may seem to make poetry rather silly, and in any event marginal to legal theory. Indeed, Stevens understood poetry as having a certain antic quality, an inherent gaudiness. This poetic "comedy," however, rests on an awareness of evil and its innate, inescapable character: the poet becomes a comedian by assimilating the idea that evil is innate, and therefore that the only "paradise" worthy of the name for beings like us must be seriously imperfect. The poet, precisely as comedian, has light to shed on legal conceptions that offer a flattering, rather frigid image of ourselves—rational, self-possessed, articulate. To appreciate these conceptions properly, it is necessary to see their slightly stilted quality, their air of unreality—their fictiveness. Poetry loosens up the model by teasing it, setting it on its head—by being antic in the presence of its solemnity.

Modeling ourselves as autonomous, free, rational, and articulate is an optimistic projection that seeks to capture what is good, or a good, in us. This model is a simplification for certain political and legal purposes, and yet it seems essential and unavoidable: we cannot but project an ideal, ennobling image of ourselves in order to get legal theory off the ground. This simplification nonetheless presents a considerable risk of distortion, of being mistaken for the essential truth about us (or, at least, the essential truth about us for purposes of legal theory). This potential for distortion seems, indeed, to be an inherent tendency of the good (any good,

---

went from being an ox to being a masterly expositor of doctrine. Stevens's progress as a poet was just the reverse—from doctrine to ox.

100. "Man Carrying Thing," *CP,* 350. On the connection between poetry and ignorance, see also "The Sense of the Sleight-of-Hand Man," *CP,* 222; "Of Bright & Blue Birds & The Gala Sun," *CP,* 248; and "Adagia," in *Opus Posthumous,* 187.

101. "The Poems of Our Climate," *CP,* 194.

the good as such) to degrade certain other things as "evil"—less valid, less real—by identifying certain qualities as especially or solely worthwhile.

The pertinence of evil, then, is partly that it stands for a more realistic complexity: it acts as a reminder of the artificiality—the provisional quality—of the idealizations needed to get legal and political theory going. "Evil" may strike us as a somewhat archaic concept: after all, it might seem that evil needs to be explained only if you are committed to the belief that the world is supposed to be good—a belief associated with the Christian world view of an all-powerful yet all-good deity. Dispense with belief in the Christian God, and you can dispense with the need to "explain" evil. Evil remains pertinent, however, even in a "postmetaphysical" era, as a corrective to a persistent tendency to simplify things—to identify a good and to marginalize whatever is left over as failing to achieve the qualities that characterize goodness.

This tendency of the good was evident, for example, in Augustine, who looked forward to a final authoritative division of the world's complexity into an unambiguous good and a clearly demarcated evil. Stevens in effect takes over the complexity of Augustine's insights, but dispenses with the idea that good will one day triumph. Evil in Stevens, then, stands for the ineluctable complexity of the world. It prevents the simplifications that good, as traditionally conceived, seems to embody and to anticipate. It is no longer the result or sign of some grave, original dislocation or miscarriage; it is not a "deficit" that implies the existence of some supervening good. As so conceived, evil is something to be embraced; it is a part of the "health" that poetry embodies.[102] Stevens treats the idealizations and simplifications of theory as satisfying a genuine appetite; this appetite, however, is only one among others, and should not predominate over the opposite desire for complexity, reality, the detailed and the centrifugal. In "The Poems of Our Climate," Stevens expressly rejects the idea that simplification *could* be a paradise, for

There would still remain the never-resting mind.[103]

Instead, Stevens claims that any paradise for beings like us must be imperfect.[104] His Mephisthophelean denial here claims that "perfection," as traditionally conceived, is not in fact the ideal it has often seemed to be. Rather than the *telos* to which we are moved by our very being, it is a desire (for simplicity) among other desires. Life does not have an ideal tra-

---

102. Stevens, "Adagia," in *Opus Posthumous,* 200.
103. "The Poems of Our Climate," III, *CP,* 194.
104. Ibid.

jectory from evil to the good, then, but is spent restlessly shuttling between different desires and their satisfactions. Any ideal must respect our
restlessness; an ideal that purports to conclude it—to put a stop to it—
cannot satisfy us.

The self, then, does not seek, even ideally, to be wholly coherent, to be
reduced to a single, rounded whole. Its vitality consists in its being "evilly
compounded."[105] Stevens expressly celebrates the proliferation of selves:
"And out of what one sees and hears and out / Of what one feels, who
could have thought to make / So many selves, so many sensuous
worlds. . . ."[106] This plurality of selves that characterizes the poet was, for
Augustine, the most telling trace of evil.

To transvalue religion—to see it as poetry unconscious of itself—is to
rethink the role of evil in human life. Poetry, in Stevens's view, inherently
rejects the idea of a final paradise, but retains it as a deep wish, one we
harbor along with other wishes. He incorporates the simplifications of
paradise within a complex pattern of desires now for the profuse, the detailed, the heterodox, and now for the grand, the simple, the eternal. He
situates simplicity within a more embracing cycle, in which the desire for
simplicity and for complexity alternate unstoppably.

I am now in a position to make the following point: the restless, poetic
mind as evoked in Stevens's poetry works in a way strikingly like the way I
have suggested *law* works. Law travels ceaselessly between a practical need
to facilitate life together in society, and an ideal need for moral authority.
In order to make life together possible, law simplifies the ethical complexity of its subjects, by reducing it to a set of reasonable rules. On the
other hand, it inevitably needs to acknowledge and incorporate some of
the complexities to avoid becoming reductive and coercive, and so illegitimate. It traces a cyclical process of returning to and departing from simplicity (an easily understood and applied rule). These alternate movements
are both aspects of law, which is distorted if we treat it solely as an autonomous system of rules. Law, too, reflects our complexity: it is an institution for imperfect beings. The self does not find its paradise in a perfect
rationality. Rather, the rationality of law is a powerful and attractive simplification of ourselves, but one that can never be wholly or finally satisfying.

So far, we have treated evil as *supplementing* ideal, simplifying concepts
with a more complex reality. But the pertinence of evil to political / legal
conceptions like autonomy, freedom, and rationality lies deeper still, for
it is also a *constituent part* of any credible formulation of them. Realist cri-

---

105. Ibid., II, *CP*, 193.
106. "Esthétique du Mal," XV, *CP*, 326; and see "A Dish of Peaches in Russia," *CP*, 224.

tiques of lofty, ideal conceptions do not finally rid us of conceptualization, nor do they yield an illusion-free close encounter with hard reality. Instead, the exposure of certain cherished super-realities leads, or ought to lead, to a more ironic, more expressly "poetic" use of these concepts. It should also introduce a greater self-consciousness, a deepened sense of one's responsibility for creating the world (or, rather, "a" world), a life-world of values and beliefs.

Stevens understood the destructive work of realism to be an attempt to correct for the inevitably idealizing work of the imagination. The realist negations amounted to the imagination reflecting on itself, correcting for its tendency to bestow an ontological super-reality on its own productions. This negation, therefore, was only the reverse of a distinctive affirmation—the imagination celebrating its own prowess and fertility. This affirmation *presupposed* the denial of transcendent realities: we only appreciate the imagination's power once we have exposed the fictiveness of its productions. This poetic celebration emerges, then, inevitably from the debunking work of realism. Stevens's effort as a poet was to find the distinctive affirmation that lurked implicitly in the staggering negations that surrounded him—the "yes" that underlay and tacitly motored the realist work of saying "no." At one level, poetry itself was the answer, for poetry was self-evidently and confessedly a fiction—a work of the imagination much like what the governing, metaphysical entities had turned out to be.

But his answer has fruitful implications as well for legal theory, and in particular for a theory of individual rights. Transience, finitude, contingency (in Stevens's language, "evil") must shape our conception of the good (autonomy, rationality—the qualities that support the idea that the individual is a bearer of rights). What would the "autonomous self" look like, once it has thoroughly assimilated its own transience, and overthrown the metaphysical trappings that once sustained it? To grasp this, we need to consider Stevens's conception of the *hero*—whose central significance lies partly in his being a conception of the good implicit in the realist critique, the "yes" lurking in the realist's "no." The hero is, in effect, Stevens's name for the postrealist self, simultaneously a realistic and an idealist conception. As a minimalist, postmetaphysical figure, the hero is what remains after the gods have been dismissed: he is what is "permitted / In an ascetic room."[107] Poetry is drawn to the hero partly because it is inherently realistic—a "destructive force" that exposes the unshakeable

---

107. "Examination of the Hero in a Time of War," VI, *CP*, 275.
108. "Montrachet-le-Jardin," *CP*, 261.

cosmic verities as human projections, feats of the imagination. The poet sings of

A hero's world in which he is the hero.
Man must become the hero of his world.[108]

At the same time, the hero captures the idea that our sense of ourselves is inevitably an idealizing projection, and inevitably entails a mythic element. The hero is "major man"—the "highest man with nothing higher / Than himself, his self, the self that embraces / The self of the hero. . . ."[109] The heroic is just this projection of the realist's sense of the self onto an ironic, self-consciously idealizing plane.

The Stevensian hero is, above all, a *fluid* conception. This poetic hero is "anonymous and cannot help it."[110] That is, Stevens's hero resists formulation, and cannot be arrested or frozen in a single form. The officially canonized, public "hero" Stevens often mocks in his poetry arrests the inherently fluid idea of the noble, and reduces it to static and banal images. This immobilizing, political conception was crystallized in the bronze statues of war heroes in public parks—for example, the statue of "General Du Puy" Stevens mocks in "Notes Toward a Supreme Fiction."

These political deformations were significantly different from the poetically conceived hero, whose intent was not to carry a single, preordained meaning, but to get past the received ways of seeing or conceiving of something. Stevens uses the image of a wave, which is not one thing, but a fusion of a wave-force and water. The wave is just the force riding across the water, constantly engaged or fused with the water through which it rides.[111] The noble, too, is like a wave: it arises more or less inevitably from the imagination's riding across reality. It can in some instances take an obviously "noble" form: Verrochio's bronze statue of Bartolommeo Colleoni in Venice is an example of this grandly noble style that Stevens cites in his lecture on "The Noble Rider and the Sound of Words." But the noble found even more revealing expression in Don Quixote—a dream of nobility immersed in a comically bathetic reality.[112] These two "noble riders," Colleoni and Don Quixote, reveal two different thrusts in the noble—its commitments both to reality and to the imagination that is a part of reality and engages with it. These different thrusts ensure that the noble (the heroic—and by extension, as I will show in the

109. "Examination of the Hero in a Time of War," XV, *CP*, 280.
110. Ibid., XIII, *CP*, 279.
111. Stevens, "Noble Rider," in *Necessary Angel*, 35–36.
112. Ibid., 7–10.

next section, the autonomous self) is not a single, univocal conception, but constantly changes as it gains, adjusts, and maintains the balance between its different commitments.

This fluid, ever-changing poetic "hero" is inextricable from tradition—the ongoing history of the different, continually evolving ways of conceiving the noble. Tradition was a crucial element in Stevens's poetic response to evil, because the experience of contingency and partialness can hardly be felt as an evil, unless a tradition exists: to experience modernity as partly "evil" is to understand oneself as an heir to a past that is no longer readily accessible to us, and which one must search out to find what was genuinely compelling in it. When the life-world crumbles, it is a part of ourselves that is passing away. Tradition, then, is to be understood not as a stock of beliefs, practices, and imperatives imposed on a generation by the past. Rather, it is a habit of continually questioning the past, and locating what remains vital and illuminating in it for contemporary experience.

The more violent the upheavals from the past, the more searching must be the scrutiny of the past. Poetry is in part a rehabilitation, a reworking of tradition, to make it newly credible. Stevens understood the poet's work as rescuing from the past what remains compelling in it. To express this complex view of tradition and the poet's relation to it, he used the image of Aeneas carrying his father Anchises out of Troy as the city goes up in flames. Aeneas became an image of the poet / hero, who continually questioned the past, and redefined it, with a view to setting the contemporary scene within a tradition now reconceived in light of contemporary experience. The effect was to present that experience in its broadest outlines, distant and impersonal. Tradition, far from being a dead hand that stifles the present, invites us to question it, as a way of learning about ourselves. Tradition, he writes, is

> A legend scrawled in a script we cannot read.[113]

Stevens's emphasis on tradition distinguishes his ideas about poetry and the imagination from those of Richard Rorty,[114] who is in many ways strikingly reminiscent of Stevens. Both present the poet as the articulator of strong languages that are at once compelling and provisional. Like Stevens, Rorty sees a vital link between poetics and politics. Rorty, however, is an optimist: his ideal society is one whose solidarity is based on the belief that, above all, cruelty must be avoided. Such a society holds that no good exists that could ever justify the use of cruelty. Poetry, then, embodies the

---

113. "Recitation after Dinner," in *Opus Posthumous,* 115.
114. Rorty, *Contingency, Irony, and Solidarity.*

absence of any final truth—the poetic, fictive character of our ideals—and thereby contributes to the solidarity of Rorty's ideal society. Rorty revisits what Plato once called the "ancient quarrel between poetry and philosophy," and resolves it in a manner strikingly opposite to Plato. Far from being condemned to exile, the poet is now the hero of Rorty's ideal republic—the democratic liberal state. Rorty's poets autonomously generate strong vocabularies, and the state stays out of their way in order that they may do so.

For Stevens, too, poetry expresses the disillusioned and ironic sense of our ongoing responsibility for imagining the world visions we inhabit. But unlike Rorty, he roots the poet more deeply in the past as retrieving from tradition whatever is still vital and compelling in it. Poetry is not the free creativity of strong minds Rorty envisions, but is in significant part burdened by the past. It is not a question of the mind's freedom, as Rorty presents it (as if poets' sole obligation were to their own imagination). Rather, the poet seeks to engage with the world, and to capture it in a vital way. The poem, Stevens writes, is an "interdependence of the imagination and reality as equals."[115] Although Stevens was far from believing that poets had an obligation to address the current political issues of their day, he nonetheless thought that the artist had a serious obligation to produce persuasive and satisfying pictures of the world. Poets, then, could fail to attain their object, which was a kind of accuracy—a more difficult ideal than Rorty's ideal of subjective, imaginative strength. In short, the artist's "autonomy," as Stevens understood it, carried a heavier burden of responsibility, a more pressing consciousness of the purely human origins of the life-world.

Autonomy, on this view, has a distinctly tragic component, for it arises from a loss of innocence, the fading of a belief in a metaphysically guaranteed cosmos. Autonomy, if we follow Stevens's line, is not so much a break or a release from the past as a distillation of it. Autonomy often appears in legal theory as a markedly antitraditional quality, one that enables the individual to assess and criticize his traditions and to endorse the good he approves. The tragic kind of autonomy, in contrast, has a depth in time; it amounts, in Stevens's vision, to a generations-old tradition of fathers and sons all alike coming to a similar sense of mortality, transience, contingency.[116] In this sense, autonomy is not synonymous with the rootlessness and self-seeking with which it has often been charged. Instead, it points to a deep solidarity among the men and

115. Stevens, "Noble Rider," in *Necessary Angel*, 27.
116. "Esthétique du Mal," XIII, CP, 324.

women of an era, and between the present and the past. In the next section I show that the conceptions of autonomy that are implicit in the case law, but that have perhaps not yet fully surfaced in legal theory, represent a similar distillation or winnowing of the past, rather than a straightforward break from it.

3. ON RIGHTS AND THE INDIVIDUAL

A theory of rights rests, most easily, on a theory of a coherent, individual self that possesses the rights, and whose integrity and autonomy are preserved by the moral claim they place on the state to refrain from infringing them. But this autonomy, the premise underlying this straightforward conception of rights, has become increasingly problematic. It no longer seems something unproblematically inherent in individuals, for the state is seen to exert a pervasive and deep influence on individuals' expectations and the control over their own lives they actually enjoy. Individual autonomy has become less a given "fact" about us, and more a public responsibility—something the state must help bring about.[117] As a result, it has become difficult to think of citizens as all essentially alike—possessing a core similarity premised on their being inherently autonomous, rational, free. Even theories—for example, Rawls's—that stress dissensus and the plurality of beliefs in our political society seem not quite plausible, when they base this plurality on a supposed uniformity, an inherent power to conceive and endorse some version of the good.

Such theories tend to de-emphasize the potent and baffling sense of deep differences (especially those of race and gender) that threaten to splinter the citizen body into different groups. Some of the most significant constitutional decisions of this century have had to do with bodily attributes—race, gender, sexuality. We have become increasingly conscious of ourselves, even for legal purposes, as physical beings. Citizens, then, are not a homogeneous body of essentially "rational agents," but parts among parts, and each one partial, contingent, heterogeneous.

These increasingly significant physical attributes are subrational: in many ways they resist not only theory, but discussion and conversation, since the realities they reflect are not articulable beliefs, but pervasive modes of being that color one's entire experience. These bodily differences can have explosive social consequences, just because they resist ar-

---

117. At least negatively, by refusing to countenance laws that prevent groups from achieving it.

ticulation.[118] To that extent, they are a "bad" from the point of view of the "good" that legal theory represents. They point to what is omitted in legal theory when we speak of "autonomous selves"—rational beings abstracted from the physical realities of race and sex. They make the idealizations legal theory needs to get off the ground look unreal.

The theory of rights has suffered as a consequence of these disturbing insights into autonomy. Louis Seidman and Mark Tushnet have recently put forth the disquieting suggestion that the basis for constitutional debate—the existence and application of rights—has been drained of meaning.[119] For it becomes difficult to say what a right is once the concept of an "individual" possessing an inviolate "core" or essence becomes implausible.

While lawyers and judges, as well as the press, scholars, and lay people, all continue to talk of rights, the beliefs that once supported the idea of rights have withered away. In consequence, according to Seidman and Tushnet, constitutional debate has grown ever more contentious and less persuasive. We are in the absurd situation of being stuck with a language—the language of rights and immunities—that is finally meaningless. Rights seem to be at best an obscuring shorthand for other, more material forces at work behind the screen of concepts. We continue to use concepts whose one-time meaning is lost to us: we have only remnants of an earlier belief that was given the coup de grâce by the legal realists. Seidman and Tushnet recall Alastair MacIntyre's famous suggestion that ethical discourse has been drained of meaning: we are left with the husks or residue of concepts whose sustaining beliefs have long since died away.[120]

This argument obviously strikes a modern nerve. Ronald Dworkin, in urging his readers to "tak[e] rights seriously," reflects the anxiety that they are no longer very plausible. It is not simply a question of rejecting one or two outmoded legal concepts; the fading of belief in rights points to a rejection of legal concepts as such. They seem to be merely distractions and mischief-makers. The realist imperative is to pierce through concepts (for example, rights) to the "real," material forces they mask. It is not that we have unfortunately lost the faith that once sustained rights;

---

118. Perhaps this is one role imaginative writers play in a democratic society—to articulate realities that are so deeply and pervasively formative that they are not easily articulated by any except those with a particular talent for language. In Habermas's formulation, writers set forth the reasons why people are in a certain state of mind.

119. Louis Michael Seidman and Mark V. Tushnet, *Remnants of Belief: Contemporary Constitutional Issues* (New York: Oxford University Press, 1996), chapter 1, esp. 23.

120. Alastair MacIntyre, *After Virtue*, 2d ed. (Notre Dame, Ind.: University of Notre Dame Press, 1984).

rather, it seems a powerful good—a sign of maturity—to dispense with them, and to look at the world with a cold and skeptical eye.

Nonetheless, if we follow through on the implications of Stevens's "poetics of evil," exposing the "mythic" elements of rights does not extinguish them, but instead reintroduces them at a different level. And, indeed, to dispense altogether with a conception of rights would be unattractive for several reasons. It would be morally crude and demeaning to conceive of ourselves in reductively materialistic terms—as though our only pertinent motivations were short-term benefits. Moreover, it would leave majority rule (conceived as a mere totalizing of haphazard preferences) as the sole possible basis for decision making, and make the well-settled practice of judicial review look inexplicable and suspect.[121] Again, such a crude reduction in our self-image would badly compromise one premise of constitutional government—that ratifying a constitution rests on people's ability and willingness at least occasionally to look further than their own narrow interests.[122]

For all these reasons, it looks like a concept of rights is indispensable, although (if we follow Stevens's lead) any plausible conception of rights should be implicit in the realist critique of the atomic "individual" that seems to underlie the straightforward but no longer very plausible conception of rights. In this section, then, I turn to see what model of rights emerges from practice—specifically, constitutional law. It is my argument that the concept of rights implicit in the case law has not yet quite surfaced in legal theories like those of Dworkin or Habermas, which remain too idealized and optimistic. Decisions like *Brown v. Board of Education*[123] and *Roe v. Wade*[124] reflect realities that are not captured by models pre-

---

121. See, e.g., Cass R. Sunstein, *The Partial Constitution* (Cambridge: Harvard University Press, 1993), 125–26, 134–35, 163–64.

122. See *The Federalist Papers,* No. 1:

> Happy will it be if our choice should be directed by a judicious estimate of our true interests, unperplexed and unbiassed by considerations not connected with the public good. But this is a thing more ardently to be wished than seriously to be expected. The plan offered to our deliberations affects too many particular interests, innovates upon too many local institutions, not to involve in its discussion a variety of objects foreign to its merits, and of views, passions, and prejudices little favorable to the discovery of truth.

Implicit in the Constitution, then, is a model of the individual as capable of now and then surmounting narrow interests when the occasion calls for it. Ratifying the Constitution reflected the disinterested view that narrow interests and short-term passions were potent, ever-present political factors, and thus required a political structure designed to minimize their disruptive power. See *The Federalist Papers,* No. 10.

123. 347 U.S. 483 (1954).

124. 410 U.S. 113 (1973).

senting law as an argumentative practice among autonomous beings. After *Brown* and *Roe,* any concept of rights, if it is to be really plausible, must be responsive to the physical aspect of citizens as beings with a race and gender. By confronting the Constitution with the sexuality of its citizens, for example—a reality that had previously been obscured or marginalized in law—*Roe* requires considerable adjustment to the legal image of ourselves as simply rational and autonomous. It points to a more complex model that situates rationality within a personality that both promotes and undermines it. Naturally, a vision of the human being as deeply sexual and therefore partly irrational is hardly a surprise in a post-Freudian era. The point is that *Roe* made sexuality relevant to an understanding of the Constitution and the political community it structures.

The realities of sex and race are not easily assimilated by theory and may seem to be merely disruptive influences. Not only do they impede rational debate; in various, subtle ways they actively resist autonomy. Especially in the case of sexuality, the very idea of autonomy can seem like an encroachment, undermining the household and the woman's traditionally dependent role within it. The realities of racial prejudice, then, and of pregnancy and childbirth, undermine a legal model that is highly abstract and presents citizens as rational, sexless and raceless, almost fungible.

Sex and race, in other words, are a "bad" from the point of view of legal theory, which locates the good—at least, a very great good—in a domain that enables citizens to reason out their life in common. To paraphrase Stevens, the challenge posed by *Brown* and *Roe* is to fashion a model that finds its good within this "bad"—a good that is evil's last invention. Race and sexuality do not preclude a model of ourselves as rational and articulate, but they situate it within a more complex reality in which rationality is an imaginative projection that is to some extent wrested from intractable materials. They call for a less optimistic jurisprudence, one that is more skeptical about rationality. Rights are like a legal analogue to Stevens's poetic conception of nobility: rights and nobility alike flow from and reflect individual dignity. Like nobility, however, rights are not static entities, but a force that persists through continuous change, and which, in any era, takes its specific character from the concrete circumstances distinguishing that time. The challenge, then, is always to see what a plausible conception of rights would look like in a particular milieu.

Because courts lack the leisure to elaborate a full theoretical doctrine, they have often fallen back on conventional and rather outmoded legal concepts in their reasoning. This was the case in *Roe,* where the court unfortunately reverted to a no longer plausible model of rights as inhering naturally in the person. In *Brown,* too, the court's reasoning was not fully adequate to the implications of the case. Sometimes, then, it is necessary to look at what courts do, and the results they reach, rather than what they expressly say. It is an important feature of law that it simplifies a complex reality. We need to ask, though: what is the more complex reality that is being simplified?

To appreciate what the *Brown* and *Roe* decisions really amounted to, and so to appreciate their implications for legal theory, it will be useful to set them within a history reaching back to the Supreme Court's notorious decision in *Lochner v. New York*[125] in 1905. *Lochner* is sometimes treated as an egregiously bad decision—narrow, unjust, out of touch. The really troubling aspect of *Lochner*, however, is that its unfortunate holding was premised on an intuitively appealing and readily intelligible model of the individual and individual rights. The bad result showed that the *Lochner* conception of the individual—whatever its appeal—was fatally outmoded. *Lochner* provides the natural starting point, therefore, in our attempt to find the conception of rights that underlies later watershed decisions like *Brown* and *Roe*.

In *Lochner*, the Supreme Court struck down a state statute that capped the number of weekly work hours in the baking industry. The Court did so based on the argument that such state-imposed limitations infringed the individual's liberty, as protected by the Fourteenth Amendment. The Court understood the individual's liberty interest to encompass the right to contract—in particular, the worker's right to agree to work as many hours per week as he judged appropriate. The state law capping the permissible work hours was viewed as a "meddlesome interference" with the rights of "grown and intelligent men"; it illegally interfered with the rights of "individuals, both employers and employés, to make contracts regarding labor upon such terms as they may think best."[126]

The majority opinion in *Lochner* was premised on a highly abstract and idealized model of the individual as existing prior to and independent of society and its institutions. Contracts represented the expression of a rational being's deliberate decision to enter into a relationship with others, and on what terms. They were binding because they were expressions of the will of free and autonomous beings.[127]

---

125. 198 U.S. 45 (1905).

126. *Lochner*, 198 U.S. at 61. See also *Coppage v. Kansas*, 236 U.S. 1, 9 (1915) (faced with a decision to quit the labor union or lose his job, a worker was "at liberty to choose what was best from the standpoint of his own interests"). For a discussion of the voluntarist conception of the self in *Lochner*, see, e.g., Michael J. Sandel, *Democracy's Discontent* (Cambridge: Harvard University Press, 1996), 194–95.

127. On the "will" theory of contract, see, from different sides of the political spectrum, Morton J. Horwitz, *The Transformation of American Law 1780–1860* (New York:

This model of an autonomous, independent self was closely inter-twined with other salient features of the *Lochner* decision. *Lochner* re-flected a view of law as merely policing from outside a free activity that went on essentially independent of it. The state statute in question, there-fore, was treated as an unwarranted "interference" with the marketplace. The market, in turn, was viewed as a natural formation in which au-tonomous selves expressed their freedom by voluntarily entering into agreements with each other. In short, society, law, and self were neatly compartmentalized: social arrangements were largely prepolitical and "natural," and the individual and law both existed essentially apart from and independent of these arrangements.

This intelligible, triadic structure seemed crucial to the concept of po-litical freedom. As the Court wrote in *Loan Association v. Topeka*,[128] there are "rights in every free government beyond the control of the State." These rights are implicitly reserved to the individual, as against the state. They "grow out of the essential nature of all free governments"; without them "the social compact could not exist."[129] This view of constitutional government underlies the constitutional stature the *Lochner* court gave to freedom of contract. Both the Constitution as a whole, and the constitu-tional freedom of contract in particular, safeguarded the "lives, the lib-erty, and the property of its citizens" from unlimited control by others.[130]

It might seem that the *Lochner* court erred mainly in extending this constitutionally protected individual domain to encompass commercial contracts: yes, a protected, exclusively private zone surrounds the individ-ual, but no, this zone does not extend to commercial contracts. On that view, the *Lochner* error could be cured simply by scaling back the pro-tected domain. The link between *Lochner* and the constitutional vision in *Loan Association,* however, shows that the problem went deeper than that. The criticisms leveled at *Lochner* ultimately made the very idea of a right problematic by calling into question the compartmentalized scheme of individual and state that found expression in the idea of a right.

Even at the time it was handed down, the model of the autonomous indi-vidual was implausible, and ignored the obvious importance the agent's

---

Oxford University Press, 1992), 180–88; and Charles Fried, *Contract as Promise* (Cambridge: Harvard University Press, 1981), 7–27. See also the accounts in P. S. Atiyah, *The Rise and Fall of Freedom of Contract* (Oxford: Clarendon Press, 1979), 405–19, 726–64; Grant Gilmore, *The Death of Contract* (Columbus: Ohio State University Press, 1974).

128. 20 Wall. 655 (1874).

129. *Loan Association v. Topeka,* 20 Wall. at 662.

130. Ibid.

economic and social milieu played in shaping his or her will. The legal realists, moreover, soon set themselves the task of showing how groundless law's
pretensions to neutrality were. They sought to demonstrate, for example,
that law in effect established and promoted the marketplace: the marketplace was not "natural" and law did not merely police it from outside.[131]

The Supreme Court later repudiated *Lochner,* but it has still not altogether dispensed with its underlying idea of an inherent autonomy—as,
for example, its decision in *Miranda* makes clear.[132] It is, after all, a demanding and elusive task fully to assimilate a view of one's own society
and world as contingent, accidental, or partial. The constitutional scholar
Cass Sunstein has recently identified a judicial stance he calls "status quo
neutrality,"[133] which views the present state of affairs as a kind of neutral
baseline from which to assess the legitimacy of state action. It reflects the
strong temptation to look upon current arrangements as somehow
"right" and natural. It is one thing to criticize "status quo neutrality"; it is
quite a different thing, however, to assimilate fully the idea that our institutions are contingent, fluid, imperfect.

Despite its wrong result, then, *Lochner* reflects some persistent trends in
legal thinking, and should alert us to the difficulty of changing our modes
of thought. *Lochner* looks in retrospect like a failure to come to grips with
the realities of labor in the Industrial Revolution. So indeed it was, but it
shows just how deep a rethinking of law, the individual, and society was necessary before a different result was conceivable. In his *Lochner* dissent,
Holmes memorably asserted that the Fourteenth Amendment did not
enact Herbert Spencer's *Social Statics.* But *Lochner* shows the hold Spencer's
vision of economic struggle had on the *Lochner* generation. Indeed, two
years after the Supreme Court handed down its opinion in 1905, William
James wrote that "half of England wants to bury [Spencer] in Westminster
Abbey," notwithstanding his manifest flaws as a thinker, "[s]imply because
we feel his heart to be *in the right place* philosophically."[134]

It is worth noting that the young Wallace Stevens himself was drawn to
this way of thinking. In 1905, the year the *Lochner* decision was handed
down, Stevens was struggling to establish himself in a profession in New
York City. There exists a famous letter from Stevens's father Garrett,

131. On the connection between *Lochner* and the rise of Progressive Legal Thought,
and later, Legal Realism, see Horwitz, *Transformation of American Law,* 33–63; Sunstein, *Partial Constitution* , 45–51.

132. See above Chapter 2, Section 1.

133. Sunstein, *Partial Constitution,* e.g. 3–7, 42–45, 75–79.

134. William James, *Pragmatism* (Buffalo, N.Y.: Prometheus, 1991), 21 (emphasis in
original). James first published *Pragmatism* in 1907.

whose advice to his poetically inclined son captures the ethos of self-reliance that imbues *Lochner*. In the letter, Stevens *père* energetically—indeed, with an odd kind of fervor—urged on his son the importance of earning his own living.[135] The idea of the autonomous worker Garrett Stevens passionately invoked underlay the dry, legal reasoning in the *Lochner* decision.

Lochner, then, had some deep roots. Besides those I have already sketched, there were still others. For example, the value the Court placed on the worker's autonomy owed much to the antislavery ideal of free labor—an ideal that helped shaped the Fourteenth Amendment whose meaning was at issue in *Lochner*.[136] More immediately, *Lochner* is a practical illustration of the link Max Weber drew between capitalism and the formal rationality of Western legal systems.[137] The Industrial Revolution brought about or accelerated the powerful ideas of (1) an atomic, freely willing self that voluntarily enters into associations with others; (2) law as a means of policing society from the outside; and (3) society as the voluntary interactions of freely willing selves. As Weber showed, industrialization required a law of contract that respected the contractual parties' judgment, and so ensured that courts would not disrupt the predictability of business arrangements by throwing out contracts.[138] *Lochner* was a vindication of this bond between capitalism, free will, and the autonomous individual.

Lochner not only illustrates Weber, however, but also supplements him, for it shows how industrialization *undermined* the very assumptions of freedom and autonomy it had called forth. The deplorable holding showed that the conception of a "free, autonomous" worker was seriously flawed. The court's insistence on workers' autonomy carried little conviction in what was obviously an exploitive situation. *Lochner* thus reflects a transitional phase; its deep structure is to be found in the contradictions of capitalism, which both requires and undermines a concept of the autonomous individual. At the same time, it expresses an ethos that had a powerful hold on people at the time, and no doubt continues to do so (albeit to a lesser extent).

135. Quoted in Holly Stevens, *Souvenirs and Prophecies: The Young Wallace Stevens* (New York: Knopf, 1977), 71.

136. Sunstein, *Partial Constitution*, 48–49.

137. Max Weber, "The General Conditions of Legal Formalism," in *Economy and Society*, ed. G. Roth and C. Wittich (New York: Bedminster Press, 1968), vol. 2, chapter 8, § v:1. See, too, the still illuminating essay by Georg Lukacs, "Reification and the Consciousness of the Proletariat," in *History and Class Consciousness*, trans. Rodney Livingstone (Cambridge: MIT Press, 1971), esp. 92–110.

138. See Horwitz, *Transformation of American Law*, 160–201.

In sum, the undesirable result in *Lochner* exposed the implausibility of the legal conceptions the Court used to generate it. Yet it demonstrates the hold these conceptions had on its generation, and points to their pervasiveness: autonomy as separateness suffused ideas not only about contract but also about the nature of constitutional government. *Lochner* was wrongly decided, to be sure; but it was correct in its implicit point that social legislation like the New York labor statute at issue there did not fit within the reigning paradigms of the individual, law, and society.

Holmes's famous dissent in *Lochner* was a trenchant, protorealist critique of the no longer plausible assumptions underlying the majority opinion. It was not until some fourteen years later, however, in his equally famous dissent in *Abrams v. United States,*[139] that Holmes went on to sketch out what amounted to an affirmative realist view of the Constitution and a conception of individual rights that incorporated realist insights and dispensed with the implausible idea of an inherent autonomy. As we will see, the conception of rights implicit in Holmes's *Abrams* dissent continues to operate in the powerful legal theories of Rawls and Habermas. Nonetheless, the realities of sex and race have outrun the synthesis Holmes achieved. The conception of rights implicit in the *Abrams* dissent, therefore, represents an intermediate stage—no longer a fully plausible theory of rights, but one that any satisfying theory must build upon.

Abrams was a case addressing the First Amendment right of free speech. The defendants in *Abrams* had been convicted under the Espionage Act, which criminalized speech opposing the production of materials necessary to prosecute the war against Germany. The defendants, all of them Russian emigrés, had circulated leaflets agitating for the Marxist cause and condemning the war effort as hostile to the workers' struggle for liberation.

Holmes objected to what he saw as the persecution of the defendants for their opinions.[140] His dissent, however, reached far beyond the particulars of the case, and made free speech central to a new and fruitful vision of the Constitution. This centrality, in turn, pointed to a new vision of rights in general:

> Persecution for the expression of opinions seems to me perfectly logical. If you have no doubt of your premises or your power and want a certain result with all your heart you naturally express your wishes in law and sweep away all opposition. To allow opposition by speech seems to indicate that you think the speech impotent . . . or that you do not care whole-

139. 250 U.S. 616, 624–31 (1919) (Holmes, J., dissenting).
140. *Abrams,* 250 U.S. at 629.

heartedly for the result, or that you doubt either your power or your premises. *But when men have realized that time has upset many fighting faiths, they may come to believe even more than they believe the very foundations of their own conduct that the ultimate good desired is better reached by free trade in ideas— that the best test of truth is the power of the thought to get itself accepted in the competition of the market, and that truth is the only ground upon which their wishes safely can be carried out.* That at any rate is the theory of our Constitution. It is an experiment, as all life is an experiment.[141]

Holmes's dissent situates the particular case within an encompassing constitutional vision, one that plainly anticipates many features of the jurisprudence of Dworkin, Rawls, and Habermas. Perhaps most striking is the similarity of the dissent to Habermas's depiction of the "postmetaphysical" condition, in which age-old verities have lost their credibility and the traditional fusion of fact and value has crumbled. For Holmes, too, the First Amendment guarantee of free speech is central, once you have a context where "fighting faiths" can no longer command unquestioning conviction. Free speech apparently rests upon a certain belatedness—an ironic perspective that looks back over the long history of faiths that have arisen and fallen. To be sure, one may still passionately hold views: Holmes's point, however, is that any such belief is now edged with the awareness that reasonable persons hold and have held views incompatible with one's own.

More deeply, and more controversially, his point is that any believer now understands that he or she may one day believe something different: truth is reached by the "free trade in ideas." This supposes that beliefs are based ultimately on reasons, at least in the sense that they are capable of adducing reasons in their support and are vulnerable to reasons showing their baselessness. Holmes's dissent, in other words, reflects a pragmatic attitude toward the truth, one that considers, so to speak, the "cash value" of a belief—how it plays out in practical terms in living one's life.[142]

The *Abrams* dissent looks back, whether consciously or not, to *Lochner.* In his *Lochner* dissent, Holmes protested that the Constitution did not enact laissez-faire economics; in *Abrams,* however, he in effect ventured that the Constitution *did* enact pragmatism. In *Lochner* he wrote that the Constitution is not tied to a particular vision of an economic marketplace (a domain of supposedly free exchanges); in *Abrams* he tied the Constitution, via the guarantee of free speech, to a kind of metaphorical marketplace— the marketplace of ideas, in which channels are kept open to ensure that

141. Ibid., 630 (emphasis added).
142. James, *Pragmatism,* 22–38.

the reasons supporting or opposing particular beliefs may be spoken.

The Constitution, as presented in the *Abrams* dissent, fundamentally protects democratic processes. These processes are not confined to the formal mechanisms of democracy: the "marketplace of ideas" seemingly includes what Habermas would later call "informal will- and opinion-formation"— media discussions and pervasive local comment and debate at all levels of society. This vision is distinctly post-*Lochner* and anti-*Lochner*, because it incorporates the fading of traditional beliefs, including beliefs in the essential, inherent autonomy of the individual. The Constitution, in other words, ensures that we may continually constitute ourselves, as seems best in the light of an ongoing exchange of ideas. We do not inaugurate the Constitution once and for all and from outside; instead we are constantly constituting ourselves within a framework that enables us to do so.

Free speech is not only central to this constitutional vision, but points to a different conception of rights. It is a remarkable fact that the First Amendment guarantee of free speech did not require or receive much attention from the Supreme Court before the First World War and the social upheavals brought about not only by the war effort, but by efforts to support and broaden communist revolution among workers. Social and political turbulence posed the question of free speech and what impediments it placed on legislation.

The "right" of free speech received attention, then, at a time when the old conception of rights—claims attaching to a person solely by right of his or her inherent, human qualities—no longer seemed adequate. The right of free speech is to an important extent a *realist* right—a right that incorporates the realist critique that had seemed to threaten the very idea of a right. It is significant that Holmes—the protorealist, the denier of brooding omnipresences, the prophet of the decline of black-letter law and the rise of social policy—should be the first great expositor of the "right to free speech."

The right of free speech does not, in the first instance, look like a right inhering in the individual. To talk is a public act, one of the most basic— if not the most basic—of social practices. Free speech, then, is not a right that serves to distinguish a "private" zone. Certainly, at least as it was posed in the *Abrams* case, free speech presupposed that one was already within a public forum. The speech protected by the First Amendment is not an area free from the state's power or action: plainly, the state creates and promotes the right of free speech, which finds its central "core" precisely in comment and debate concerning government affairs. The "clear and present danger" test Holmes formulated, whatever its flaws may be, reflects the fact that the right of free speech is understood as existing and exercised within a concrete situation: speech can be regulated when the combination of a particular speech and a particular situation poses an immediate, obvious danger of harm. Rather than a stable quality inhering in individuals even before they act, then, a right exists in the engagements between self and society.

Habermas in effect generalizes Holmes's point: the "conversation" that constitutes the solidarity of a political community presupposes the autonomy and dignity of participants. Individual rights ("private autonomy") arise along with the decision to work out discursively the rules to govern life together in society ("public autonomy"). In other words, the idea of a polity as a conversation (of free and equal citizens freely speaking to one another) brings about as a necessary corollary the idea of each citizen as autonomous and rights-bearing. Only when citizens are understood in this way does the idea of an ongoing, community-wide "conversation" make sense.[143] Although Holmes does not get into theoretical elaborations of this kind, his *Abrams* dissent nonetheless suggests that free speech is a paradigm for a new, realist conception of rights.

It is significant that Holmes elaborated his speech-centered vision of the Constitution in response to communist agitation—political statements, in other words, that called into question the very premises of constitutional government (as inevitably serving the interests of the moneyed classes—a charge that had undeniable force after *Lochner*).[144] Holmes situated his First Amendment jurisprudence within a grand vision of democracy, one that corrected the *Lochner* court's misreading of the Constitution and offered a better account of constitutional government—in effect, that it allowed communist agitation to occur, and trusted that the

143.   Even closer to Habermas's later philosophical elaboration is Justice Brandeis's opinion in *Whitney v. California*, 274 U.S. 357, 372 (1927). Sunstein has argued that it is the Brandeis opinion in *Whitney*, rather than Holmes's dissent in *Abrams*, that offers the more compelling account of democracy. See Cass R. Sunstein, *Democracy and the Problem of Free Speech* (New York: The Free Press, 1993), 23–28. The differences between the *Abrams* dissent and Brandeis's *Whitney* concurrence, however, are a question more of emphasis than of substance.

144.   One of the leaflets, for example, said that the "President's cowardly silence" about the intervention in Russia "reveal[ed] the hypocrisy of the plutocratic gang in Washington." It went on to say "that there is only one enemy of the workers of the world and that is CAPITALISM." It ended "Awake! Awake, you Workers of the World! Revolutionists." Quoted in *Abrams*, 250 U.S. at 620. While the defendants in *Abrams* had been found guilty under the Espionage Act, Holmes wrote that the severe, twenty-year sentence they received for distributing leaflets suggested that they were being punished for their beliefs. See ibid., 629.

free speech licensed by the Constitution would refute the reasons given in behalf of communism.[145]

As Holmes wrote in a later dissent, "If in the long run the beliefs expressed in proletarian dictatorship are destined to be accepted by the dominant forces of the community, the only meaning of free speech is that they should be given their chance and have their way."[146] Constitutional government, therefore, not only was an experiment, but found one of its strongest justifications in its experimental character. Even an opinion we "loathe" and believe to be "fraught with death," therefore, ought not to be suppressed unless it "so imminently threaten[s] immediate interference with the lawful and pressing purposes of the law that an immediate check is required to save the country."[147]

Because of its experimental character, the Constitution allows discussion and criticism even of its own premises. It anticipates and trumps communism because it facilitates discussion of the comparative merits of the two systems. It is not just a partisan opponent to communism; it encompasses or outflanks it. That is because the Constitution is not based on a particular, substantive vision (for example, laissez-faire economics, as the *Lochner* majority presumed). It is premised rather on skepticism about any final truths—a willingness to let truth emerge from robust public discussion, and ultimately (it seems implicit) to let the back-and-forth in the marketplace of ideas be so much of the truth as we will have. It is a strong point in favor of the Constitution, in effect, that it allows citizens to discuss the possibility even of a communist regime opposed to the very premises of the Constitution.

This experimentality, however disorienting or disheartening initially, in fact "grounds" the Constitution more surely than the metaphysical conceptions of *Lochner* could do. Notwithstanding its powerful realism, Holmes's vision of the Constitution evades the troubling picture of the state as a "part among parts." Because "all life is an experiment,"[148] the experimental nature of the Constitution in fact roots it in nature itself—that is, the "natural," experimental process of debate, trial, and assessment. Holmes's brand of ironic pragmatism—the sense that all of one's beliefs

---

145. This is not to say, of course, that communists have not been punished by the United States. The Supreme Court, moreover, has in fact upheld on several occasions the constitutionality of statutes criminalizing communist advocacy. See, e.g., *Dennis v. United States,* 341 U.S. 494 (1951). The point, however, is that the rise of communism threw light on what the core of a liberal democracy in fact was.

146. *Gitlow v. New York,* 268 U.S. 652, 673 (1925) (J. Holmes, dissenting).

147. *Abrams,* 250 U.S. at 630 (J. Holmes, dissenting).

148. Ibid.

are contingent and changeable—partly ensured that the Constitution would not itself be immersed in politics, but would stand apart from it as the structure facilitating political struggle. It is just this supposed separability of state and citizen—public and private—that subsequent historical developments made implausible.

Holmes's First Amendment jurisprudence, then, made free speech central to his vision of constitutional democracy, and did so in a case involving communist agitation. This bears a telling resemblance to Stevens's poetic, developed in the late 1930s and early 1940s, some years after the *Abrams* dissent. For Stevens, too, communism posed an especially troubling challenge to poetry, for it represented the imagination on a truly massive scale, and therefore threatened to marginalize poetry (as the expression of the merely individual imagination) and to make it appear trivial and irrelevant. As we can now see, Stevens's defense proceeded along the lines Holmes had already laid down. Holmes rejected the model of liberal democracy that tied it to a model of the self existing apart from or independent of the social milieu. So, too, Stevens's poetic rejected the idea of a poet as a vatic outsider and assimilated him to the politician (the one who understands what people are thinking before even they are aware of it). Both legal theory and poetics respond to that sense of immanence—of being deeply immersed within a world—that gave Marxism much of its force and credibility.

Communism was a "fighting faith" in which many—like the defendants in *Abrams*—believed with the most passionate fervor. But free speech reflected the yet deeper belief that any belief, however passionately held, may pass away. It is the principle that underlies the rise and fall of the fighting faiths and endures throughout the succession of beliefs. So, too, Stevens deconstructed political and religious belief into the ongoing and interminable poetic articulation of desire. Free speech and poetry, then, are what the long history of creeds comes to in the end: they are different offshoots of belief, once it has become aware of its true nature. For Stevens, autonomy arises in the first instance from the disenchantment of the world, and the consequent sense of one's own contingency. Holmes's view of free speech—of citizens as rational speakers—is similarly tethered to a disenchanted sense of the contingency of all beliefs.

In this way, both Holmes and Stevens sought to outflank communism. The poetic imagination is political (it intuits what people are thinking), but offers deeper satisfactions than the massive, political imagination is capable of providing. Even in a communist regime, Stevens believed, poetry would flourish because it alone addressed the full scope of human desires. Similarly, the right of free speech outflanks communism because it allows it to be discussed.

Stevens's poetic does not merely parallel Holmes's jurisprudence; it deepens it and points toward a more satisfying conception of rights. Before showing that, however, it will be worthwhile to reflect further on this parallel between Holmes's conception of free speech and Stevens's conception of the poetic imagination. For this parallel suggests that some of the most far-reaching constitutional decisions have an ineliminable poetic element; they cannot be construed as simply expounding a legal text—a reading off from the text of conclusions supposedly implicit in it. "That, at any rate, is the theory of our Constitution," Holmes wrote in his *Abrams* dissent, but it would be mistaken to suppose that he thought the Framers were philosophical pragmatists *avant la lettre*. It seems clear that the ironic sense of belatedness Holmes reflects is not something literally "in" the Constitution. His view of the Constitution was a self-conscious reinterpretation of it, along lines that anticipated legal realism, and certainly reflected his skepticism about the existence or usefulness of fixed essences like "will" or "contract" as real things having distinct properties and determinate consequences. Holmes, then, is articulating what constitutional theory must look like if the Constitution is to remain authoritative. He is doing what the Stevensian poet does; that is, he works over the tradition that has formed him and distills from it what remains credible and compelling in it. In this way, he shows himself to be a faithful "son" of the father-like tradition.

What makes some constitutional decisions extraordinary in legal terms is just that they are *not* principally construing this or that clause, but instead situating the text as a whole within a world view in which the Constitution can remain pertinent. A Constitution necessarily presupposing an autonomous individuality is bound to become outmoded, once the beliefs supporting such a concept have faded. A Constitution, in contrast, that rests on the possible obsolescence of any belief—however fundamental and apparently necessary—seems better able to endure. Rather than "reading" his opinion off from the text of the First Amendment, then, Holmes was elaborating a vision of the individual and society in which the Constitution remains authoritative, partly because it is now seen to be premised on free speech. He created a context in which the Constitution could continue to be foundational and central.

The Constitution cannot be adequately understood as a kind of flat blueprint for government or a list of stipulated rights, because it has an important *self-reflexive* quality: it implies a model of its own relation to the citizen body, and ultimately a model of the individual as citizen. This self-reflexivity is essential to its being a constitution, which is, in the first instance, law made aware of itself as something manmade. A constitution reflects the attempt to maintain law's authority within a more realistic, disenchanted sense of law's immanence.

The Constitution is tied to a sense of its source in autonomous citizens ("we, the people"): this source is the grounds for the Constitution's authority. Although it addresses what government must do in order to respect autonomy, the Constitution does not take into account the determinants of autonomy: that is, it does not look too deeply behind or into autonomy to see what nurtures or underwrites it. The Constitution must nonetheless adapt to evolving perceptions of autonomy if it is to remain, so to speak, constitutive.

Autonomy is most readily understood as a kind of rationality and independence: citizens are then modeled as enacting the Constitution in a free act of self-commitment, "ordain[ing] and establish[ing] this Constitution for the United States of America." Once that model of autonomy had come to seem seriously incomplete, autonomy had to be rethought and the relation between the Constitution and its autonomous sources (we, the people) adjusted. Certain opinions by the Supreme Court are in significant part attempts to readjust the Constitution's implicit, self-reflective model of autonomy and of its relation to autonomous citizens. I have suggested that Holmes's *Abrams* dissent was one such opinion. Granted, the *Abrams* dissent was an important moment for the understanding of the Free Speech clause. Even more fundamentally, however, Holmes's dissent shows that the "right" of free speech was paradigmatic for the kind of thing a right—any right—must be. At this level, Holmes was not so much interpreting a clause within the Constitution as situating the Constitution as a whole within a new conceptual model of the relations between the state and its citizens.

As Robert Post has trenchantly observed, "constitutional interpretation is not merely about the Constitution, but about the more radical and profound question of how we stand in connection to the Constitution."[149] An account of the practice of constitutional interpretation must therefore "situate constitutional authority. . .in the *relationship* obtaining between participants in that practice and the Constitution."[150] Constitutional adjudication at this level has what I shall call a poetic quality: it calls less for expertise in interpreting specific legal language, and consists rather in finding a credible paradigm for the relation between the individual and the state.

---

149. Robert C. Post, *Constitutional Domains: Democracy, Community, Management* (Cambridge: Harvard University Press, 1995), 39.
150. Ibid. (emphasis in original).

This poetic aspect of constitutional law seems unavoidable, because part of the point of any constitution is the relationship between the citizens and the state they establish (and because this relationship is susceptible to change over time). Decisions with this poetic quality can hardly be mandated by this or that clause within the text, since their whole point is to locate the text as a whole within a paradigm of the relation between state and citizen. Such decisions can therefore seem unfounded—and, indeed, so they are, if by "unfounded" we mean "not plainly authorized by a specific clause within the Constitution."

However, such decisions are not unprincipled. Identifying a paradigm for the relation between state and citizen may be a matter of articulating what is implicit in legislative efforts to address social issues. So, for example, the labor laws at issue in *Lochner* pointed to a model in which autonomy was no longer inherent in citizens, and was partly something brought about (or withheld) by the state. In 1905, it was difficult to see how such a model could be reconciled with the Constitution (given the prevalent constitutional vision in which free, autonomous individuals established the state). The *Lochner* court's error lay in its failure to heed the new relation between state and citizen implicit in labor laws, and in its use of an outmoded paradigm to strike down the laws.

The doctrine of judicial review teaches that the courts are authorized to pronounce on the compatibility of legislative enactments with the Constitution. What the discussion so far suggests, however, is that the relation between the judiciary and the legislature is more complex. Courts do not simply weigh legislation against specific provisions of the Constitution. At times they might ask whether the kinds of laws being enacted point to a new or emerging model of the relation between the Constitution and citizens, and modify their conception of this relation accordingly. (It is significant, in this regard, that the labor laws scrutinized in *Lochner* would be wholly unobjectionable under Holmes's "free speech" model of rights.)

Thus, Post seems to me a little misleading when he suggests that adjudication entailing the relationship between the Constitution and citizens amounts to an assessment of the national character. "[I]n the absence of consensus the frank ambition of responsive interpretation to 'speak for' the character of the nation, while expressive of the outlook of some, will necessarily constitute a hegemonic imposition upon others."[151] Rather than doing anything so nebulous as reading the nation's ethos (a task for which the courts are not especially suited), courts construe the relation between the Constitution and citizens, based on what actually goes on be-

---

151. Post, *Constitutional Domains*, 43.

tween the state and individuals—above all, ongoing legislative activity. These legislative developments feed back into the self-reflexive sense of the Constitution, and revise the sense of what individual autonomy entails. On this view, judicial review is not a one-way street (in which judges apply the Constitution as a kind of standard to assess the acceptability of laws); rather, it entails a far more complex process of mutually referring legislation and Constitution to each other: the Constitution is a standard against which legislative enactments are assessed, but the enactments, for their part, contribute to a sense of what the Constitution is, and how citizens stand in relation to it.

Holmes's *Abrams* dissent reflects a still powerful model of the relationship between citizens and the state. Holmes modeled citizens as rational speakers, capable of articulating reasons for their beliefs and therefore able to enter a discussion concerning them. This view of law continues to be an influential one, but seems too optimistic in its assumption that articulate beliefs lie at the root of human motivation and behavior. Despite its anti-*Lochner* quality, moreover, Holmes's model still appears premised on an inherent autonomy (consisting now, however, in citizens' ability to articulate their beliefs and desires). But this runs counter to the realist sense (which became clearer after Holmes wrote his *Abrams* dissent) that law actively forms its citizens—that autonomy is not something inherent, but something learned.

This feature of autonomy found its most fateful expression in *Brown v. Board of Education*,[152] which struck down laws mandating segregated public school systems. More to my purpose here, *Brown* reflected a far more flexible model of the individual as vulnerable to his or her environment. The segregation laws, the court wrote, generated a "feeling of inferiority as to [black children's] status in the community that may affect their hearts and minds in a way unlikely ever to be undone."[153] Justice Warren seemed to suggest that the result in *Brown* was called for by increased knowledge about the psychological effects of segregation.[154] The Court, however, need not have pinned its decision on specific psychological studies. *Brown* reflected the more realistic sense that autonomy is not inherent, but something achieved over the course of a lifetime. It depends on a host of environmental factors, and consists partly in a contingent and vulnerable orientation toward oneself: it contains an important component of self-respect. It was not that psychological knowledge had improved, but

152. 347 U.S. 483 (1954).
153. *Brown*, 347 U.S. at 494.
154. Ibid., 494 and n. 11.

rather that psychology had become relevant: citizens were not born autonomous, but educated into it.

Brown implicitly but powerfully transcends the dichotomy between self and society by illustrating how the self—a rational, autonomous center—is to an important degree the product of society and social practices. The children educated by the state were a paradigmatic case that clarified one feature of the relationship, more generally, between all citizens and their laws, and the way autonomy is achieved in and through a society shaped by law. Social slights and dishonor actively impede the ability of individual citizens to achieve autonomy. Segregation bruises the self-respect that is essential to it.[155] This dishonoring of the individual takes on yet graver consequences when it is sanctioned by law.

Brown undermined the *Abrams* conception of autonomy in another, more disturbing way as well. The segregation laws at issue in *Brown* showed that law, far from reflecting or promoting autonomy, was being conscripted actively to prevent or frustrate it. Insofar as they are racial beings, citizens do not universally or reliably embrace autonomy; they tend to resist it in others as a way of holding on to power. The segregation laws were not occasional aberrations or sporadic miscarriages of majority rule, but entrenched and pervasive features in American legal and social life. They deeply resisted a vision of a rational, deliberative community.

Even more disturbingly, autonomy, far from embodying what is prepolitical in the individual—a guarantee of the individual's inviolate integrity—is itself an object of political struggle. Individual autonomy became a controversial good that had to be achieved, often in the face of pervasive forces whose deep tendency was to frustrate it. Race is a powerful realist force. After *Brown*, the vision of an autonomous body of free and equal citizens necessarily seems less "natural" and more partisan—opposed to some deeply entrenched attitudes and beliefs many wished to see enshrined in law. Constitutional law could no longer purport (as it could, say, in the constitutional vision sketched in Holmes's *Abrams* dissent) merely to facilitate debate. It became involved in a political struggle to ensure the predominance of its own distinctive vision of autonomy. To paraphrase Stevens, it now became a "destructive force." That the decision in *Brown* would foment violence by overthrowing expectations could not ultimately count against its rightness, once it was recognized that law was an important shaper of expectations.

155. On the autonomous self as socially produced, see Post, *Constitutional Domains,* chapter 2 ("The Social Foundations of Privacy: Community and Self in the Common Law Tort"), 51–88.

Brown thus undermined Holmes's persisting laissez-faire sense in *Abrams* that the Constitution leaves the marketplace of ideas alone. One of the Constitution's great strengths, according to Holmes, was that it was so accommodating—compatible with anything that seemed best to the deliberative community of free speakers. This remains a powerful conception. Rawls presents the constitutional state as a module that can be "plugged into" any number of reasonable beliefs. The Constitution, moreover, can supposedly "coexist" with social formations in which autonomy is unimportant or actively discouraged. The Free Exercise and Establishment clauses of the First Amendment inscribe this compatibility within the constitutional text itself.

Brown, in contrast, reflects the sense that law (and, in particular, the Constitution), far from leaving things alone, actively forms citizens and that citizens resist the constitutional vision of autonomy. Constitutional law partly becomes a more aggressive force—a sword rather than a shield—a tool to bring about the kind of citizen body it apparently assumes. This is a disturbing vision, the more so since it is at odds with the broad compatibility that seems to be a central feature of the Constitution.

The sense that the Constitution does not leave things alone is what most distinguishes *Brown* from its notorious predecessor, *Plessy v. Ferguson,*[156] in which the Supreme Court held that segregation did not violate the Equal Protection Clause of the Fourteenth Amendment. The Court reached this result by distinguishing between law and society: law merely policed from outside the social formations that exist in their own right. "If the two races are to meet upon terms of social equality," the Court wrote, "it must be the result of natural affinities, a mutual appreciation of each other's merits, and a voluntary consent of individuals." Law, the *Plessy* court wrote, could not reform nature: legislation was "powerless to eradicate racial instincts or to abolish distinctions based upon physical differences." Any attempt to use law to do so would "only result in accentuating the difficulties of the present situation."[157]

Viewed from a century's distance, it is difficult to understand how the *Plessy* court could possibly have found that segregation laws did not impose separation on the races. Our latter-day response to *Plessy,* however, shows how deeply we have assimilated the realist critique and how incredible the supposed distinction between law and society now appears. Because law was not supposed to upset social expectations—because it was supposed to leave things alone—the very commonness of the segrega-

---

156. 163 U.S. 537 (1896).
157. *Plessy,* 163 U.S. at 551.

tion statutes argued in favor of their constitutionality. The state did not stigmatize blacks by enacting segregation laws, since the laws were intended merely to keep the peace (based on the deep social formations that kept blacks separate from whites). In that sense the segregation laws served the interests of blacks (as the potential victims of white violence) as well as of whites. To use the law to force integration, as the *Plessy* court expressly noted, could only exacerbate a difficult situation.

In striking contrast to *Plessy*, *Brown* reflects an evolving realist understanding that law in general, and the Constitution in particular, are powerful shapers of social and individual reality. This understanding, however, does not easily coexist with the Constitution's "accommodating" quality, its compatibility with a host of different and inconsistent social and economic arrangements. This compatibility is a decidedly mixed blessing. At one level, it is one of the great, enduring strengths of the Constitution. At another level, however, it means that the Constitution does not denounce evils like segregation with the unambiguous force we might desire. While it was possible to understand the Constitution as implicitly antislavery before the Civil War amendments, the Constitution was far from compelling this result, and seemed rather to countenance slavery. Even after the passage of the Fourteenth Amendment, segregation of the races was not plainly ruled out by that amendment's guarantee of equal protection. *Brown* thus impressed Learned Hand as an unprincipled decision, because it lacked a solid basis in the text of the Constitution.[158] Herbert Wechsler, too, understood the *Brown* court as upholding the associational preferences of blacks (who sought association with whites) over those of whites (who sought to avoid such association). He was unable to articulate a "neutral principle" of law that would generate such a conclusion.[159]

On the other hand, *Brown* has achieved a nearly universal approval rating, despite the challenge it presents to received notions of the Constitution and individual autonomy. This is no doubt due to the recognition of the deep injustice of segregation. But to see racial prejudice as *injustice* (rather than, say, merely an unfortunate fact of life) entails a profound readjustment in the sense of the relation between law and citizen. To affirm the separate-but-equal doctrine of *Plessy* would have been, in effect,

158. Learned Hand, *The Bill of Rights* (Cambridge: Harvard University Press, 1958), 54–55.
159. Herbert Wechsler, "Toward Neutral Principles of Constitutional Law," *Harvard Law Review* 73 (1959): 1, 34. On the response of Hand and Wechsler to *Brown*, see Horwitz, *Transformation of American Law*, 258–68.

to reject a half century's lessons about law and its complex relation to the self and society. It would have tied the Constitution to an outmoded, implausible model of autonomy. To put it differently, the Constitution loses much of its relevance to modern society *unless* the Equal Protection clause rules out segregation. The Constitution prohibits segregation partly because unless it did so it would be simply irrelevant to a matter at the heart of modern society.

Brown illustrates the point (made above in connection with Holmes's dissent in *Abrams*) that constitutional adjudication cannot be solely and always a matter of "reading off" determinate meanings from a text. At times, judges reread the Constitution in light of changing perceptions of autonomy and the relations among law, the individual, and society. Even though it lacked a solid, uncontroversial basis in the text of the Constitution, *Brown* was not an unprincipled decision, as Hand charged. The principle underlying it was not a specific clause within the Constitution, but the Constitution's self-reflective model of the relation between it and the citizen body. Autonomy was no longer natural or inherent, but something the law had to encourage: citizens had to be educated into it; they also had to be prevented from blocking or frustrating it in others. In *Brown*—and in *Roe,* as we shall see—the Court was not striking down legislation it didn't like, but rather taking into account a new, more realistic sense of the complex relations between law and citizen, and, in particular, of the way law actively promotes (or disserves) autonomy. Because segregated public schools thwarted the autonomy presupposed by the Constitution, the laws enforcing them were unconstitutional.

Brown suggests that rights have not become mere remnants of belief, as Seidman and Tushnet suggest, but that they have become more complex.[160] On the one hand, certain rights seem to belong to the individual as an autonomous member of the political community. On the other hand, however, a right also exists to *become* a full-fledged member of the political community. This is a right to the greatest possible measure of equal individual liberties.[161] The Constitution spells out only the former kind of rights (those that result from membership in the political community). These "membership" rights presuppose that the citizen is autonomous, and are, in essence, so many specifications of that autonomy. The Constitution does not, however, examine the preconditions to au-

160.   One of the distinguishing features of critical race theory, as opposed to critical legal theory, is its recognition of the continued importance of rights. See the Introduction to Kimberle Creshaw et al., eds., *Critical Race Theory: The Key Writings* (New York: New Press, 1995), xiii–xxxii, esp. xxiii–xxiv.

161.   See Habermas, *Between Facts and Norms,* 122–24.

tonomy, and seems for the most part simply to assume it exists naturally. The latter kind of right emerges, however, only once membership in the political community is seen to be problematic. Once that happens, the Constitution is threatened with irrelevance to the extent that it fails to address obstacles to autonomy, especially legal obstacles.

In American constitutional jurisprudence, the second kind of right—the right to the greatest possible amount of equal individual liberties—is linked to the Equal Protection clause. As construed by *Brown,* however, that clause is far more than a guarantee of neutrality. "Protection" was in effect conceived more actively as *bringing about* the equality some deep social forces conspired to prevent. The Constitution became a means of forming the kind of political community that, at another level, it simply presupposed. In other words, it had to construct the sources of its own legitimacy.

The second kind of right, then, can be linked to the Equal Protection clause, but it arises from the need to keep the Constitution pertinent— that is, to incorporate into it the evolving sense of the way law and citizens are related. It reflects a paradigm shift of the kind Holmes sketched out in his *Abrams* dissent, but now taking into account a more radical conception of the state's formative influence on citizens and on individual autonomy.

Brown, then, was an instance of "poetic" judgment—one that reread tradition in light of the present, and then situated the present within this reinterpreted constitutional history. More deeply, perhaps, it showed the dynamic, "poetic" character of rights. These are no longer credibly based on stable qualities supposedly inhering in the individual as such. They are "poetic"—qualities we imaginatively "see in" ourselves and then attempt to bring about. Like the Stevensian concept of the heroic or the noble, rights need to be continually reconceived, for they reflect the ongoing relationship between the individual and society. The idea of a right, like the poetic idea of the noble, is like a wave-force that persists through continual change, and takes its character partly from a perpetually shifting environment. The idea of rights emerging from the discussion so far represents (to invoke Stevens) a "yes" lurking in the realist "no." No—autonomy is not a given, universal, inherent quality. It is something that needs to be energetically cultivated if it is to exist at all. The state cannot plausibly claim to respect it simply by leaving it alone, or by remaining neutral in regard to it. But that realist negation gives rise to a new conception of rights, as imperatives requiring the state to root out practices discouraging autonomy and its flourishing in individuals.

This new paradigm points to a complex relationship between the self and the state, in which the self is at once deeply formed by the state and yet apart from it, with claims over against it. The state—in its relation to the citizen—is something like the mythic sculptor Pygmalion, who shaped stone into a human being, whom he had then to respect as an equal. This relation is far more intricate than the straightforward, implausibly simple relation envisioned in *Lochner.* To appreciate its manifold complexities, we need first to consider *Roe v. Wade*,[162] the deeply controversial decision that ensured women's access to abortion.

Equal protection—in the strong sense indicated by *Brown*—seems to be at the heart, too, of *Roe.* Although the Court based its holding on the controversial "right of privacy," *Roe* is more plausibly understood as ensuring that law not be used as a tool to prevent women from participating fully in the political, social, and economic life of the community.[163] The abortion laws at issue in *Roe* necessarily tended to confine women to traditional, dependent roles as mothers and wives, and to that extent prevented them from becoming autonomous, full-fledged possessors of rights. Laws requiring a woman to bear a baby she did not want affronted her autonomy by taking responsibility away from her, and imposing state force, in a matter fundamentally shaping her life. They also frustrated it by tending to keep her in the traditional sexual role of dependency.

Autonomy seems to comport, at the least, a certain control over one's life. *Roe* rests on the new and troubling perception that this control has a hidden sexual aspect, and that it tends to be a feature more of male lives than of female ones. As traditionally conceived, individual autonomy silently reflected the sovereignty of each male citizen in his own home: autonomy, as so conceived, tacitly harbored and rested in part on hierarchically ordered formations that militated against the autonomy of some. As women's opportunities expanded, however, the household inevitably appeared to an important extent at odds with the constitutional vision of a political community of autonomous citizens. When seen against this background, the laws restricting access to abortion looked like ways of ensuring that women would not achieve the control over their lives that au-

---

162. 410 U.S. 113 (1973).

163. I have not set out detailed arguments for reading *Roe* as an Equal Protection case, since it has been amply done by others. As Sunstein notes (*Partial Constitution*, 395 n. 21): "There appears to be a mounting consensus that equality arguments are better than liberty arguments with respect to abortion generally." On *Roe* as an Equal Protection decision, see Sunstein, ibid., 270–85; and Kenneth Karst, *Law's Promise, Law's Expression: Visions of Power in the Politics of Race, Gender and Religion* (New Haven, Conn.: Yale University Press, 1993), 53. See also Catherine MacKinnon, "Reflections on Sex Equality under Law," *Yale Law Journal* 100 (1991): 1281, 1307–24; Ruth Bader Ginsburg, "Some Thoughts on Autonomy and Equality in Relation to *Roe v. Wade,*" *North Carolina Law Review* 63 (1985): 275, 282–83; and Sylvia Law, "Rethinking Sex and the Constitution," *University of Pennsylvania Law Review* 132 (1984): 955.

tonomy requires. They had the constitutionally suspect tendency to keep some citizens outside the public forum. *Roe* in effect states that the Constitution cannot countenance state laws that obstruct a citizen's power to achieve autonomy.

On this reading, *Roe* stands in the same line as *Brown,* and its strong reading of the Equal Protection clause. Women in *Roe,* like the children in *Brown,* are paradigms of one aspect of the relation, more generally, between citizens and their laws. They are situated in a way that demonstrates with special clarity how law actively creates the shape of the political community and the individual lives within it. Just as important, the abortion laws at issue in *Roe,* like the segregation laws in *Brown,* show how autonomy is not only not natural, but deeply resisted. The constitutional vision that emerges from *Roe* and *Brown* is not quite that of a political community deliberating about the terms and conditions of life together, but rather of a deliberative community being constructed, or wrested, from often intractable materials.

As in *Brown,* autonomy emerges from *Roe* as something partisan and contested. The majority opinion in *Roe* struck down the abortion laws at issue in the name of privacy, and in the interests of keeping the government out of necessarily intimate decisions. But preventing states from legislating against abortion did not secure state neutrality. First, by assuring women control over their reproductive functions, *Roe* leveled the playing field for males and females in the public sector. It also modified the family's internal dynamics in the interests of securing individual autonomy: parents, for example, cannot use law to veto a minor's decision to have an abortion.[164] More deeply, by holding that states could not take away from women the ability to choose, *Roe* made it likelier that women would be autonomous individuals able to govern their own lives rationally.

In other words, *Roe* did not so much respect an independently existing autonomy in women as help to produce it, and to do so in the face of deep and pervasive social forces that resisted it. It reflects a troubling view of the Constitution as an aggressive force, bringing about the autonomy it presupposes. *Roe* and *Brown,* then, both undermine Holmes's vision of the Constitution as facilitating debate, but existing essentially independent of it. The Constitution, as construed in these cases, is necessarily partisan—immersed in the political fray, and struggling to bring about its own version of the good.

164. States may require a minor seeking an abortion to obtain the consent of a parent or guardian, but only provided that there exists an adequate "judicial bypass" procedure. See *Planned Parenthood of Southeastern Pennsylvania v. Casey,* 505 U.S. 833, 898 (1992); *Bellotti v. Baird,* 443 U.S. 622, 643–44 (1979).

Although *Roe* seems better understood in terms of equal protection, the Court in fact premised its holding on an individual right to privacy.[165] While this right is problematic (and, I think, plainly insufficient to explain *Roe*), it nonetheless represents a relevant dimension of the case, and one that makes it even more illuminating (and disturbing) than *Brown* about the nature of political autonomy. It will be useful first to set forth reasons why the right of privacy seems unpersuasive as the rationale really underlying *Roe*. First, the Constitution nowhere speaks of a "right of privacy," and, while the Supreme Court has on several occasions recognized the existence of such a right, its basis in the Constitution remains vague. Moreover, the pre-*Roe* cases recognizing a right of privacy did not clearly support a right of access to abortion, and the Court's reasoning in this regard was notoriously perfunctory.

More deeply, the idea of a privacy right inherent in women prior to any social or political arrangements reverted to an outmoded *Lochner*-type model of autonomous, independent agents. This was especially inappropriate, because such a model could accommodate the realities of pregnancy and childbirth only with difficulty, and made them look puzzling and uncanny—a liminal phenomenon that did not quite fit anywhere. This inadequate conceptualization foreordained the Court's controversial result. The Court in effect allocated the pregnancy between the two entities (individual and state) made relevant by its model: part of the gestation period was the individual woman's exclusive preserve, and part was susceptible to state regulation.

The apparent reversion to *Lochner* was not so much inept as reflective of the difficulty the state has often encountered when confronting the household. *Roe* replicates in a highly sophisticated, latter-day setting the conflict between state and household that drove (for example) the *Oresteia*, in which a legal system was based on the denial of the woman's role in procreation. The state stands for equality, generality, and legality, while the family embodies specificity, hierarchy, and authority. The citizen has a certain fungibility, for (s)he is conceived abstractly—that is, apart from the concrete particulars that constitute the individual identity of the person within the household. The citizen, too, has a certain atemporal quality: young and old citizens, *qua* citizens, are equals. The family, in contrast, is deeply rooted in time and change: age is a highly significant difference among its members, and the household is in a continuing process of generation, growth, and decline.

165. *Roe*, 410 U.S. at 152–53; *accord, Casey*, 505 U.S. at 846 (constitutional protection of the woman's decision to terminate her pregnancy derives from the Due Process clause of the Fourteenth Amendment).

The two principles—household and state—therefore exist in marked tension. They are not simply opposed principles, however, for the family is the source of citizens, and provides the discipline and moral training the state requires. The state is based on the household, and yet seeks inevitably to limit its influence.[166] *Roe* reflects this ancient conflict between household and state: the polarized categories of individual and state the majority opinion used—unexceptional in some contexts—could not do justice to the realities posed by the family.

The decision in *Roe* need not have been tied to an outmoded model of self and state. It challenged the Court to rethink the relation between the Constitution and "we, the people" once the people were understood to be sexed and sexual beings. The individual was now seen to be constituted in an important way by emotional needs and by a capacity for intimate rapport with others. She or he now became more deeply *interiorized*. The right of privacy in *Roe* hailed from a line of cases relating to marriage and the family: because of the right to privacy, for example, the state cannot enact laws forbidding interracial marriage or blocking access to contraception.[167] The right restricts a state's ability to intervene in decisions concerning child rearing and education.[168] Although access to abortion did not fit quite so easily into these earlier cases, they nonetheless pointed to an area of intimate decision making about one's life and body that ought to be kept free of state coercion.

The ethic infusing *Lochner* had presented the individual as self-reliant wage-earner. *Roe* and the line of privacy cases leading up to it evinced a rather different ethos that emphasized sexual and emotional desires and needs. It reflected a deepening or interiorization of the legally relevant self: citizens' "private" activity was not confined to earning a living, but extended now to achieving such non-economic goods as self-expression and emotional satisfaction. It was no longer simply a question of (by and large male) citizens supporting a family, but of citizens (male and female) securing happiness together. The shifting paradigm of the legally relevant

166. On the claims of household and state, see Costas Douzinas and Ronnie Warrington, "Antigone's Law," in *Politics, Postmodernity and Critical Legal Sudies: The Legality of the Contingent,* ed. Costas Douzinas, Peter Goodrich, and Yifat Hachamovitch (London: Routledge, 1994), 187–223, esp. 202–5.

167. See *Loving v. Virginia,* 388 U.S. 1 (1967) (state may not prohibit interracial marriage); *Eisenstadt v. Baird,* 405 U.S. 438 (1972) (state may not block access to contraception); *Griswold v. Connecticut,* 381 U.S. 479 (1965) (state may not deny married couples access to contraceptives).

168. See *Pierce v. Society of Sisters,* 268 U.S. 510 (1925) (striking down state law requiring students to attend state schools); *Meyer v. Nebraska,* 262 U.S. 390 (1923) (state could not prohibit the teaching of foreign languages).

self naturally reflects a variety of social changes—among them a rising standard of living and greater economic opportunities for women.

This deepened, interiorized self presents a yet more compelling case for the government to steer clear of the individual's domain: plainly, decisions touching the most intimate aspects of one's life should be outside the reach of majority politics. But this imperative clashed with the realist, *Brown*-type insight that the state never simply "steers clear" of a naturally existing zone of privacy. In other words, as the case for government neutrality became more compelling, the ability to realize neutrality became ever more questionable.

Here, then, we see a far more complex model of the relation between state and citizen than anything the *Lochner* court had envisioned. In *Roe*, we are presented with the following paradox: on the one hand, the law partly produces the individual, and does so by loosening the hierarchies that have traditionally structured the household and assigned women a subordinate role. (This is the "equal protection" aspect of the case, which seems to provide the most compelling rationale underlying *Roe*. It grows from the need to bring about the individual autonomy apparently presupposed in the Constitution, if the Constitution is to remain relevant.) On the other hand, the individual, once produced, stands apart from the state, with claims over against it.

We might call this the "Pygmalion" paradox. It has several dimensions. First, as the "equal protection" reading of *Roe* suggests, the individual's dignity, and the respect the state must give it, flow from different and not altogether compatible sources. On the one hand, this dignity rests on the individual being an integrated, autonomous center—a self. The state must strike down laws that perpetuate social formations militating against individual autonomy (e.g., women's subordinate and dependent role in the household). On the other hand, the individual's dignity flows in large part from his or her capacity for affective ties and intimate emotional bonds with others—and above all, the family. The autonomous individual emerges from the household, but at the same time the value of autonomy and individuality finds an important source in the household.

This bears a striking resemblance to the picture of law I have tried to present in this book: law simplifies a complex ethical reality in the interests of facilitating life together, but continually draws on the complexity to maintain its legitimacy. Similarly, here, law produces the autonomous individual—singular, raceless, sexless—from out of a host of concrete physical conditions, which nonetheless remain an important feature of the individual's integrity.

The legal model of the person can no longer be conceptualized as a single thing—the rational individual. Rather, we should think of a stroboscopic image, which blurs together a series of "moments" as the individual emerges from and refers back to the household—emerges into an abstract citizenship, and refers back again to the concrete particulars of his or her existence. The problem with Justice Blackmun's opinion in *Roe*, on this reading, is that it ignored the more disturbing, realist aspects of the case, and oversimplified it as a situation where the government must simply "steer clear" of the individual. This fails to do justice to the complex, not to say snarled, relations between state and citizen. On the one hand, the state must not trespass on the individual's domain (this has been the traditional understanding of rights). On the other hand, the state cannot help but shape individual lives. This points to a new aspect of rights—call them "rights$_2$,"—as claims on the state to remove the legal impediments to attaining full autonomy. The relation between the individual and the state is now inevitably inconsistent and shifting. Rights had been thought of as timeless, articulating the essentially static relation between the self and the state.

After *Brown* and *Roe*, however, rights not only are timeless, but also have a propulsive character: they drive law forward in order to make it less untrue to the Constitution's idealized assumption of autonomous citizens. That means, among other things, that constitutional adjudication cannot be confined to "reading off" the rights specifically named in the Constitution. Decisions that cannot be reduced to outcomes determined by a specific clause are not for that reason unprincipled; they are attempts to adjust the relationship between the Constitution and citizens to reflect the realities of life within the political community. Courts do not step outside their judicial role in assessing these new realities, for they are implicit in the way state and citizens actually interact.

Roe represents the culmination (at least for now) of a development in which autonomy becomes ever more problematic, and increasingly difficult to reconcile with perceptions of the individual's vulnerability to circumstance and his or her deeply formative relations with others, above all in the household. Properly understood, *Roe*—like *Brown*—points to a "poetic" conception of autonomy, in the severe and interesting sense of that word reflected in Stevens. This post-*Roe* autonomy is poetic in the negative sense that it does not inhere in the individual as something actually or demonstrably present. It is poetic in the deeper, affirmative sense that it is self-consciously aware of its origins in what is in important ways its opposite. We emerge into autonomy and away from the household and partly at its expense. At the same time, the household is a chief source of any individual's value, the reason why she or he must be respected by the state.

This complex, unstable view of autonomy does not lend itself easily—or at all—to expression in legal opinions. *Roe* crystallizes the argument in this book that law simplifies a complex reality it nonetheless acknowledges and seeks to incorporate. The *Roe* court rested its decision on a rough-and-ready idea of rights, even though the case implicitly points to a far more intricate model of the relation between citizen and state. *Roe* also suggests the relevance of literature to law—as articulating rather more clearly and centrally the complex ethical realities that are then simplified in law.

4. LAW AS AN "IMAGINATION OF THE NORMAL"

Poetry, in one of Stevens's most intriguing formulations, is an imagination of the normal.[169] This description points to a deep affinity between poetry and law, whose legitimacy, I suggest, partly consists in its also being an "imagination of the normal." But first, what did Stevens mean?

He offered this description of poetry in the course of a postwar lecture on the role of the lyric poet in a world characterized everywhere by violence. The momentous upheavals of the world war and its aftermath had apparently extinguished forever people's sense of a stable, predictable normality. Poets, then, helped people live their lives in a warlike world by "imagining the normal." This formulation may seem paradoxical for an audience reared on Foucault, who uses "normality" as a pejorative term for the forces bent on imposing a sterile conformity. Richard Rorty, too, has celebrated the importance and the edifying power of "abnormal" discourse, which is any discourse that lacks agreed-upon criteria for reaching agreement.[170] Such discourse is "edifying" because it aims at finding "new, better, more interesting, more fruitful ways of speaking"—rather than purporting to describe more accurately an objective truth.[171] Abnormal discourse is not confined to any particular discipline: it may consist, for example, "in the 'poetic' activity of thinking up such new aims, new words, or new disciplines." The idea is to "de-normalize" our surroundings—to reinterpret them in unfamiliar terms.[172] Rorty recalls the injunc-

---

169. Stevens, "Imagination as Value," in *Necessary Angel*, 153–56. Stevens delivered his lecture at Columbia University in 1948.

170. Richard Rorty, *Philosophy and the Mirror of Nature* (Princeton, N.J.: Princeton University Press, 1979), 11.

171. Ibid., 360.

172. Ibid.

tion of the Russian formalists, to "make it strange." Edifying discourse, he writes, "is *supposed* to be abnormal, to take us out of our old selves by the power of strangeness, to aid us in becoming new beings."[173] In this way, abnormal discourse prevents the "freezing-over" of culture that the search for objective truth (and, God forbid, the achievement of it) threatens to impose.[174] It breaks the "crust of convention," and "prevent[s] man from deluding himself with the notion that he knows himself, or anything else, except under optional descriptions."[175] What gets edified in abnormal discourse—built up, nourished, fortified—is *ourselves,* and our ability to conduct a fruitful and ongoing conversation with each other.

Rorty seems at times to be describing the poetic of Wallace Stevens, one of whose aspirations, like that of Rorty's "edifying philosophers" was:

> to keep space open for the sense of wonder which poets can sometimes cause—wonder that there is something new under the sun, something which is *not* an accurate representation of what was already there, something which (at least for the moment) cannot be explained and can barely be described.[176]

Rorty here captures that aspect of Stevens that celebrated ignorance and aphasia. Stevens wrote, "The poem must resist the intelligence / Almost successfully"[177]—that is, it should *not* fit easily into the familiar molds of "normal discourse." Foucault and Rorty capture the sense that the abnormal is a powerful good, in the promise it offers of refreshing and vitalizing a culture that tends to staleness. It is one of the most engaging features of Stevens' poetry, too, that it affords this bracing freshness.

Nonetheless, Stevens insists that poetry is an imagination of the *normal.* The "normal," for Stevens, is not some conventional and irretrievable "normality" of years past. Rather, he is pointing out something that threatens to get lost in celebrations (like Rorty's) of the abnormal as such, and corrects a potential misreading of his own poetry. To identify the imagination solely with the abnormal, Stevens writes, would be like "identifying liberty with those that abuse it."[178] The destabilizing, "abnormal" poetic imagination can easily seem to be nothing more than a knack possessed by a few unorthodox souls. It threatens to disintegrate into an

---

173. Ibid. (emphasis in original).
174. Ibid., 377.
175. Ibid., 379.
176. Ibid., 370 (emphasis in original).
177. Stevens, "Man Carrying Thing," *CP,* 350.
178. Stevens, "Imagination as Value," in *Necessary Angel,* 153.

atomic kind of individualism, and to rob public discourse of any vitality. It is not clear, in Rorty's terms, exactly *how* abnormal discourse keeps the conversation going; it seems just as capable of sliding into a hermetic, conversation-stopping privacy.

Abnormality, in other words, ought to be a stage or a phase—a "no" that looks forward to completion in some "yes". For Stevens, the poetic imagination was not the fanciful or capricious invention of a singular talent. Rather, it was a serious attempt to arrive at what he called an "agreement with reality"—a counterpressure the mind exerts against the pressure of events on it.[179] It was not simply creative but responsive[180]— the mode par excellence in which human beings register events in the world and express or synthesize their significance. The centrality of the imagination should reflect the recognition that values, beliefs, ideals are crucial to our knowing the world at all, and navigating our way through it.

Stevens's was a "normal" poetically conceived: the poet "perceiv[ed] the normal in the abnormal, the opposite of chaos in chaos."[181] Poetry's peculiar merit was to see the noble, even in the midst of violence. It lifted to its highest level the human trait of "seeing in"—of seeing values, significance, goodness within a transient, conflicted and violent world. This "seeing in" is, I think, what Stevens meant when he spoke of the "instinctive integrations" that constitute "imagining the normal." These integrations, Stevens boldly claims, are the real reason for living.[182] For those in the immediate grip of misery they represent a saving consciousness of something other than evil. "Is evil normal or abnormal?" Stevens provocatively asks.[183] His point seems to be that the poet's task is to penetrate down to what is perennial, nurturing, and good within the upheavals and turbulence of warlike times.

If we dwell on this, its pertinence to legal theory should become clear. The "normal" is the background to one's own life; it provides the orientation needed to chart one's course. It is not simply that which is by and large the case, but is deeply hued with normativity; it is felt, to a considerable degree, to be the way things *should* be. It consists above all of the familiar—the deeply assimilated practical knowledge that sustains and

179. On the poem as an "agreement with reality," see Stevens, "The Figure of the Youth as Virile Poet," in *Necessary Angel,* 54. On the poem as a "counterpressure," see "Noble Rider," in *Necessary Angel,* 12–23.

180. On the imagination as both responsive and creative, see Charles Larmore, *The Legacy of Romanticism* (New York: Columbia University Press, 1996), 7–16.

181. Stevens, "Imagination as Value," in *Necessary Angel,* 153.

182. Ibid., 154–55.

183. Ibid., 154.

informs anyone's conduct. The normal, then, is in large part our "contents"—the store of background beliefs, attitudes, lore, and knowledge that constitutes the self. This is a central point of communitarians like Michael Sandel: the self comes "encumbered" with a store of familiar beliefs and attitudes. In other words, the self is deeply constituted by the normal—which amounts to community and the traditions that make it up. The self's pleasures, its conception of what is good, its desire for the good, then, are not so much the deliberate products of rational choice as "expressions of belonging to a given form of life."[184]

Stevens's challenging and fruitful point is partly that this normal is no longer simply given to us: an earlier fusion of the "is" and the "ought" has crumbled, as the world has revealed itself ever more insistently as a violent place. Stevens reveals a weakness in some contemporary communitarian thought, which tends to present the formative past (the "normal") as unproblematically available to us. Rather, he suggests, the normal almost exceeds our grasp: the familiar is now something we create, or into which we breathe life by continually reconceiving it. Our communities are now no less imagined than real.[185] It is the mark of the serious artist that he or she discovers / invents a normal, which society needs in order to function. The poet's individual self-development is not done in defiance of society. His or her attempts to discover the fictions that will suffice (at a time when traditional beliefs have come unraveled) provide society with that orienting sense of the normal that it deeply needs.

The poet characteristically seeks to reach down to the images that have always and everywhere touched people, so that he or she may write poetry older than the oldest poems of the earth. The normality that poetry affords, then, is in part the "ur-familiar"—the sun, the moon, the weather. These age-old lyric themes become newly vital, as affording a deepened, more seasoned sense of the familiar, as old beliefs wither away. Poetry's task is to valorize the familiar, and to unleash its orienting powers, so that it can spread its leavening influence throughout one's life. This is especially so in violent times: for those who live in the grip of troubles poetry provides an imagination of something other than evil. Its imagination of the normal soothes the tormented and abased imagination war inflicts on its immediate victims. For those who witness war and its effects from a distance, poetry destroys the stale imaginings of the past, and goes on to construct provisional, but compelling "life-worlds"—imagined communities.

184. Larmore, *Legacy of Romanticism*, 58.
185. Ibid., 61. See also Benedict Anderson, *Imagined Communities*, rev. ed. (London: Verso, 1991), 1–7.

Law too unleashes the stabilizing and wholesome properties of the normal, and does so by discovering how they subsist under conditions of pluralism and the fading away of old verities. Law is a predominant part of our public "normal"—a powerful fashioner of anyone's sense of "the way things are," and a major contributor to what Habermas calls the "life-world." The legal "normal" includes ideas of autonomy, rationality, a coherent self. To speak of "imagining" this normal, however, means that these ideas are never realized, and retain always a strong vestige of the ideal. They become more explicitly what, in retrospect, they always were—ideal visions that a society does not in fact embody, but to which it must attempt to live up. They take their position ahead of us, beckoning us forward. To think of law as an imagining of reality, then, corrects the undue optimism of much recent legal theory. For it suggests the difficulty of achieving "normality": it corrects the sense that the normal is easily available to us, or that it can be more than a provisional, and changeable, construct. Habermas, for example, has pointed out the fictive, ideal character of private autonomy, but he suggests that this character is simply given once a society undertakes to work out in common the rules that will govern public life. But an ideal like the "rational, autonomous individual" is a conception at once fluid and perennial: it changes continually, in order to maintain a precarious equilibrium between ideal and reality. It requires powerful and seasoned legal imaginations to detect what visions of individual dignity, rationality, and autonomy are implicit in new historical shifts—to see the normal in the abnormal.

But to present law as an "imagination of the normal" is also to correct for the tendency in realist approaches to level law into sheer factuality—to treat law, for example, as though it were simply policy, or essentially a way of gaining or entrenching power. The ideal is a crucial part of our "normal"—that was Habermas's point. To show the considerable injustices lurking in a legal system's particular "normal"—indeed, to go deeper and show the injustice intrinsic in the very idea of social norms and the "normal" itself—is not to extinguish the need for the ideal. One of the problems with Foucault's sweeping critique of law is that, however telling his points, law remains an inescapable necessity if we are to get on. The question posed by Foucault's critique, therefore, is not so much what will replace law: nothing will, law is here to stay. Rather, the question is how to make the necessary evil a little less evil—an Augustinian formulation. To show the repressive tendencies of the "normal," then, should lead us to cast normative ideals as self-conscious fictions, but fictions that have a genuine claim on us.

The obligations imposed by law, construed as an imagination of the normal, have a certain *ironic* quality: law is entitled to citizens' concern and respect partly because of the pressing need for normality—a peaceful and at least roughly equitable order that will facilitate life. But this peaceful order—this normal—is something we have imagined; it can no longer plausibly claim to be inscribed in the cosmos, or deeply within our own intrinsic nature. We are obliged now to acknowledge, as Larmore puts it, the limits of fundamental moral commitments we cannot imagine giving up. We hold back from commitments, even as we affirm them.[186] This ironic sense of obligations is a mark of maturity: it entails the ability to step back from one's commitment to a particular belief and appreciate how it could have been different, or to consider it objectively, from the viewpoint of a disinterested observer.[187]

As an imagining of the normal, law is a precarious enterprise. One of the points I have tried to make in this book is that law traces out a cycle between simplifying ethical complexities and incorporating them. *Brown* and *Roe* reflect models of the self that are troubling in their complexity. *Roe* in particular presents us with a view of autonomy as something the state produces, and (at the same time) something inherent in the person, which the state must respect. Historical developments have delivered the courts to this complexity, but it remains awkward and rather intractable: it muddies the clarity of language and concept that remains a powerful legal ideal. Our legal system now requires a considerable degree of sophistication, an ironic stance that simultaneously affirms and stands back from one's commitments. But that troubles the aspiration of law to be clear and straightforward. The precariousness of law, then, resides to a large extent in the fact that we have a variety of commitments—things we want to see reflected in law, but which are to a painful degree inconsistent with each other. Moreover, there is no guarantee that our legal intelligence will be strong enough to discern what visions of dignity and autonomy are implicit in new historical shifts. The most serious flaw in *Lochner* was the court's imposition of a stale ideal on an economic reality it no longer fit: the court refused to be guided by social developments. *Brown* and *Roe,* in contrast, sought to incorporate history's lessons about the relationship between citizens and the state, but neither decision quite articulated the relationship or what it portended for constitutional jurisprudence.

186. Larmore, *Legacy of Romanticism,* 70, 76; see also 81: "Irony is not the absence of commitment. It is, on the contrary, impossible without it. Irony is not the single-minded flight from commitment. It is instead the state of being of two minds, committed and reserved, at the same time."
187. Ibid., 81.

To call law an imagination of the normal, in sum, is another way of saying that it is an institution for the imperfect. It is informed by ideals that it can never really possess, and that often resist efforts to articulate them. These are serious flaws, for they make unclear why law should exert any authority, above and beyond the need to avoid its punishments. One of the pressing problems for jurisprudence is to find a place for this imperfection in legal theory, and to give it its due—to take the full measure of law's deficits and to show how such a seriously flawed institution nonetheless has a claim to citizens' respect.

The contribution of literature to legal theory is twofold. It shows the ethical complexity law can never hope fully to reflect, but which it is continually obliged to revisit and to attempt to incorporate. It points to the serious imperfections of law—the ranges of human experience and aspirations to which law can never really do justice. Beyond that, literature helps out legal theory by showing the depth and centrality of the fictive and the ideal in human life, and the way ideals get conceived within historical circumstances and are continually modified by them. Literature shows the *reality* of the fictive, and the depths of our immersion in it. It shows, in other words, how exposing the fictiveness of law's ideals does not prevent them from truly obligating us.

Conclusion: Law's Interior

Law is a practice, not a system. This terse formula is meant to capture several features of the law explored in this book. First, law is not a body of commands, nor is it a system of rules animated by certain underlying principles. Ultimately, law does not possess the virtues of a system— for example, coherence, stability, or predictability. But to demonstrate that law lacks these qualities does not "expose" it as mere politics or demonstrate that it is illusory (or, worse, hypocritical). To model law as a system is to present it as something that exists outside us and, so to speak, on its own legs, autonomously. This, however, is to underestimate the depth and intimacy of our connection with law. Better to understand it as a practice we cannot help but carry on. (Come to think of it, "Carry on, Counsel!" would not be a bad subtitle for this book.)

Law is a practice one of whose points is to contain or sideline the ethical quandaries of life in the hope of enabling society to function. It can never succeed entirely in doing this, however. In fact, it must acknowledge this complexity in order to show its legitimacy—that is, to show that it is an institution that truly serves an authentic human good. Law is heir to all our indecisions and ambivalence, our conflicted commitments within social life. This ambivalence entails a commitment, on the one hand, to keeping our relations and the rules structuring them as lapidary and determinate as possible; and, on the other hand, to ensuring that they reflect the nuances and idiosyncrasies of the particular case. Law bears our allegiance at once to simplicity and complexity. As such, it is not separate from morality, but one especially important and pervasive site in which this split in our ethical ideals gets played out.

Time is another essential feature of law as practice, and one that gets ignored in approaches that treat law as a system. If the pervasive ambivalence of law does not make it merely incoherent, that is largely thanks to the fact that it is carried on across time. Law is characterized by its well-settled procedures for ensuring that it is continually referred to the past and that the present, *mutatis mutandis,* will be continued into the future. The familiarity of the law is a powerful stabilizing force—more important, certainly, than theoretical justifications of the justice or integrity of the legal system. The "futurity" of law is another essential attribute. For justice and integrity, rather than qualities the law actually possesses, are ideals that continually beckon law forward, and ensure that it remains always a practice, never a finished product.

The persistence of law across time is not to say that its progress is always steady and sure. Even when the pace of cultural change is rapid, however, the challenge is to discover the way the past bears on the present—or, to invoke Stevens, to see the "normal" in the unfamiliar and "abnormal." This requires imagination and a certain creativity. Law's creativity, however, is of a distinctive kind, for its grandest aspirations aim at the commonsensical; it is a creativity of the familiar.

Because law is a practice we carry on, rather than a system of rules that exists independent of us, it reflects certain ideas about the person or the self. Such is law's "interior"—its reflexive reference to the kind of beings that carry on the practice. This is most clearly the case with rights, for law—at least the way *we* do law—presupposes that it is the practice of autonomous, rational beings. Law seems to require this rather simplified model of ourselves; certainly, it feels most comfortable with it. Where the facts of a case undermine this "pellet-like" self, however—individual, well-bounded, resourceful in defending its boundaries—courts have had a difficult time. The case law of custodial confessions is a history of attempts to reconcile the fascinating psychological complexities of interrogation and confession with the law's commitment to the model of a rational, rights-bearing self.

More troubling yet is that this model of a rights-bearing self has not stayed still: deep currents in American society in the twentieth century, and the new centrality of race and gender, have made the abstract model of an innately autonomous agent outmoded and even subtly oppressive. The autonomous self retains its grip on our legal imagination, but it needs to be seasoned now by a realistic sense that before the state can "respect" the autonomous person, it must first bring about the autonomy it will then respect.

One disturbing feature in constitutional developments over the last fifty years, then, is that autonomy, far from being an innate quality of persons, has emerged as a controversial political good. Rather than shielding certain unambiguously cherished rights, the Constitution has become a more aggressive tool—a sword—to bring about the autonomy it envisions, and to do so in opposition to some powerful and deeply rooted social forces militating against it. More than once in the last half century, the Constitution has prompted Americans to violence.

This new realistic sense of rights in turn calls for some changes in the way we think of constitutional jurisprudence. By and large, the Constitution is a legal document that stipulates certain rights that should be applied to specific cases. But the Constitution cannot be confined to that. It self-reflexively expresses the relation between the people and itself, and as that relation changes, so the understanding of the Constitution must change. Some few, momentous legal decisions possess a "poetic" quality in which the court revises and recharacterizes this internal relation between the Constitution and the people who constitute it. This new relation is not something spelled out in the text of the Constitution; instead it is imaginatively constructed from the way the Constitution works in practice, and from the ongoing and shifting relationships among the branches (executive, legislative, and judicial) stipulated in the Constitution. Judicial review ought not to be understood, then, as though courts were holding up a specific enactment to the decisive constitutional language. Rather, courts need to look at ongoing—especially legislative—developments to see how the Constitution plays out in a changing social environment. The Constitution is to be explicated not only by a close reading of its text—and not only by the judicial history of close readings—but also by reference to the way the system inaugurated by the Constitution in fact functions, and the relation between people and Constitution implicit in such functioning.

Law as a practice, law as bound up with human lives, law as reflecting our complexity even as (or just because) it tries to escape it—these are some of the features of law that make comparison with literature so suggestive and illuminating. For literature is, arguably, an exploration of our own complexity. It is drawn to situations that defy or challenge our usual moral conceptions and legal categories. It enables us to feel emotions, explore states of mind, and linger over memories in a way we normally don't and can't in our actual lives, where the press of commitments and duties and distractions compels us to move speedily ahead. If law's point is (at least partly) to simplify us, the effect of literature is to enable us to dwell on the complexity that we usually ignore in daily life. Seen this way, law and literature supplement each other. I have stressed the way literary treatments illuminate the complexity that law tries to escape (but can never quite succeed in escaping). But the converse is just as true: literature, and the delectation of the unique, the heterodox, the particular represents but one commitment in a human life. Law, and its simplifying, imperative mode reflect another.

Jurisprudence is not only a fascinating subject, but an important one in a democracy that prides itself on being a government of laws. Literature, I think, can be used to dramatize issues in legal philosophy and to show their human content. In doing so, literary works point to a model of law potentially more persuasive than the often abstruse and highly idealized picture offered by legal philosophy. Rather than presenting law as an autonomous discipline, I have tried to present it as a vital practice with deep and significant affinities with other human pursuits—most especially, literature. It is not simply that law is a humane pursuit; properly understood, law throws light on the ambivalence of humane pursuits—the way we alternatively seek, in our laws and letters, both individuality and solidarity, rules and principles, self and other.

Index